Spring MVC

A Tutorial

Paul Deck

Spring MVC: A Tutorial
Copyright © 2014 Brainy Software Inc.
First Edition: April 2014

ISBN: 978-0-9808396-5-4

Book and Cover Designer: Mona Setiadi

Technical Reviewer: Budi Kurniawan
Indexer: Chris Mayle

Trademarks
Oracle and Java are registered trademarks of Oracle and/or its affiliates.
UNIX is a registered trademark of The Open Group.
Microsoft Internet Explorer is either a registered trademark or a trademark of Microsoft
Corporation in The United States and/or other countries.
Apache is a trademark of The Apache Software Foundation.
Firefox is a registered trademark of the Mozilla Foundation.
Google is a trademark of Google, Inc.

Throughout this book the printing of trademarked names without the trademark symbol is
for editorial purpose only. We have no intention of infringement of the trademark.

Warning and Disclaimer
Every effort has been made to make this book as accurate as possible. The author and the
publisher shall have neither liability nor responsibility to any person or entity with respect
to any loss or damages arising from the information in this book.

Table of Contents

Introduction

Welcome to *Spring MVC: A Tutorial*.

Spring MVC is a module in the Spring Framework (or Spring for short) for rapidly developing web applications. The MVC in Spring MVC stands for Model-View-Controller, a design pattern widely used in Graphical User Interface (GUI) development. This pattern is not only common in web development, but is also used in desktop technology like Java Swing.

Sometimes called Spring Web MVC, Spring MVC is one of the most popular web frameworks today and a most sought-after skill. This book is for you if you want to learn how to develop Java-based web applications with Spring MVC.

Learning Spring MVC will be much easier if you already master the Spring Framework as well as Servlet and JavaServer Pages (JSP), the two Java technologies upon which Spring MVC is based. If you're new to Spring, Chapter 1 presents a short tutorial on the Spring Framework. If you are not familiar with Servlet and JSP, don't despair. You can find two crash courses that will help: Appendix B, "Servlet" and Appendix C, "JavaServer Pages." If you are interested to know more about Servlet and JSP, I would recommend *Servlet and JSP: A Tutorial* (ISBN 978-0980839623) by Budi Kurniawan.

The rest of this introduction talks about HTTP, web programming with Servlet and JSP, and the content of the book.

The Hypertext Transfer Protocol (HTTP)

The HTTP protocol enables web servers and browsers to exchange data over the Internet or an intranet. The World Wide Web Consortium (W3C), an international community that develops standards, is responsible for revising and maintaining this protocol. The first version of HTTP was HTTP 0.9, which was then replaced by HTTP 1.0. Superseding HTTP 1.0 is HTTP 1.1, the current version. HTTP 1.1 is defined in the W3C's Request for Comments (RFC) 2616, which can be downloaded from http://www.w3.org/Protocols/HTTP/1.1/rfc2616.pdf.

A web server runs 24x7 waiting for HTTP clients (normally web browsers) to connect to it and ask for resources. In HTTP it is always the client that initiates a connection, a server is never in a position to contact a client.

Note
It is worth noting that in 2011 the Internet Engineering Task Force (IETF), a standards body, standardized the WebSocket protocol as RFC 6455. The protocol allows an HTTP connection to be upgraded to a WebSocket, which will allow the connection to send messages in both directions. This means, using the WebSocket protocol a server can initiate conversations with its WebSocket clients.

To locate a resource, an Internet user would click a link that contains a Uniform Resource Locator (URL) or enter one in the Location box of his/her browser. Here are two examples of URLs:

```
http://google.com/index.html
```

```
http://facebook.com/index.html
```

The first part of the URLs is **http**, which identifies the protocol. Not all URLs use HTTP. For instance, these two URLs are valid even though they are not HTTP-based URLs:

```
mailto:joe@example.com
```

```
ftp://marketing@ftp.example.org
```

In general an HTTP-based URL has this format:

```
protocol://[host.]domain[:port][/context][/resource][?query string
| path variable]
```

or

```
protocol://IP address[:port][/context][/resource][?query string |
path variable]
```

The parts in square brackets are optional, therefore a URL can be as simple as http://yahoo.ca or http://192.168.1.9. An Internet Protocol (IP) address, by the way, is a numerical label assigned to a computer or another device. In other words, instead of typing http://google.com, you can use its IP address: http://173.194.46.35. To find out the IP address of a domain, use the **ping** program on your computer console:

```
ping google.com
```

An IP address is hard to remember, so people prefer to use the domain. A computer may host more than one domain, so multiple domains can have the same IP address. And, did you know that you can't buy example.com or example.org because they are reserved for documentation purpose?

The host part of a URL may be present and identify a totally different location on the Internet or an intranet. For instance, http://yahoo.com (no host) brings you to a different location than http://mail.yahoo.com (with a host). Over the years www has been the most popular host name and become the default. Normally, http://www.*domainName* is mapped to http://*domainName*.

80 is the default port of HTTP. Therefore, if a web server runs on port 80, you don't need the port number to reach the server. Sometimes, however, a web server doesn't run on port 80 and you need to type the port number. For example, Tomcat by default runs on port 8080, so you need to supply the port number when requesting a resource:

```
http://localhost:8080/index.html
```

localhost is a reserved name typically used to refer to the local computer, i.e. the same computer the web browser is running on.

The context part of a URL refers to the application name, but this is also optional. A web server can run multiple contexts (applications) and one of them can be configured to be the default context. To request a resource in the default context, you skip the context part in a URL.

Finally, a context can have one or more default resources (ordinarily index.html or index.htm or default.htm). A URL without a resource name is considered to identify a default resource. Of course, if more than one default resource exists in a context, the one with the highest priority will always be returned when a client does not specify a resource name.

After a resource name comes one or more query string or path variable. A query string is a key/value pair that can be passed to the server to be processed. Two query strings are separated by an ampersand (&). A path variable is like a query string, but contains only the value part. Two path variables are separated with a forward slash (/).

The following subsections discuss HTTP requests and responses in more detail.

The HTTP Request

The HTTP request consists of three components:

- Method—Uniform Resource Identifier (URI)—Protocol/Version
- Request headers
- Entity body

Here is a sample HTTP request:

```
POST /examples/default.jsp HTTP/1.1
Accept: text/plain; text/html
Accept-Language: en-gb
Connection: Keep-Alive
Host: localhost
User-Agent: Mozilla/5.0 (Macintosh; U; Intel Mac OS X 10.5; en-US;
rv:1.9.2.6) Gecko/20100625 Firefox/3.6.6
Content-Length: 30
Content-Type: application/x-www-form-urlencoded
Accept-Encoding: gzip, deflate

lastName=Blanks&firstName=Mike
```

The method—URI—protocol version appears as the first line of the request.

```
POST /examples/default.jsp HTTP/1.1
```

Here **POST** is the request method, **/examples/default.jsp** the URI, and **HTTP/1.1** the Protocol/Version section.

An HTTP request can use one of the many request methods specified in the HTTP standards. HTTP 1.1 supports seven request types: GET, POST, HEAD, OPTIONS, PUT, DELETE, and TRACE. GET and POST are the most commonly used in Internet applications.

The URI specifies an Internet resource. It is usually interpreted as being relative to the server's root directory. Thus, it should always begin with a forward slash /. A Uniform Resource Locator (URL) is actually a type of URI (See http://www.ietf.org/rfc/rfc2396.txt).

In an HTTP request, the request header contains useful information about the client environment and the entity body of the request. For instance, it may contain the language the browser is set for, the length of the entity body, and so on. Each header is separated by a carriage return/linefeed (CRLF) sequence.

Between the headers and the entity body is a blank line (CRLF) that is important to the HTTP request format. The CRLF tells the HTTP server where the entity body begins. In some Internet programming books, this CRLF is considered the fourth component of an HTTP request.

In the previous HTTP request, the entity body is simply the following line:

```
lastName=Blanks&firstName=Mike
```

The entity body can easily be much longer in a typical HTTP request.

The HTTP Response

Similar to the HTTP request, the HTTP response also consists of three parts:

- Protocol—Status code—Description
- Response headers
- Entity body

The following is an example of an HTTP response:

```
HTTP/1.1 200 OK
Server: Apache-Coyote/1.1
Date: Thu, 29 Sep 2013 13:13:33 GMT
Content-Type: text/html
Last-Modified: Wed, 28 Sep 2013 13:13:12 GMT
Content-Length: 112

<html>
<head>
<title>HTTP Response Example</title>
```

```
</head>
<body>
Welcome to Brainy Software
</body>
</html>
```

The first line of the response header is similar to the first line of the request header. It tells you that the protocol used is HTTP version 1.1, and that the request succeeded (200 is the success code).

The response headers contain useful information similar to the headers in an HTTP request. The entity body of the response is the HTML content of the response itself. The headers and the entity body are separated by a sequence of CRLFs.

Status code 200 is only issued if the web server was able to find the resource requested. If a resource cannot be found or the request cannot be understood, the server sends a different request code. For instance, 401 is the status code for an unauthorized access and 405 indicates that the HTTP method is not allowed. For a complete list of HTTP status codes, refer to this online document.

```
http://www.w3.org/Protocols/rfc2616/rfc2616-sec10.html
```

Servlet and JSP Overview

Java Servlet technology, or Servlet for short, is the underlying technology for developing web applications in Java. Sun Microsystems released it in 1996 to compete with the Common Gateway Interface (CGI), the then standard for generating dynamic content on the web. The main problem with the CGI was the fact that it spawned a new process for every HTTP request. This made it difficult to write scalable CGI programs because creating a process took a lot of CPU cycles. A servlet, on the other hand, is much faster than a CGI program because a servlet stays in memory after serving its first request, waiting for subsequent requests.

Since the day Servlet emerged, a number of Java-based web frameworks have been developed to help programmers write web applications more rapidly. These frameworks let you focus on the business logic and spend less time writing boilerplate code. However, you still have to understand the nuts and bolts of Servlet. And JavaServer Pages (JSP), which was later released to make writing servlets easier. You may be using a great framework like Spring MVC, Struts 2, or JavaServer Faces. However, without excellent knowledge of Servlet and JSP, you won't be able to code effectively and efficiently. Servlets, by the way, are Java classes that run on a servlet container. A servlet container or servlet engine is like a web server but has the ability to generate dynamic contents, not just serve static resources. Servlet 3.1, the current version, is defined in Java Specification Request (JSR) 340 (http://jcp.org/en/jsr/detail?id=340). It requires Java Standard Edition 6 or later. JSP 2.3 is specified in JSR 245 (http://jcp.org/en/jsr/detail?id=245). This book assumes you know Java and object-oriented programming. If you're new to Java, I recommend *Java 7: A Beginner's Tutorial (Third Edition)*, ISBN 978-0-9808396-1-6.

A servlet is a Java program. A servlet application consists of one or more servlets. A JSP page is translated and compiled into a servlet.

A servlet application runs inside a servlet container and cannot run on its own. A servlet container passes requests from the user to the servlet application and responses from the servlet application back to the user. Most servlet applications include at least several JSP pages. As such, it's more appropriate to use the term "servlet/JSP application" to refer to a Java web application than to leave JSP out.

Web users use a web browser such as Internet Explorer, Mozilla Firefox, or Google Chrome to access servlet applications. A web browser is referred to as a web client. Figure I.1 shows the architecture of a servlet/JSP application.

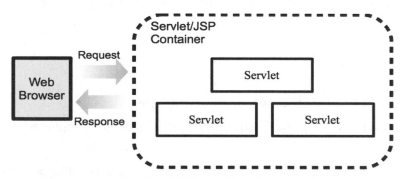

Figure I.1: Servlet/JSP application architecture

The web server and the web client communicate in a language they both are fluent in: the Hypertext Transfer Protocol (HTTP). Because of this, a web server is also called an HTTP server.

A servlet/JSP container is a special web server that can process servlets as well as serve static contents. In the past, people were more comfortable running a servlet/JSP container as a module of an HTTP server such as the Apache HTTP Server because an HTTP server was considered more robust than a servlet/JSP container. In this scenario the servlet/JSP container would be tasked with generating dynamic contents and the HTTP server with serving static resources. Today servlet/JSP containers are considered mature and widely deployed without an HTTP server. Apache Tomcat and Jetty are the most popular servlet/JSP containers and are free and open-source. You can download them from http://tomcat.apache.org and http://jetty.codehaus.org, respectively.

Servlet and JSP are two of a multitude of technologies defined in the Java Enterprise Edition (EE). Other Java EE technologies include Java Message Service (JMS), Enterprise JavaBeans (EJB), JavaServer Faces (JSF), and Java Persistence. The complete list of technologies in the Java EE version 7 (the current version) can be found here.

`Http://www.oracle.com/technetwork/java/javaee/tech/index.html`

To run a Java EE application, you need a Java EE container, such as GlassFish, Jboss, Oracle WebLogic, and IBM WebSphere. You can deploy a servlet/JSP application in a Java EE container, but a servlet/JSP container is sufficient and is more lightweight than a Java EE container. Tomcat and Jetty are not Java EE containers, so they cannot run EJB or JMS.

About This Book

This section presents an overview of each chapter.

Chapter 1, "The Spring Framework" introduces the popular open source framework.

Chapter 2, "Model 2 and the MVC Pattern" discusses the pattern on which Spring MVC was built.

Chapter 3, "Introduction to Spring MVC" presents a gentle introduction to Spring MVC. In this chapter you learn to write your first Spring MVC application.

Chapter 4, "Annotation-Based Controllers" discusses one of the main pillars of the MVC pattern, the controller. In this chapter you learn how to write annotation-based controllers, an approach introduced in Spring MVC 2.5.

Chapter 5, "Data Binding and the Form Tags" discusses one of the most powerful features in Spring MVC and how to use it to repopulate form fields.

Chapter 6, "Converters and Formatters" talks about two object types that help with data binding, the converter and the formatter.

Chapter 7, "Validators" teaches you how to validate user input by building validators.

Chapter 8, "The Expression Language" explains one of the most important features added in JSP 2.0, the Expression Language (EL). The EL aims to make it possible to author script-free JSP pages and can help you write shorter and more effective JSP pages. In this chapter you will learn to use the EL to access JavaBeans and scoped objects.

Chapter 9, "JSTL" explains the most important libraries in the JavaServer Pages Standard Tag Library (JSTL), a collection of custom tag libraries for solving common problems such as iterating over a map or collection, conditional testing, XML processing, and even database access and data manipulation.

Chapter 10, "Internationalization" shows how to build multi-language web sites using Spring MVC.

Chapter 11, "File Upload" shows how to write controllers that can handle uploaded files. Two approaches are discussed.

Chapter 12, "File Download" explains how to send a resource to the browser programmatically.

Appendix A, "Tomcat" explains how to install and configure Tomcat and run it in multiple operating systems.

Appendix B, "Servlet" introduces the Servlet API and presents several simple servlets. This chapter focuses on two of the four Java packages in the Servlet API, the **javax.servlet** and **javax.servlet.http** packages.

JavaServer Pages (JSP) is a technology that complements Servlet. Appendix C, "JavaServer Pages" covers the JSP syntax, including its directives, scripting elements, and actions.

Appendix D, "The Deployment Descriptor" explains how to configure your Spring MVC applications for deployment.

Downloading the Sample Applications

You can download the zipped sample applications used in this book from this web page.

```
http://books.brainysoftware.com/download
```

Chapter 1
The Spring Framework

The Spring Framework (or Spring for short) is an open source framework for developing enterprise applications. It is a light-weight solution composed of about twenty different modules. This book covers Spring's Core and Beans modules as well as Spring MVC. Spring MVC is of course the subject of this book and a subframework within Spring.

This chapter explains the Core and Beans modules and how they provide solutions for dependency injection. For the uninitiated, the concept of dependency injection is also discussed in detail. You will use the skills you acquire in this chapter to configure the Spring MVC applications developed in the next chapters.

Dependency InjectionDependency injection has been widely used in the past few years as a solution to, among others, code testability. In fact, dependency injection is behind great frameworks like Spring and Google Guice. So, what is dependency injection?

Many people use the terms dependency injection and Inversion of Control (IoC) interchangeably, even though Martin Fowler argues that they are not the same in his excellent article on the subject.

`http://martinfowler.com/articles/injection.html`

For those in a hurry, the short explanation of dependency injection is this.

If you have two components, **A** and **B**, and **A** depends on **B**, you can say **A** is dependent on **B** or **B** is a dependency of **A**. Suppose **A** is a class that has a method called **importantMethod** that uses **B**, as defined in the following code fragment.

```
public class A {
    public void importantMethod() {
        B b = ... // get an instance of B
```

```
        b.usefulMethod();
        ...
    }
    ...
}
```

A must obtain an instance of **B** before it can use **B**. While it is as straightforward as using the **new** keyword if **B** is a concrete class, it can be problematic if **B** is an interface with many implementations. You will have to choose an implementation of **B** and by doing so you reduce the reusability of **A** because you cannot use **A** with the implementations of **B** that you did not choose.

Dependency injection deals with this kind of situation by taking over object creation and injecting dependencies to an object that needs them. In this case, a dependency injection framework like Spring would create an instance of **A** and an instance of **B** and inject the latter to the former.

To make it possible for a framework to inject a dependency, you have to create a set method or a special constructor in the target class. For example, to make **A** injectable with an instance of **B**, you would modify **A** to this.

```
public class A {
    private B b;
    public void importantMethod() {
        // no need to worry about creating B anymore
        // B b = ... // get an instance of B
        b.usefulMethod();
        ...
    }
    public void setB(B b) {
        this.b = b;
    }
}
```

In the revised version of **A**, there is a setter method that can be called to inject an instance of **B**. Since dependency injection provides dependencies for an object, the **importantMethod** method in **A** no longer needs to create an instance of **B** before being allowed to call its **usefulMethod** method.

Alternatively, if you prefer a constructor, you could modify class **A** to this.

```
public class A {
```

```
    private B b;

    public A(B b) {
        this.b = b;
    }

    public void importantMethod() {
        // no need to worry about creating B anymore
        // B b = ... // get an instance of B
        b.usefulMethod();
        ...
    }
}
```

In this case, Spring would create an instance of **B** before it creates an instance of **A** and injects the former to the latter.

Note
Objects that Spring manages are called beans.

Spring gives you a way to intelligently manage dependencies of your Java objects by providing an Inversion of Control (IoC) container (or a dependency injection container, if you wish). The beauty of Spring is your classes do not need to know anything about Spring, nor do they need to import any Spring types.

Spring supports both setter-based and constructor-based dependency injection since version 1. Starting from Spring 2.5, field-based dependency injection is also made possible via the use of the **Autowired** annotation type. The drawback of using **@Autowired** is you have to import the **org.springframework.beans.factory.annotation.Autowired** annotation type in your class, which makes it dependent on Spring. In such scenarios, porting the application to another dependency injection container would not be straightforward.

With Spring, you practically hand over the creation of all important objects to it. You configure Spring to tell it how it should inject dependencies. There are two types of configuration in Spring, by using an XML file and by employing annotations. You would then create an **ApplicationContext**, which essentially represents a Spring IoC container. The **org.springframework.context.ApplicationContext** interface comes with several implementations, including

ClassPathXmlApplicationContext and
FileSystemXmlApplicationContext. Both expect an XML document or
multiple XML documents that contain information on the beans that it will
manage. A **ClassPathXmlApplicationContext** will try to find the
configuration files in the class path whereas a
FileSystemXmlApplicationContext will try to find them in the file system.

For example, here is code to create an **ApplicationContext** that
searches for **config1.xml** and **config2.xml** files in the class path.

```
ApplicationContext context = new ClassPathXmlApplicationContext(
        new String[] {"config1.xml", "config2.xml"});
```

To obtain a bean from the **ApplicationContext**, call its **getBean** method.

```
Product product = context.getBean("product", Product.class);
```

The **getBean** method above looks for a bean with the id **product** that is of
type **Product**.

Note
Ideally, you only need to create an **ApplicationContext** in a test
class, and your application should not know that it is being managed
by Spring. With Spring MVC you do not deal with
ApplicationContext directly. Instead, you use a Spring servlet to
handle the **ApplicationContext**.

XML-Based Spring Configuration

Spring supports XML-based configuration since version 1.0 as well as
annotation-based configuration starting version 2.5. The following section
discusses how an XML configuration file would look like. The root element
of a Spring configuration file is always **beans**.

```
<?xml version="1.0" encoding="UTF-8"?>
<beans xmlns="http://www.springframework.org/schema/beans"
  xmlns:xsi="http://www.w3.org/2001/XMLSchema-instance"
  xsi:schemaLocation="http://www.springframework.org/schema/beans
  http://www.springframework.org/schema/beans/spring-beans-3.0.xsd">

  ...
```

```
</beans>
```

You can add more schemas to the **schemaLocation** attribute if you need more Spring functionality in your application. In addition, you can split your XML configuration file into multiple files to make it more modular. Implementations of **ApplicationContext** are designed to read multiple configuration files. Alternatively, you can have a main XML configuration file that imports other configuration files.

Here is an example of importing three other XML configuration files from a main configuration file.

```xml
<?xml version="1.0" encoding="UTF-8"?>
<beans xmlns="http://www.springframework.org/schema/beans"
  xmlns:xsi="http://www.w3.org/2001/XMLSchema-instance"
  xsi:schemaLocation="http://www.springframework.org/schema/beans
  http://www.springframework.org/schema/beans/spring-beans-3.0.xsd">

    <import resource="config1.xml"/>
    <import resource="module2/config2.xml"/>
    <import resource="/resources/config3.xml"/>
  ...
</beans>
```

You learn the other subelements of <beans> in the next section.

Using the Spring IoC Container

In this section you learn how to use Spring to manage your objects and dependencies.

Creating A Bean Instance with A Constructor

To get an instance of a bean, call the **getBean** method on the **ApplicationContext**. For example, the XML configuration file in Listing 1.1 contains the definition of a single bean named **product**.

Listing 1.1: A simple configuration file

```xml
<?xml version="1.0" encoding="UTF-8"?>
<beans xmlns="http://www.springframework.org/schema/beans"
```

```
        xmlns:xsi="http://www.w3.org/2001/XMLSchema-instance"
        xsi:schemaLocation="http://www.springframework.org/schema/beans
        http://www.springframework.org/schema/beans/spring-beans-3.0.xsd">

        <bean name="product" class="app01a.bean.Product"/>

</beans>
```

The bean declaration will tell Spring to instantiate the **Product** class using its no-argument (default) constructor. If such a constructor does not exist (because the author of the class defined another constructor and did not explicitly define the default constructor), Spring will throw an exception. The no-argument constructor does not have to be public for Spring to create an instance of the class.

Note that you use the **name** or **id** attribute to identify a bean. To use Spring to create an instance of **Product**, call the **ApplicationContext**'s **getBean** method, passing the bean name or id and its class.

```
ApplicationContext context =
        new ClassPathXmlApplicationContext(
        new String[] {"spring-config.xml"});
Product product1 = context.getBean("product", Product.class);
product1.setName("Excellent snake oil");
System.out.println("product1: " + product1.getName());
```

Creating A Bean Instance with A Factory Method

Most classes will be instantiated using one of their constructors. However, Spring is equally happy if it has to call a factory method to instantiate a class.

The following bean definition specifies a factory method for instantiating **java.util.Calendar**.

```
<bean id="calendar" class="java.util.Calendar"
    factory-method="getInstance"/>
```

Note that instead of the **name** attribute, I used the **id** attribute to identify the bean. You can then use **getBean** to get an instance of **Calendar**.

```
ApplicationContext context =
        new ClassPathXmlApplicationContext(
```

```
            new String[] {"spring-config.xml"});
Calendar calendar = context.getBean("calendar", Calendar.class);
```

Using A Destroy Method

Some classes come with methods that should be called before instances of
the classes are put for garbage collection. Spring supports this notion too. In
your bean declaration, you can use the **destroy-method** attribute to name a
method that should be invoked before the object is decommissioned.

For example, the following **bean** element instructs Spring to create an
instance of **java.util.concurrent.ExecutorService** by calling the static
method **newCachedThreadPool** on the **java.util.concurrent.Executors**
class. The bean definition defines the **shutdown** method as the value of its
destroy-method attribute. As a result, Spring will call **shutdown** before
destroying the **ExecutorService** instance.

```
<bean id="executorService" class="java.util.concurrent.Executors"
    factory-method="newCachedThreadPool"
    destroy-method="shutdown"/>
```

Passing Arguments to a Constructor

Spring can pass arguments to a class constructor if using the constructor is
how it is intended to instantiate the class. Consider the **Product** class in
Listing 1.2.

Listing 1.2: The Product class

```
package app01a.bean;
import java.io.Serializable;

public class Product implements Serializable {
    private static final long serialVersionUID = 748392348L;
    private String name;
    private String description;
    private float price;

    public Product() {
    }

    public Product(String name, String description, float price) {
```

```
            this.name = name;
            this.description = description;
            this.price = price;
    }
    public String getName() {
        return name;
    }
    public void setName(String name) {
        this.name = name;
    }
    public String getDescription() {
        return description;
    }
    public void setDescription(String description) {
        this.description = description;
    }
    public float getPrice() {
        return price;
    }
    public void setPrice(float price) {
        this.price = price;
    }
}
```

The following **bean** definition passes arguments to the **Product** class by name.

```
<bean name="featuredProduct" class="app01a.bean.Product">
    <constructor-arg name="name" value="Ultimate Olive Oil"/>
    <constructor-arg name="description"
        value="The purest olive oil on the market"/>
    <constructor-arg name="price" value="9.95"/>
</bean>
```

In this case, Spring will use the following constructor of the **Product** class.

```
public Product(String name, String description, float price) {
    this.name = name;
    this.description = description;
    this.price = price;
}
```

Passing arguments by name is not the only way to do business in Spring. Spring allows you to pass argument by index. Here is how the **featuredProduct** bean can be rewritten.

```
<bean name="featuredProduct2" class="app01a.bean.Product">
    <constructor-arg index="0" value="Ultimate Olive Oil"/>
    <constructor-arg index="1"
        value="The purest olive oil on the market"/>
    <constructor-arg index="2" value="9.95"/>
</bean>
```

If you choose to pass arguments to a constructor, you must pass all the arguments required by the constructor. An incomplete list of arguments will not be accepted.

Setter-based Dependency Injection

Consider the **Employee** class in Listing 1.3 and the **Address** class in Listing 1.4.

Listing 1.3: The Employee class

```
package app01a.bean;

public class Employee {
    private String firstName;
    private String lastName;
    private Address homeAddress;

    public Employee() {
    }

    public Employee(String firstName, String lastName, Address
        homeAddress) {
        this.firstName = firstName;
        this.lastName = lastName;
        this.homeAddress = homeAddress;
    }

    public String getFirstName() {
        return firstName;
    }

    public void setFirstName(String firstName) {
        this.firstName = firstName;
    }

    public String getLastName() {
```

```
        return lastName;
    }

    public void setLastName(String lastName) {
        this.lastName = lastName;
    }

    public Address getHomeAddress() {
        return homeAddress;
    }

    public void setHomeAddress(Address homeAddress) {
        this.homeAddress = homeAddress;
    }

    @Override
    public String toString() {
        return firstName + " " + lastName
                + "\n" + homeAddress;
    }

}
```

Listing 1.4: The Address class

```
package app01a.bean;

public class Address {
  private String line1;
    private String line2;
    private String city;
    private String state;
    private String zipCode;
    private String country;

    public Address(String line1, String line2, String city,
            String state, String zipCode, String country) {
        this.line1 = line1;
        this.line2 = line2;
        this.city = city;
        this.state = state;
        this.zipCode = zipCode;
        this.country = country;
    }

    // getters and setters omitted
```

```
@Override
public String toString() {
    return line1 + "\n"
            + line2 + "\n"
            + city + "\n"
            + state + " " + zipCode + "\n"
            + country;
    }
}
```

Employee depends on **Address**. To make sure that every **Employee** instance contains an instance of **Address**, you can configure Spring with these two **bean** elements.

```
<bean name="simpleAddress" class="app01a.bean.Address">
    <constructor-arg name="line1" value="151 Corner Street"/>
    <constructor-arg name="line2" value=""/>
    <constructor-arg name="city" value="Albany"/>
    <constructor-arg name="state" value="NY"/>
    <constructor-arg name="zipCode" value="99999"/>
    <constructor-arg name="country" value="US"/>
</bean>

<bean name="employee1" class="app01a.bean.Employee">
    <property name="homeAddress" ref="simpleAddress"/>
    <property name="firstName" value="Junior"/>
    <property name="lastName" value="Moore"/>
</bean>
```

The **simpleAddress** bean instantiates **Address** and passes values to its constructor. The **employee1** bean uses **property** elements to inject values to its setter methods. Of special interest is the **homeAddress** property, which is given the reference of **simpleAddress**.

The bean declaration of a dependency does not have to appear before the declarations of the beans that use it. In this example, **employee1** may appear before **simpleAddress**.

Constructor-based Dependency Injection

Since the **Employee** class in Listing 1.3 provides a constructor that can take values, you can inject an **Address** to an instance of **Employee** through its

constructor. For instance, these bean definitions create an instance of
Employee and inject three values to its constructor.

```
<bean name="employee2" class="app01a.bean.Employee">
    <constructor-arg name="firstName" value="Senior"/>
    <constructor-arg name="lastName" value="Moore"/>
    <constructor-arg name="homeAddress" ref="simpleAddress"/>
</bean>

<bean name="simpleAddress" class="app01a.bean.Address">
    <constructor-arg name="line1" value="151 Corner Street"/>
    <constructor-arg name="line2" value=""/>
    <constructor-arg name="city" value="Albany"/>
    <constructor-arg name="state" value="NY"/>
    <constructor-arg name="zipCode" value="99999"/>
    <constructor-arg name="country" value="US"/>
</bean>
```

Summary

In this chapter you learned about dependency injection and how to use the
Spring IoC container. You will apply what you learned in this chapter to
configure Spring applications in the chapters to come.

Chapter 2
Model 2 and the MVC Pattern

There are two models in Java web application design, conveniently called Model 1 and Model 2. Model 1 is page-centric and suitable for very small applications only. Model 2 is based on the Model-View-Controller (MVC) design pattern and the recommended architecture for all but the simplest Java web applications.

This chapter discusses Model 2 and provides three Model 2 sample applications. The first application features a basic Model 2 application with a servlet as the controller. The second one introduces the use of controller classes. The third one introduces a validator component for validating user input.

Model 1 Overview

When you first learn JSP, your very first applications would normally enable navigation from one page to another by providing links to the JSP pages. While this navigation method is straightforward, in medium-sized or large applications with significant numbers of pages, this approach can cause a maintenance headache. Changing the name of a JSP page, for instance, could force you to rename the links to the page in many other pages. As such, Model 1 is not recommended unless your application will only have two or three pages.

Model 2 Overview

Model 2 is based on the Model-View-Controller (MVC) design pattern, the central concept behind the Smalltalk-80 user interface. As the term "design pattern" had not been coined at that time, it was called the MVC paradigm.

An application implementing the MVC pattern consists of three modules: model, view, and controller. The view takes care of the display of the application. The model encapsulates the application data and business logic. The controller receives user input and commands the model and/or the view to change accordingly.

Note
The paper entitled *Applications Programming in Smalltalk-80(TM): How to use Model-View-Controller (MVC)* by Steve Burbeck, Ph.D. discusses the MVC pattern. You can find it at http://st-www.cs.illinois.edu/users/smarch/st-docs/mvc.html.

In Model 2, you have a servlet or a filter acting as the controller. All modern web frameworks are Model 2 implementations. Frameworks such as Spring MVC and Struts 1 employ a servlet controller in their MVC architectures, whereas Struts 2, another popular framework, uses a filter. Generally JSP pages are employed as the views of the application, even though other view technologies are supported. As the models, you use POJOs (POJO is an acronym for Plain Old Java Object). POJOs are ordinary objects, as opposed to Enterprise JavaBeans (EJB) or other special objects. Many people choose to use a JavaBean (plain JavaBean, not EJB) to store the states of a model object and move business logic to an action class. A JavaBean must have a no-argument constructor and get/set methods for accessing properties. In addition, a JavaBean should be serializable.

Figure 2.1 shows the diagram of a Model 2 application.

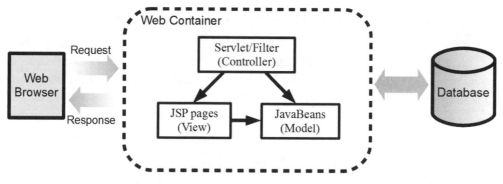

Figure 2.1: Model 2 architecture

In a Model 2 application, every HTTP request must be directed to the controller. The request's Uniform Request Identifier (URI) tells the controller what action to invoke. The term "action" refers to an operation that the application is able to perform. The Java object associated with an action is called an action object. A single action class may be used to serve different actions (as in Spring MVC and Struts 2) or a single action (as in Struts 1).

A seemingly trivial operation may take more than one action. For instance, adding a product to a database would require two actions:

1. Display an "Add Product" form for the user to enter product information.
2. Save the product information in the database.

As mentioned above, you use the URI to tell the controller which action to invoke. For instance, to get the application to send the "Add Product" form, you would use a URI like this:

```
http://domain/appName/product_input
```

To get the application to save a product, the URI would be:

```
http://domain/appName/product_save
```

The controller examines the URI to decide what action to invoke. It also stores the model object in a place that can be accessed from the view, so that server-side values can be displayed on the browser. Finally, the controller uses a **RequestDispatcher** to forward to a view (JSP page). In the JSP page, you use the Expression Language expressions and custom tags to display values.

Note that calling **RequestDispatcher.forward()** does not prevent the code below it from being executed. Therefore, unless the call is the last line in a method, you need to return explicitly.

Model 2 with A Servlet Controller

This section presents a simple Model 2 application to give you a general idea of what a Model 2 application looks like. In real life, Model 2 applications are far more complex than this.

The application can be used to enter product information and is named **app02a**. The user fills in a form like the one in Figure 2.2 and submits it. The application then sends a confirmation page to the user and display the details of the saved product. (See Figure 2.3)

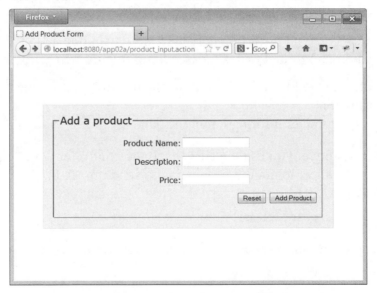

Figure 2.2: The Product form

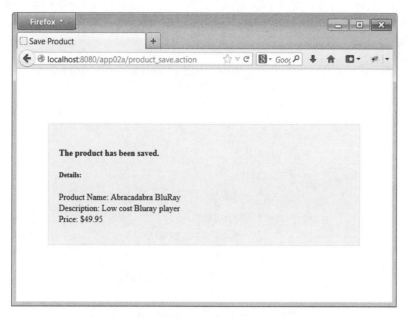

Figure 2.3: The product details page

The application is capable of performing these two actions:

1. Display the "Add Product" form. This action sends the entry form in Figure 2.2 to the browser. The URI to invoke this action must contain the string **product_input**.
2. Save the product and returns the confirmation page in Figure 2.3. The URI to invoke this action must contain the string **product_save**.

The **app02a** application consists of the following components:

1. A **Product** class that is the template for product domain objects. An instance of this class contains product information.
2. A **ProductForm** class, which encapsulates the fields of the HTML form for inputting a product. The properties of a **ProductForm** are used to populate a **Product**.
3. A **ControllerServlet** class, which is the controller of this Model 2 application.
4. An action class named **SaveProductAction**.
5. Two JSP pages (**ProductForm.jsp** and **ProductDetails.jsp**) as the views.

6. A CSS file that defines the styles of the views. This is a static resource.

The directory structure of this application is shown in Figure 2.4.

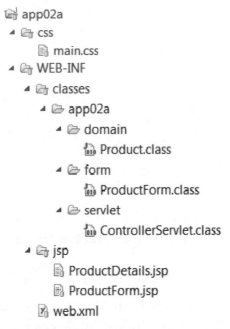

Figure 2.4: The directory structure of app02a

Note that all JSP pages are stored in a directory under **WEB-INF** so they cannot be accessed directly.

Let's take a closer look at each component in **app02a**.

The Product Class

A **Product** instance is a JavaBean that encapsulates product information. The **Product** class (shown in Listing 2.1) has three properties: **productName**, **description**, and **price**.

Listing 2.1: The Product class

```
package app02a.domain;
import java.io.Serializable;
```

```
public class Product implements Serializable {
    private static final long serialVersionUID = 748392348L;
    private String name;
    private String description;
    private float price;

    public String getName() {
            return name;
    }
      public void setName(String name) {
            this.name = name;
    }
    public String getDescription() {
        return description;
    }
    public void setDescription(String description) {
        this.description = description;
    }
    public float getPrice() {
        return price;
    }
    public void setPrice(float price) {
        this.price = price;
    }
}
```

The **Product** class implements **java.io.Serializable** so that its instances can be stored safely in the **HttpSession**. As an implementation of **Serializable**, **Product** should have a **serialVersionUID** field.

The ProductForm Class

A form class is mapped to an HTML form. It is the representation of the HTML form on the server. The **ProductForm** class, given in Listing 2.2, contains the **String** values of a product. At a glance the **ProductForm** class is similar to the **Product** class and you might question why **ProductForm** needs to exist at all. A form object, as you can see in the section "Validators" later in this chapter, saves passing the **ServletRequest** to other components, such as validators. **ServletRequest** is a servlet-specific type and should not be exposed to the other layers in the application.

The second purpose of a form object is to preserve and redisplay user input in its original form if input validation fails. You will learn how to do this in the section "Validators" later in this chapter.

Note that most of the time a form class does not have to implement **Serializable** as form objects are rarely stored in an **HttpSession**.

Listing 2.2: The ProductForm class

```
package app02a.form;
public class ProductForm {
    private String name;
    private String description;
    private String price;

    public String getName() {
        return name;
    }
    public void setName(String name) {
        this.name = name;
    }
    public String getDescription() {
        return description;
    }
    public void setDescription(String description) {
        this.description = description;
    }
    public String getPrice() {
        return price;
    }
    public void setPrice(String price) {
        this.price = price;
    }
}
```

The ControllerServlet Class

The **ControllerServlet** class (presented in Listing 2.3) extends the **javax.servlet.http.HttpServlet** class. Both its **doGet** and **doPost** methods call the **process** method, which is the brain of the servlet controller.

I am probably raising a few eyebrows here by naming the servlet controller **ControllerServlet**, but I'm following the convention that says all servlet classes should be suffixed with **Servlet**.

Listing 2.3: The ControllerServlet Class

```java
package app02a.servlet;
import java.io.IOException;

import javax.servlet.RequestDispatcher;
import javax.servlet.ServletException;
import javax.servlet.http.HttpServlet;
import javax.servlet.http.HttpServletRequest;
import javax.servlet.http.HttpServletResponse;

import app02a.domain.Product;
import app02a.form.ProductForm;

public class ControllerServlet extends HttpServlet {

    private static final long serialVersionUID = 1579L;

    @Override
    public void doGet(HttpServletRequest request,
            HttpServletResponse response)
            throws IOException, ServletException {
        process(request, response);
    }

    @Override
    public void doPost(HttpServletRequest request,
            HttpServletResponse response)
            throws IOException, ServletException {
        process(request, response);
    }

    private void process(HttpServletRequest request,
            HttpServletResponse response)
            throws IOException, ServletException {

        String uri = request.getRequestURI();
        /*
         * uri is in this form: /contextName/resourceName,
         * for example: /app10a/product_input.
         * However, in the event of a default context, the
         * context name is empty, and uri has this form
         * /resourceName, e.g.: /product_input
         */
        int lastIndex = uri.lastIndexOf("/");
        String action = uri.substring(lastIndex + 1);
```

```java
            // execute an action
            if (action.equals("product_input.action")) {
                // no action class, there is nothing to be done
            } else if (action.equals("product_save.action")) {
                // create form
                ProductForm productForm = new ProductForm();
                // populate action properties
                productForm.setName(request.getParameter("name"));
                productForm.setDescription(
                        request.getParameter("description"));
                productForm.setPrice(request.getParameter("price"));

                // create model
                Product product = new Product();
                product.setName(productForm.getName());
                product.setDescription(productForm.getDescription());
                try {
                    product.setPrice(Float.parseFloat(
                            productForm.getPrice()));
                } catch (NumberFormatException e) {
                }

                // code to save product

                // store model in a scope variable for the view
                request.setAttribute("product", product);
            }

            // forward to a view
            String dispatchUrl = null;
            if (action.equals("product_input.action")) {
                dispatchUrl = "/WEB-INF/jsp/ProductForm.jsp";
            } else if (action.equals("product_save.action")) {
                dispatchUrl = "/WEB-INF/jsp/ProductDetails.jsp";
            }
            if (dispatchUrl != null) {
                RequestDispatcher rd =
                        request.getRequestDispatcher(dispatchUrl);
                rd.forward(request, response);
            }
        }
    }
```

Note that if you're using Servlet 3.0, you can also annotate your servlet class so that you don't have to map it in the deployment descriptor.

```
...
import javax.servlet.annotation.WebServlet;
...

@WebServlet(name = "ControllerServlet", urlPatterns = {
        "/product_input", "/product_save" })
public class ControllerServlet extends HttpServlet {
    ...
}
```

The **process** method in the **ControllerServlet** class processes all incoming requests. It starts by obtaining the request URI and the action name.

```
String uri = request.getRequestURI();
int lastIndex = uri.lastIndexOf("/");
String action = uri.substring(lastIndex + 1);
```

The value of **action** in this application can be either **product_input** or **product_save**.

The **process** method then continues by performing these steps:

1. Create and populate a form object with request parameters. There are three properties in the **product_save** action: **name**, **description**, and **price**. Next, create a domain object and populate its properties from the form object.
2. Perform business logic to handle the domain object, such as saving it to a database.
3. Forward the request to a view (JSP page).

The part of the **process** method that determines what action to perform is in the following **if** block:

```
// execute an action
if (action.equals("product_input")) {
    // there is nothing to be done
} else if (action.equals("product_save")) {
    ...
    // code to save product
}
```

There is no action class to instantiate for action **product_input**. For **product_save**, the **process** method creates a **ProductForm** and a **Product** and copies values from the former to the latter. At this stage, there's no guarantee all non-string properties, such as **price**, can be copied successfully, but we'll deal with this later in the section "Validators."

The **process** method then instantiates the **SaveProductAction** class and calls its **save** method.

```
// create form
ProductForm productForm = new ProductForm();
// populate action properties
productForm.setName(request.getParameter("name"));
productForm.setDescription(
        request.getParameter("description"));
productForm.setPrice(request.getParameter("price"));

// create model
Product product = new Product();
product.setName(productForm.getName());
product.setDescription(product.getDescription());
try {
    product.setPrice(Float.parseFloat(
            productForm.getPrice()));
} catch (NumberFormatException e) {
}
// execute action method
SaveProductAction saveProductAction =
        new SaveProductAction();
saveProductAction.save(product);

// store model in a scope variable for the view
request.setAttribute("product", product);
```

The **Product** is then stored in the **HttpServletRequest** so that the view for this action can access it.

```
// store action in a scope variable for the view
request.setAttribute("product", product);
```

The **process** method concludes by forwarding to a view. If **action** equals **product_input**, control is forwarded to the **ProductForm.jsp** page. If **action** is **product_save**, control is forwarded to the **ProductDetails.jsp** page.

```
// forward to a view
String dispatchUrl = null;
```

```
    if (action.equals("Product_input")) {
        dispatchUrl = "/WEB-INF/jsp/ProductForm.jsp";
    } else if (action.equals("Product_save")) {
        dispatchUrl = "/WEB-INF/jsp/ProductDetails.jsp";
    }
    if (dispatchUrl != null) {
        RequestDispatcher rd =
                request.getRequestDispatcher(dispatchUrl);
        rd.forward(request, response);
    }
```

The Views

The application utilizes two JSP pages for the views of the application. The first page, **ProductForm.jsp**, is displayed if the action is **product_input**. The second page, **ProductDetails.jsp**, is shown for **product_save**. **ProductForm.jsp** is given in Listing 2.4 and **ProductDetails.jsp** in Listing 2.5.

Listing 2.4: The ProductForm.jsp page

```
<!DOCTYPE HTML>
<html>
<head>
<title>Add Product Form</title>
<style type="text/css">@import url(css/main.css);</style>
</head>
<body>

<div id="global">
<form action="product_save.action" method="post">
    <fieldset>
        <legend>Add a product</legend>
        <p>
            <label for="name">Product Name: </label>
            <input type="text" id="name" name="name"
                    tabindex="1">
        </p>
        <p>
            <label for="description">Description: </label>
            <input type="text" id="description"
                    name="description" tabindex="2">
        </p>
        <p>
```

```
              <label for="price">Price: </label>
              <input type="text" id="price" name="price"
                     tabindex="3">
        </p>
        <p id="buttons">
              <input id="reset" type="reset" tabindex="4">
              <input id="submit" type="submit" tabindex="5"
                     value="Add Product">
        </p>
     </fieldset>
</form>
</div>
</body>
</html>
```

Listing 2.5: The ProductDetails.jsp page

```
<!DOCTYPE HTML>
<html>
<head>
<title>Save Product</title>
<style type="text/css">@import url(css/main.css);</style>
</head>
<body>
<div id="global">
    <h4>The product has been saved.</h4>
    <p>
        <h5>Details:</h5>
        Product Name: ${product.name}<br/>
        Description: ${product.description}<br/>
        Price: $${product.price}
    </p>
</div>
</body>
</html>
```

The **ProductForm.jsp** page contains an HTML form for entering product details. I have taken the effort to avoid using an HTML table to lay out the HTML elements. Instead, the elements are styled using CSS styles in the main.css file in the **css** directory.

The **ProductDetails.jsp** page uses the Expression Language (EL) to access the **product** scoped-object in the **HttpServletRequest**. You'll learn more about the EL in Chapter 8, "The Expression Language."

In this application, as is the case for most Model 2 applications, you need to prevent the JSP pages from being accessed directly from the browser. There are a number of ways to achieve this, including:

- Putting the JSP pages under **WEB-INF**. Anything under **WEB-INF** or a subdirectory under **WEB-INF** is protected. If you put your JSP pages under **WEB-INF** you cannot access them directly from the browser, but the controller can still dispatch requests to those pages. This method is chosen for this application.
- Using a servlet filter and filter out requests for JSP pages.
- Using security restriction in the deployment descriptor. This is easier than using a filter since you do not have to write a filter class.

Testing the Application

Assuming you are running the application on port 8080 of your local machine, you can invoke the application using the following URL:

```
http://localhost:8080/app02a/product_input.action
```

You will see something similar to Figure 2.2 in your browser.

When you submit the form, the following URL will be sent to the server:

```
http://localhost:8080/app02a/product_save.action
```

Using a servlet controller allows you to use the servlet as a welcome page. This is an important feature since you can then configure your application so that the servlet controller will be invoked simply by typing your domain name (such as http://example.com) in the browser's address box. You can't do this with a filter.

Isolating Code in Controller Classes

The business logic in **app02a** was written in the servlet controller. You guess right, the servlet can easily become bloated as the application grows more complex. To prevent this from happening, you should isolate business logic in separate classes called controller classes.

The **app02b** application is a revised version of **app02a**. In **app02b** you have two controller classes (**InputProductController** and **SaveProductController**) in a directory named **controller**. The application's directory structure is given in Figure 2.5.

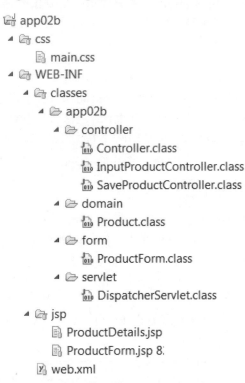

Figure 2.5: The directory structure of app02b

Both controllers in **app02b** implement the **Controller** interface in Listing 2.6. This interface has only one method, **handleRequest**, which allows access to the **HttpServletRequest** and **HttpServletResponse** of the current request to the implementing class.

Listing 2.6: The Controller interface

```
package app02b.controller;

import javax.servlet.http.HttpServletRequest;
import javax.servlet.http.HttpServletResponse;

public interface Controller {
```

```
        String handleRequest(HttpServletRequest request,
                HttpServletResponse response);
}
```

The **InputProductController** class (given in Listing 2.7) simply returns a path to the **ProductForm.jsp** page. The **SaveProductController** class (shown in Listing 2.8) reads the request parameters to populate a **ProductForm**, and then use the **ProductForm** to populate a new **Product** object before returning the path to the **ProductDetails.jsp** page.

Listing 2.7: The InputProductController class

```java
package app02b.controller;

import javax.servlet.http.HttpServletRequest;
import javax.servlet.http.HttpServletResponse;

public class InputProductController implements Controller {
    @Override
    public String handleRequest(HttpServletRequest request,
            HttpServletResponse response) {

        return "/WEB-INF/jsp/ProductForm.jsp";
    }
}
```

Listing 2.8: The SaveProductController class

```java
package app02b.controller;

import javax.servlet.http.HttpServletRequest;
import javax.servlet.http.HttpServletResponse;

import app02b.domain.Product;
import app02b.form.ProductForm;

public class SaveProductController implements Controller {

    @Override
    public String handleRequest(HttpServletRequest request,
            HttpServletResponse response) {
        ProductForm productForm = new ProductForm();
        // populate form properties
        productForm.setName(
                request.getParameter("name"));
        productForm.setDescription(
```

```
                       request.getParameter("description"));
        productForm.setPrice(request.getParameter("price"));

        // create model
        Product product = new Product();
        product.setName(productForm.getName());
        product.setDescription(productForm.getDescription());
        try {
            product.setPrice(Float.parseFloat(
                        productForm.getPrice()));
        } catch (NumberFormatException e) {
        }

        // insert code to add product to the database

        request.setAttribute("product", product);
        return "/WEB-INF/jsp/ProductDetails.jsp";
    }
}
```

The positive effect of migrating business logic to controller classes is that the controller servlet has now become very slim, just as intended. It now acts more like a dispatcher than a controller and I've changed its name to **DipatcherServlet**. The **DispatcherServlet** class, printed in Listing 2.9, checks each URI, creates the appropriate controller, and calls the controller's **handleRequest** method.

Listing 2.9: The DispatcherServlet class

```
package app02b.servlet;

import java.io.IOException;
import javax.servlet.RequestDispatcher;
import javax.servlet.ServletException;
import javax.servlet.http.HttpServlet;
import javax.servlet.http.HttpServletRequest;
import javax.servlet.http.HttpServletResponse;
import app02b.controller.InputProductController;
import app02b.controller.SaveProductController;

public class DispatcherServlet extends HttpServlet {

    private static final long serialVersionUID = 748495L;

    @Override
```

```java
public void doGet(HttpServletRequest request,
        HttpServletResponse response)
        throws IOException, ServletException {
    process(request, response);
}

@Override
public void doPost(HttpServletRequest request,
        HttpServletResponse response)
        throws IOException, ServletException {
    process(request, response);
}

private void process(HttpServletRequest request,
        HttpServletResponse response)
        throws IOException, ServletException {

    String uri = request.getRequestURI();
    /*
     * uri is in this form: /contextName/resourceName,
     * for example: /app10a/product_input.
     * However, in the event of a default context, the
     * context name is empty, and uri has this form
     * /resourceName, e.g.: /product_input
     */
    int lastIndex = uri.lastIndexOf("/");
    String action = uri.substring(lastIndex + 1);

    String dispatchUrl = null;
    if (action.equals("product_input.action")) {
        InputProductController controller =
                new InputProductController();
        dispatchUrl = controller.handleRequest(request,
                response);
    } else if (action.equals("product_save.action")) {
        SaveProductController controller =
                new SaveProductController();
        dispatchUrl = controller.handleRequest(request,
                response);
    }

    if (dispatchUrl != null) {
        RequestDispatcher rd =
                request.getRequestDispatcher(dispatchUrl);
        rd.forward(request, response);
    }
```

```
        }
}
```

To test the application, direct your browser to this URL.

```
http://localhost:8080/app02b/product_input.action
```

Validators

Input validation is an important step when performing an action. Validation ranges from simple tasks like checking if an input field has a value to more complex ones like verifying a credit card number. In fact, validation play such an important role that the Java community has published JSR 303, "Bean Validation" and JSR 349, "Bean Validation 1.1" to standardize input validation in Java. Modern MVC frameworks often offer both programmatic and declarative validation methods. In programmatic validation, you write code to validate user input. In declarative validation, you provide validation rules in an XML document or properties file.

The following example features a new application (**app02c**) that extends the servlet controller-based Model 2 application in **app02b**.

Figure 2.6 shows the directory structure of **app02c**.

The new application is similar to **app02b**, except that it incorporates a **ProductValidator** class and two JSTL JAR files in its **WEB-INF/lib** directory. JSTL is discussed in Chapter 9, "JSTL." For now, it suffices to say that it helps with the displaying of validation error messages in the **ProductForm.jsp** page.

The **ProductValidator** class is given in Listing 2.10.

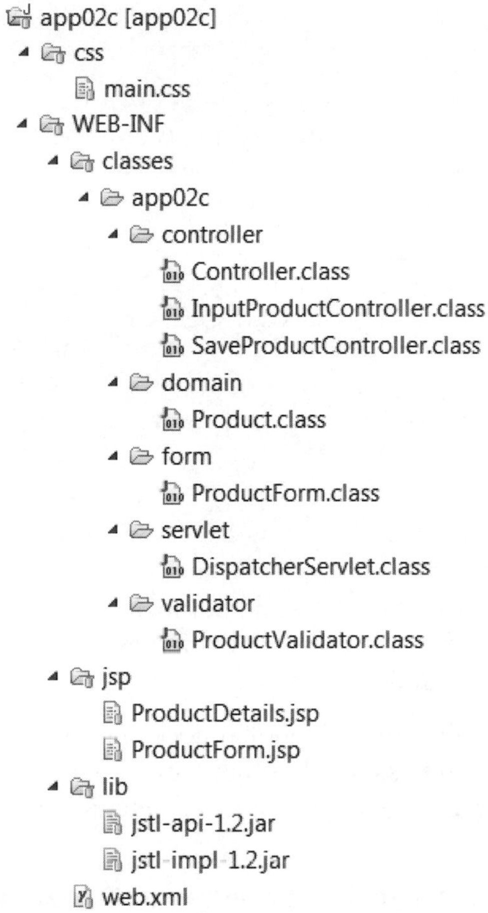

```
🖳 app02c [app02c]
  ▲ 🗁 css
        📄 main.css
  ▲ 🗁 WEB-INF
      ▲ 🗁 classes
          ▲ 🗁 app02c
              ▲ 🗁 controller
                    🗿 Controller.class
                    🗿 InputProductController.class
                    🗿 SaveProductController.class
              ▲ 🗁 domain
                    🗿 Product.class
              ▲ 🗁 form
                    🗿 ProductForm.class
              ▲ 🗁 servlet
                    🗿 DispatcherServlet.class
              ▲ 🗁 validator
                    🗿 ProductValidator.class
      ▲ 🗁 jsp
            📄 ProductDetails.jsp
            📄 ProductForm.jsp
      ▲ 🗁 lib
            📄 jstl-api-1.2.jar
            📄 jstl-impl-1.2.jar
        📄 web.xml
```

Figure 2.6: The directory structure of app02c

Listing 2.10: The ProductValidator class

```java
package app02c.validator;

import java.util.ArrayList;
import java.util.List;
import app02c.form.ProductForm;

public class ProductValidator {

    public List<String> validate(ProductForm productForm) {
        List<String> errors = new ArrayList<String>();
        String name = productForm.getName();
```

```
            if (name == null || name.trim().isEmpty()) {
                errors.add("Product must have a name");
            }
            String price = productForm.getPrice();
            if (price == null || price.trim().isEmpty()) {
                errors.add("Product must have a price");
            } else {
                try {
                    Float.parseFloat(price);
                } catch (NumberFormatException e) {
                    errors.add("Invalid price value");
                }
            }
            return errors;
        }
    }
}
```

The **ProductValidator** class in Listing 2.10 offers a **validate** method that works on a **ProductForm**. The validator makes sure that a product has a non-empty name and its price is a valid number. The **validate** method returns a **List** of **String**s containing validation error messages. An empty **List** means successful validation.

The only place in the application that needs product validation is when the product information is saved. In other words, in the **SaveProductController** class. Let's now change the class to incorporate the **ProductValidator**.

Listing 2.11 shows the revised **SaveProductController** class.

Listing 2.11: The SaveProductController class in app02c

```
package app02c.controller;

import java.util.List;
import javax.servlet.http.HttpServletRequest;
import javax.servlet.http.HttpServletResponse;
import app02c.domain.Product;
import app02c.form.ProductForm;
import app02c.validator.ProductValidator;

public class SaveProductController implements Controller {

    @Override
    public String handleRequest(HttpServletRequest request,
```

```
        HttpServletResponse response) {
    ProductForm productForm = new ProductForm();
    // populate action properties
    productForm.setName(request.getParameter("name"));
    productForm.setDescription(request.getParameter(
            "description"));
    productForm.setPrice(request.getParameter("price"));

    // validate ProductForm
    ProductValidator productValidator = new ProductValidator();
    List<String> errors =
            productValidator.validate(productForm);
    if (errors.isEmpty()) {
        // create Product from ProductForm
        Product product = new Product();
        product.setName(productForm.getName());
        product.setDescription(productForm.getDescription());
        product.setPrice(Float.parseFloat(
                productForm.getPrice()));

        // no validation error, execute action method
        // insert code to save product to the database

        // store product in a scope variable for the view
        request.setAttribute("product", product);
        return "/WEB-INF/jsp/ProductDetails.jsp";
    } else {
        //store errors and form in a scope variable for the view
        request.setAttribute("errors", errors);
        request.setAttribute("form", productForm);
        return "/WEB-INF/jsp/ProductForm.jsp";
    }
    }
}
```

The new **SaveProductController** class in Listing 2.11 inserts code that instantiates the **ProductValidator** class and calls its **validate** method.

```
    // validate ProductForm
    ProductValidator productValidator = new ProductValidator();
    List<String> errors =
            productValidator.validate(productForm);
```

If there is a validation error, the **handleRequest** method in **SaveProductController** forwards to the **ProductForm.jsp** page.

Otherwise, it creates a **Product** object, populates its properties, and returns
/WEB-INF/jsp/ProductDetails.jsp.

```
if (errors.isEmpty()) {
    // create Product from ProductForm
    Product product = new Product();
    product.setName(productForm.getName());
    product.setDescription(productForm.getDescription());
    product.setPrice(Float.parseFloat(
            productForm.getPrice()));

    // no validation error, execute action method
    // insert code to save product to the database

    // store product in a scope variable for the view
    request.setAttribute("product", product);
    return "/WEB-INF/jsp/ProductDetails.jsp";
} else {
    //store errors and form in a scope variable for the view
    request.setAttribute("errors", errors);
    request.setAttribute("form", productForm);
    return "/WEB-INF/jsp/ProductForm.jsp";
}
```

Of course, in a real-world application, there must be code that actually saves
the **Product** in a database or some form of storage. For now, let's focus on
input validation.

The **ProductForm.jsp** page in **app02c** has been modified to give it the
capability of showing error messages and redisplaying invalid values.
Listing 2.12 shows the **ProductForm.jsp** in **app02c**.

Listing 2.12: The ProductForm.jsp page in app02c

```
<%@ taglib uri="http://java.sun.com/jsp/jstl/core" prefix="c" %>
<!DOCTYPE HTML>
<html>
<head>
<title>Add Product Form</title>
<style type="text/css">@import url(css/main.css);</style>
</head>
<body>

<div id="global">
<c:if test="${requestScope.errors != null}">
        <p id="errors">
```

```
        Error(s)!
        <ul>
        <c:forEach var="error" items="${requestScope.errors}">
            <li>${error}</li>
        </c:forEach>
        </ul>
        </p>
</c:if>
<form action="product_save.action" method="post">
    <fieldset>
        <legend>Add a product</legend>
            <p>
                <label for="name">Product Name: </label>
                <input type="text" id="name" name="name"
                    tabindex="1">
            </p>
            <p>
                <label for="description">Description: </label>
                <input type="text" id="description"
                    name="description" tabindex="2">
            </p>
            <p>
                <label for="price">Price: </label>
                <input type="text" id="price" name="price"
                    tabindex="3">
            </p>
            <p id="buttons">
                <input id="reset" type="reset" tabindex="4">
                <input id="submit" type="submit" tabindex="5"
                    value="Add Product">
            </p>
    </fieldset>
</form>
</div>
</body>
</html>
```

You can test **app02c** by invoking the **product_input** action:

```
http://localhost:8080/app02c/product_input.action
```

If the Product form contains an invalid value when you submit it, an error message will be displayed along with the incorrect value. Figure 2.7 shows two validation error messages.

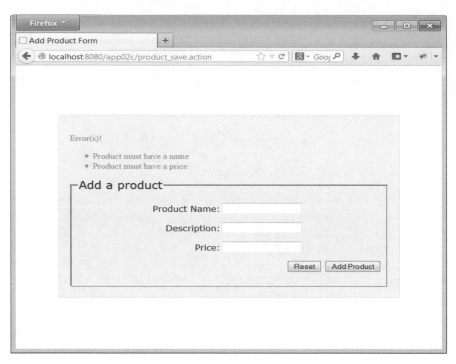

Figure 2.7: The ProductForm with error mesages

The Back End

Applications **app02a**, **app02b**, and **app02c** demonstrated how to deal with the front end. Now, what about the back end? Surely you need one for dealing with the database and so on.

Using MVC, you can call the back end business logic from your controller classes. Normally, you would want several Service classes that encapsulate the complexity of the back end stuff. From a Service class, you would instantiate a DAO class for accessing the database. In a Spring environment, as demonstrated in later chapters, Service objects can be automatically injected to controller instances and DAO objects to Service objects.

Summary

In this chapter you learned about the Model 2 architecture, which is based on the MVC pattern, and how to write Model 2 applications. In a Model 2 application, JSP pages are often used as the view, even though other technologies such as Apache Velocity and FreeMarker can also be used. If JSP pages are used as the view in a Model 2 architecture, those pages are used to display values only and no scripting elements should be present in them.

In this chapter you also built a simple MVC framework incorporating such components as a validator.

Chapter 3
Introduction to Spring MVC

In Chapter 2, "Model 2 and the MVC Pattern" you learned that the widely used design of modern web applications follow the MVC pattern. You also learned the advantages of the Model 2 architecture and how to build Model 2 applications. Spring MVC is a framework that helps developers write MVC applications more rapidly.

This chapter starts by discussing the benefits of Spring MVC and how it expedites Model 2 application development. It also discusses some basic components of Spring MVC, such as the Dispatcher Servlet, and teaches you how to write "old-style" controllers that were the only way of writing controllers in older versions of Spring prior to version 2.5. Another type of controller is covered in Chapter 4, "Annotation-based Controllers." The old style controller is discussed here because you might still have to work with legacy code written with older versions of Spring. For new developments, however, you should use annotation-based controllers.

Introducing Spring MVC configuration is another objective of this chapter. Most Spring MVC applications will have an XML file for declaring various beans that are used in the applications.

The Benefits of Spring MVC

When writing a Model 2 application without a framework, it is your responsibility to write a dispatcher servlet and controller classes. Your dispatcher servlet must be capable of doing these things:

1. Determine from the URI what action to invoke.
2. Instantiate the correct controller class.
3. Populate a form bean with request parameter values.

4. Call the correct method in the controller object.

5. Forward control to a view (JSP page).

Spring MVC is an MVC framework that employs a dispatcher servlet that invokes methods in controllers and forwards control to a view. This is the first benefit of using Spring MVC: You don't need to write your own dispatcher servlet. Here is the list of features that Spring MVC is equipped with to make development more rapid.

- Spring MVC provides a dispatcher servlet, saving your writing one.
- Spring MVC employs an XML-based configuration file that you can edit without recompiling the application.
- Spring MVC instantiates controller classes and populates beans with user inputs.
- Spring MVC automatically binds user input with the correct type. For example, Spring MVC can automatically parse a string and sets a property of type float or decimal.
- Spring MVC validates user input and redirects the user back to the input form if validation failed. Input validation is optional and can be done programmatically or declaratively. On top of that, Spring MVC provides built-in validators for most of the tasks you may encounter when building a web application.
- Spring MVC is part of the Spring framework. You get everything Spring has to offer.
- Spring MVC supports internationalization and localization. This means, you can display messages in multiple languages depending on the user locale.
- Spring MVC supports multiple view technologies. Most of the time you'll be using JSP, but other technologies are supported, including Velocity and FreeMarker.

Spring MVC DispatcherServlet

Recall that in Chapter 2, "Model 2 and the MVC Pattern" you built a simple MVC framework that consisted of a servlet that acted as a dispatcher. With Spring MVC, you don't have to do that. Spring MVC comes with a

dispatcher servlet that you can instantly use. Its fully qualified name is
org.springframework.web.servlte.DispatcherServlet.

To use this servlet, you need to configure it in your deployment
descriptor (**web.xml** file) using the **servlet** and **servlet-mapping** elements,
like this.

```
<servlet>
    <servlet-name>springmvc</servlet-name>
    <servlet-class
        org.springframework.web.servlet.DispatcherServlet
    </servlet-class>
    <load-on-startup>1</load-on-startup>
</servlet>

<servlet-mapping>
    <servlet-name>springmvc</servlet-name>
    <!-- map all requests to the DispatcherServlet -->
    <url-pattern>/</url-pattern>
</servlet-mapping>
```

The **load-on-startup** element under **<servlet>** is optional. If it is present, it
will load the servlet and call its **init** method when the application is started.
Without the **load-on-startup** element, the servlet will be loaded when it is
first requested.

By itself the dispatcher servlet will use many default components that
come with Spring MVC. In addition, at initialization it will look for a
configuration file in the **WEB-INF** directory of the application. The name
of the XML file must conform to this pattern

servletName-servlet.xml

where *servletName* is the name given to the Spring dispatcher servlet in the
deployment descriptor. If you have given the servlet the name **springmvc**,
you will need to have a **springmvc-servlet.xml** file under the **WEB-INF**
directory of your application directory.

However, you can place your Spring MVC configuration file anywhere
within your application directory as long as you tell the dispatcher servlet
where to find it. You do this by using an **init-param** element under the
servlet declaration. The **init-param** element would have a **param-name**
element that has the value **contextConfigLocation**. It would also have a

param-value element containing the path to your configuration file. For example, you can change the default name and location of the configuration file to **/WEB-INF/config/simple-config.xml** by using this **init-param** element.

```
<servlet>
    <servlet-name>springmvc</servlet-name>
    <servlet-class>
        org.springframework.web.servlet.DispatcherServlet
    </servlet-class>
    <init-param>
        <param-name>contextConfigLocation</param-name>
        <param-value>/WEB-INF/config/simple-config.xml</param-value>
    </init-param>
    <load-on-startup>1</load-on-startup>
</servlet>
```

The Controller Interface

Prior to Spring 2.5, the only way to write a controller was by implementing the **org.springframework.web.servlet.mvc.Controller** interface. This interface exposes a **handleRequest** method that must be overidden by implementing classes. Here is the signature of the method.

```
ModelAndView handleRequest(HttpServletRequest request,
        HttpServletResponse response)
```

An implementation has access to the **HttpServletRequest** and **HttpServletResponse** of the corresponding request. The implementation must also return a **ModelAndView** that contains a view path or a view path and a model.

A controller implementing the **Controller** interface can only handle one single action. On the other hand, an annnotation-based controller can house many request-handling methods and do not have to implement any interface. You will learn about the latter in Chapter 4, "Annotation-based Controllers."

Your First Spring MVC Application

The **app03a** sample application showcases a basic Spring MVC application. The application is very similar to the **app02b** application you learned in Chapter 2. It was deliberately made so to show you how Spring MVC works. The **app03a** application also has two controllers that are similar to the ones in **app02b**.

The Directory Structure

Figure 3.1 shows the directory structure of **app03a**. Note that the **WEB-INF/lib** directory contains all the jar files required by Spring MVC. Of special interest is the **spring-webmvc-x.y.z.jar** file, which contains the **DispatcherServlet** class. Also note that Spring MVC depends on the Apache Commons Logging component and without it your Spring MVC applications won't work. You can download this component from this site.

```
http://commons.apache.org/proper/commons-loggins/
download_logging.cgi
```

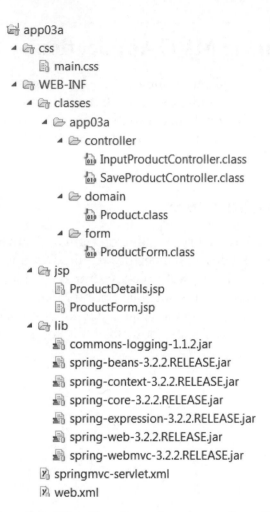

Figure 3.1: The directory structure of app03a

The JSP pages for this application are stored under **/WEB-INF/jsp** to keep them from direct access.

The Deployment Descriptor and Spring MVC Configuration File

Now look at the deployment descriptor (**web.xml** file) in Listing 3.1.

Listing 3.1: The deployment descriptor for app03a

```xml
<?xml version="1.0" encoding="UTF-8"?>
<web-app version="3.0"
    xmlns="http://java.sun.com/xml/ns/javaee"
    xmlns:xsi="http://www.w3.org/2001/XMLSchema-instance"
    xsi:schemaLocation="http://java.sun.com/xml/ns/javaee
http://java.sun.com/xml/ns/javaee/web-app_3_0.xsd">

    <servlet>
        <servlet-name>springmvc</servlet-name>
        <servlet-class>
            org.springframework.web.servlet.DispatcherServlet
        </servlet-class>
        <load-on-startup>1</load-on-startup>
    </servlet>

    <servlet-mapping>
        <servlet-name>springmvc</servlet-name>
        <!-- map all requests to the DispatcherServlet -->
        <url-pattern>/</url-pattern>
    </servlet-mapping>

</web-app>
```

Nothing spectacular here. You're just telling the servlet/JSP container that you want to use the Spring MVC dispatcher servlet and map it to all URLs by using / in the **url-pattern** element. Since there is no **init-param** element under the **servlet** element, the Spring MVC configuration file is assumed to be under **/WEB-INF** and follow the usual naming convention.

Next, examine the Spring MVC configuration file (**springmvc-servlet.xml** file) in Listing 3.2.

Listing 3.2: The Spring MVC configuration file

```xml
<?xml version="1.0" encoding="UTF-8"?>
<beans xmlns="http://www.springframework.org/schema/beans"
  xmlns:xsi="http://www.w3.org/2001/XMLSchema-instance"
  xsi:schemaLocation="http://www.springframework.org/schema/beans
  http://www.springframework.org/schema/beans/spring-beans-3.0.xsd">

    <bean name="/product_input.action"
        class="app03a.controller.InputProductController"/>
    <bean name="/product_save.action"
```

```
        class="app03a.controller.SaveProductController"/>

</beans>
```

Here you declare two controller classes, **InputProductController** and **SaveProductController**, and map them to **/product_input.action** and **/product_save.action**, respectively. The controllers are discussed in the next section.

The Controllers

The **app03a** application has two "old-style" controllers, **InputProductController** and **SaveProductController**. Both implement the **Controller** interface. The **InputProductController** class is given in Listing 3.3 and **SaveProductControler** in Listing 3.4.

Listing 3.3: The InputProductController class

```
package app03a.controller;

import javax.servlet.http.HttpServletRequest;
import javax.servlet.http.HttpServletResponse;
import org.apache.commons.logging.Log;
import org.apache.commons.logging.LogFactory;
import org.springframework.web.servlet.ModelAndView;
import org.springframework.web.servlet.mvc.Controller;

public class InputProductController implements Controller {

    private static final Log logger = LogFactory
            .getLog(InputProductController.class);

    @Override
    public ModelAndView handleRequest(HttpServletRequest request,
            HttpServletResponse response) throws Exception {
        logger.info("InputProductController called");
        return new ModelAndView("/WEB-INF/jsp/ProductForm.jsp");
    }
}
```

The **handleRequest** method of the **InputProductController** class simply returns a **ModelAndView** that contains a view with no model. In this case, the request will be forwarded to the **/WEB-INF/jsp/ProductForm.jsp** page.

Listing 3.4: The SaveProductController class

```
package app03a.controller;

import javax.servlet.http.HttpServletRequest;
import javax.servlet.http.HttpServletResponse;
import org.apache.commons.logging.Log;
import org.apache.commons.logging.LogFactory;
import org.springframework.web.servlet.ModelAndView;
import org.springframework.web.servlet.mvc.Controller;
import app03a.domain.Product;
import app03a.form.ProductForm;

public class SaveProductController implements Controller {

    private static final Log logger = LogFactory
            .getLog(SaveProductController.class);

    @Override
    public ModelAndView handleRequest(HttpServletRequest request,
            HttpServletResponse response) throws Exception {
        logger.info("SaveProductController called");
        ProductForm productForm = new ProductForm();
        // populate action properties
        productForm.setName(request.getParameter("name"));
        productForm.setDescription(request.getParameter(
                "description"));
        productForm.setPrice(request.getParameter("price"));

        // create model
        Product product = new Product();
        product.setName(productForm.getName());
        product.setDescription(productForm.getDescription());
        try {
            product.setPrice(
                    Float.parseFloat(productForm.getPrice()));
        } catch (NumberFormatException e) {
        }

        // insert code to save Product

        return new ModelAndView("/WEB-INF/jsp/ProductDetails.jsp",
                "product", product);
```

```
    }
}
```

The **handleRequest** method in the **SaveProductController** class creates a **ProductForm** object and populates it using the request parameters. It then creates a **Product** object that gets its property values from the **ProductForm**. Since the **price** property of the **ProductForm** is a **String** and its counterpart in the **Product** class is a float, some parsing is necessary. In the next chapters you will learn how Spring MVC eliminates the need for form beans like **ProductForm** and makes things much simpler.

The **handleRequest** method in **SaveProductController** concludes by returning a **ModelAndView** that contains a view path, a model name, and a model (the Product object). The model added to the **ModelAndView** object will be available to the target view for display.

The View

The **app03a** application comes with two JSP pages, the **ProductForm.jsp** page (given in Listing 3.5) and the **ProductDetails.jsp** page (printed in Listing 3.6).

Listing 3.5: The ProductForm.jsp page

```
<!DOCTYPE HTML>
<html>
<head>
<title>Add Product Form</title>
<style type="text/css">@import url(css/main.css);</style>
</head>
<body>

<div id="global">
<form action="product_save.action" method="post">
    <fieldset>
        <legend>Add a product</legend>
        <label for="name">Product Name: </label>
        <input type="text" id="name" name="name" value=""
            tabindex="1">
        <label for="description">Description: </label>
        <input type="text" id="description" name="description"
            tabindex="2">
        <label for="price">Price: </label>
        <input type="text" id="price" name="price" tabindex="3">
        <div id="buttons">
```

```
            <label for="dummy"> </label>
            <input id="reset" type="reset" tabindex="4">
            <input id="submit" type="submit" tabindex="5"
                value="Add Product">
        </div>
    </fieldset>
</form>
</div>
</body>
</html>
```

This is not a place to discuss HTML and CSS, but I'd like to stress here that the HTML in Listing 3.5 has been written with proper design in mind. Among others, I did not use <table> to lay out the input fields.

Listing 3.6: The ProductDetails.jsp page

```
<!DOCTYPE HTML>
<html>
<head>
<title>Save Product</title>
<style type="text/css">@import url(css/main.css);</style>
</head>
<body>
<div id="global">
    <h4>The product has been saved.</h4>
    <p>
        <h5>Details:</h5>
        Product Name: ${product.name}<br/>
        Description: ${product.description}<br/>
        Price: $${product.price}
    </p>
</div>
</body>
</html>
```

The **ProductDetails.jsp** page has access to the **Product** object passed by the **SaveProductController** with the model attribute name **product**. I used the JSP Expression Language expressions to display various properties of the **Product** object. You will learn about the JSP EL in Chapter 8, "The Expression Language."

Testing the Application

To test the application, direct your browser to this URL:

```
http://localhost:8080/app03a/product_input.action
```

You will see the familiar Product form like the one in Figure 3.2. Type in values in the empty fields and click the Add Product button. You will see the product properties are shown in the next page.

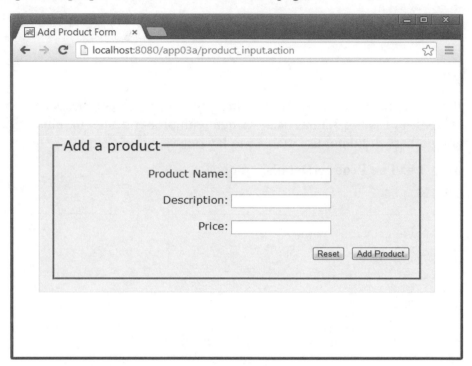

Figure 3.2: The Product form in app03a

The View Resolver

The view resolver in Spring MVC is responsible for resolving views. To use and configure the view resolver, declare a **viewResolver** bean in your configuration file, such as this one.

```
<bean id="viewResolver" class="org.springframework.web.servlet.
➥view.InternalResourceViewResolver">
    <property name="prefix" value="/WEB-INF/jsp/"/>
    <property name="suffix" value=".jsp"/>
</bean>
```

The **viewResolver** bean above configures two properties, **prefix** and **suffix**. As a result, your view paths will be shorter. Instead of setting the view path to **/WEB-INF/jsp/myPage.jsp**, for example, you just write **myPage** and the view resolver will prefix and suffix the string.

As an example, consider the **app03b** application, which is similar to **app03a**. However, the name and the location of the configuration file have been changed. In addition, it configures the default view resolver to add a prefix and a suffix to all view paths.

Figure 3.3 shows the directory structure of **app03b**.

Figure 3.3: The directory structure of app03b

In **app03b** the Spring MVC configuration file has been renamed
springmvc-config.xml and moved to **/WEB-INF/config**. In order to tell
Spring MVC where to find it, you need to pass the location of the file to the
Spring MVC dispatcher servlet. Listing 3.7 shows the deployment
descriptor (**web.xml** file) for **app03b**.

Listing 3.7: The deployment descriptor for app03b

```
<?xml version="1.0" encoding="UTF-8"?>
<web-app version="3.0"
    xmlns="http://java.sun.com/xml/ns/javaee"
    xmlns:xsi="http://www.w3.org/2001/XMLSchema-instance"
    xsi:schemaLocation="http://java.sun.com/xml/ns/javaee
    http://java.sun.com/xml/ns/javaee/web-app_3_0.xsd">

    <servlet>
        <servlet-name>springmvc</servlet-name>
        <servlet-class>
            org.springframework.web.servlet.DispatcherServlet
        </servlet-class>
        <init-param>
            <param-name>contextConfigLocation</param-name>
            <param-value>
                /WEB-INF/config/springmvc-config.xml
            </param-value>
        </init-param>
        <load-on-startup>1</load-on-startup>
    </servlet>

    <servlet-mapping>
        <servlet-name>springmvc</servlet-name>
        <url-pattern>*.action</url-pattern>
    </servlet-mapping>
</web-app>
```

Pay special attention to the **init-param** element in the **web.xml** file. To
refer to a configuration file that is not using the default naming and location,
you need to use the **contextConfigLocation** initial parameter. Its value
should be the path to the configuration file, relative to the application
directory.

The configuration file for **app03b** is given in Listing 3.8.

Listing 3.8: The Spring MVC configuration file for app03b

```xml
<?xml version="1.0" encoding="UTF-8"?>

<beans xmlns="http://www.springframework.org/schema/beans"
  xmlns:xsi="http://www.w3.org/2001/XMLSchema-instance"
  xsi:schemaLocation="http://www.springframework.org/schema/beans
  http://www.springframework.org/schema/beans/spring-beans-3.0.xsd">

    <bean name="/product_input.action"
          class="app03b.controller.InputProductController"/>
    <bean name="/product_save.action"
          class="app03b.controller.SaveProductController"/>
    <bean id="viewResolver"
          class="org.springframework.web.servlet.view.
➥InternalResourceViewResolver">
        <property name="prefix" value="/WEB-INF/jsp/"/>
        <property name="suffix" value=".jsp"/>
    </bean>
</beans>
```

To test the application, direct your browser to this URL:

```
http://localhost:8080/app03b/product_input.action
```

You will see a form similar to Figure 3.2.

Summary

This chapter is a gentle introduction to Spring MVC. It teaches you how to write simple applications similar to the examples in Chapter 2. You don't need to write your own dispatcher servlet in Spring MVC and controllers can be written by implementing the **Controller** interface. This is the old style controller. In Spring 2.5 and later, there is a better way of writing controllers, i.e. by using annotations. Chapter 4, "Annotation-Based Controllers" discusses this type of controller.

Chapter 4
Annotation-Based Controllers

In Chapter 3, "Introduction to Spring MVC" you built two simple Spring MVC applications using some old style controllers. The controllers were classes that implemented the **Controller** interface. Spring 2.5 introduced a new way of creating controllers: by using the **Controller** annotation type.

This chapter discusses annotation-based controllers and the various annotation types that can be beneficial to your applications.

Spring MVC Annotation Types

There are several advantages of using annotation-based controllers. For one, a controller class can handle multiple actions. (By contrast, a controller that implements the **Controller** interface can only handle one action.) This means, related actions can be written in the same controller class, thus reducing the number of classes in your application.

Secondly, with annotation-based controllers request mappings do not need to be stored in a configuration file. Using the **RequestMapping** annotation type, a method can be annotated to make it a request-handling method.

Controller and **RequestMapping** annotation types are two most important annotation types in the Spring MVC API. This chapter focuses on these two and briefly touches on some other less popular annotation types.

The Controller Annotation Type

The **org.springframework.stereotype.Controller** annotation type is used to annotate a Java class to indicate to Spring that instances of the class are controllers. Here is an example of a class annotated with **@Controller**.

```
package com.example.controller;

import org.springframework.stereotype;
...

@Controller
public class CustomerController {

    // request-handling methods here

}
```

Spring uses a scanning mechanism to find all annotation-based controller classes in an application. To ensure Spring can find your controllers, there are two things you need to do. First, you need to declare the **spring-context** schema in your Spring MVC configuration file, like so:

```
<beans
    ...
    xmlns:context="http://www.springframework.org/schema/context"
    ...
>
```

Second, you need to use a **<component-scan/>** element in your configuration file:

```
context:component-scan base-package="basePackage"/>
```

In your **<component-scan/>** element, specify the base package of your controller classes. For example, if you put all your controller classes under **com.example.controller** and its subpackages, you need to write a **<component-scan/>** element like so.

```
<context:component-scan base-package="com.example.controller"/>
```

Integrating **<component-scan/>**, your configuration file would look like this:

```
<?xml version="1.0" encoding="UTF-8"?>
<beans xmlns="http://www.springframework.org/schema/beans"
    xmlns:xsi="http://www.w3.org/2001/XMLSchema-instance"
    xmlns:p="http://www.springframework.org/schema/p"
    xmlns:context="http://www.springframework.org/schema/context"
    xsi:schemaLocation="
        http://www.springframework.org/schema/beans
        http://www.springframework.org/schema/beans/spring-beans.xsd
        http://www.springframework.org/schema/context
        http://www.springframework.org/schema/context/spring-
    context.xsd">

    <context:component-scan base-package="com.example.controller"/>

    <!-- ... -->
</beans>
```

You would want to make sure all controller classes are part of the base package. At the same time, you don't want to specify a base package that is too wide (say, by specifying **com.example** instead of **com.example.controller**) because this would make Spring MVC scan irrelevant packages.

The RequestMapping Annotation Type

Inside a controller class you write request handling methods that each will handle an action. To tell Spring which method handles which action, you need to map URIs with methods using the **org.springframework.web.bind.annotation.RequestMapping** annotation type.

The **RequestMapping** annotation type does what its name implies: map a request and a method. You can use **@RequestMapping** to annotate a method or a class.

A method annotated with **@RequestMapping** becomes a request-handling method and will be invoked when the dispatcher servlet receives a request with a matching URI.

Here is a controller class with a **RequestMapping**-annotated method.

```
package com.example.controller;
```

```
import org.springframework.stereotype.Controller;
import org.springframework.web.bind.annotation.RequestMapping;
...

@Controller
public class CustomerController {

    @RequestMapping(value = "/customer_input")
    public String inputCustomer() {

        // do something here

        return "CustomerForm";
    }
}
```

You specify the URI mapped to the method using the **value** attribute in the **RequestMapping** annotation. In the example above, the URI **customer_input** is mapped with the **inputCustomer** method. This means, the **inputCustomer** method can be invoked using a URL having this pattern.

```
http://domain/context/customer_input
```

Since the **value** attribute is the default attribute of the **RequestMapping** annotation type, you can omit the attribute name if it is the only attribute used in the **RequestMapping** annotation. In other words, these two annotations have the same meaning.

```
@RequestMapping(value = "/customer_input")
```

```
@RequestMapping("/customer_input")
```

However, if more than one attributes appear in **@RequestMapping**, you must write the **value** attribute name.

The value of a request mapping can be an empty string, in which case the method is mapped to the following URL:

```
http://domain/context
```

RequestMapping has other attributes besides **value**. For instance, the **method** attribute takes a set of HTTP methods that will be handled by the corresponding method.

For example, the **processOrder** method below can only be invoked with the HTTP POST or PUT method.

```
...
import org.springframework.stereotype.Controller;
import org.springframework.web.bind.annotation.RequestMapping;
import org.springframework.web.bind.annotation.RequestMethod;
...
    @RequestMapping(value="/order_process",
            method={RequestMethod.POST, RequestMethod.PUT})
    public String processOrder() {

        // do something here

        return "OrderForm";
    }
```

If there is only one HTTP request method assigned to the **method** attribute, the bracket is optional. For instance,

```
@RequestMapping(value="/order_process", method=RequestMethod.POST)
```

If the **method** attribute is not present, the request-handling method will handle any HTTP method.

The **RequestMapping** annotation type can also be used to annotate a controller class like this:

```
import org.springframework.stereotype.Controller;
...

@Controller
@RequestMapping(value="/customer")
public class CustomerController {
```

In this case, request mappings in all methods will be deemed relative to the class-level request mapping. For instance, consider the following **deleteCustomer** method

```
...
import org.springframework.stereotype.Controller;
import org.springframework.web.bind.annotation.RequestMapping;
import org.springframework.web.bind.annotation.RequestMethod;
...
@Controller
@RequestMapping("/customer")
```

```
public class CustomerController {

    @RequestMapping(value="/delete",
            method={RequestMethod.POST, RequestMethod.PUT})
    public String deleteCustomer() {

        // do something here

        return ...;
    }
```

Because the controller class is mapped with "/customer" and the
deleteCustomer method with "/delete", the method can be invoked using a
URL with this pattern.

```
http://domain/context/customer/delete
```

Writing Request-Handling Methods

A request-handling method can have a mix of argument types as well as one
of a variety of return types. For example, if you need access to the
HttpSession object in your method, you can add **HttpSession** as an
argument and Spring will pass the correct object for you:

```
@RequestMapping("/uri")
public String myMethod(HttpSession session) {
    ...
    session.addAttribute(key, value);
    ...
}
```

Or, if you need the client locale and the **HttpServletRequest**, you can
include both as method arguments like this.

```
@RequestMapping("/uri")
public String myOtherMethod(HttpServletRequest request,
        Locale locale) {
    ...
    // access Locale and HttpServletRequest here
    ...
}
```

Here is the list of argument types that can appear as arguments in a request-handling method.

- **javax.servlet.ServletRequest** or **javax.servlet.http.HttpServletRequest**
- **javax.servlet.ServletResponse** or **javax.servlet.http.HttpServletResponse**
- **javax.servlet.http.HttpSession**
- **org.springframework.web.context.request.WebRequest** or **org.springframework.web.context.request.NativeWebRequest**
- **java.util.Locale**
- **java.io.InputStream** or **java.io.Reader**
- **java.io.OutputStream** or **java.io.Writer**
- **java.security.Principal**
- **HttpEntity<?>** parameters
- **java.util.Map** / **org.springframework.ui.Model** / **org.springframework.ui.ModelMap**
- **org.springframcwork.web.servlet.mvc.support.RedirectAttributes**
- **org.springframework.validation.Errors** / **org.springframework.validation.BindingResult**
- Command or form objects
- **org.springframework.web.bind.support.SessionStatus**
- **org.springframework.web.util.UriComponentsBuilder**
- Types annotated with **@PathVariable**, **@MatrixVariable**, **@RequestParam**, **@RequestHeader**, **@RequestBody**, or **@RequestPart**.

Of special importance is the **org.springframework.ui.Model** type. This is not a Servlet API type, but rather a Spring MVC type that contains a **Map**. Every time a request-handling method is invoked, Spring MVC creates a **Model** object and populates its **Map** with potentially various objects.

A request-handling method can return one of these objects.

- A **ModelAndView** object
- A **Model** object
- A **Map** containing the attributes of the model
- A **View** object

- A **String** representing the logical view name
- void
- An **HttpEntity** or **ResponseEntity** object to provide access to the Servlet response HTTP headers and contents
- A **Callable**
- A **DeferredResult**
- Any other return type. In this case, the return value will be considered a model attribute to be exposed to the view

You'll learn how to write request-handling methods in the sample applications given later in this chapter.

Using An Annotation-Based Controller

The **app04a** application, a rewrite of the sample applications in Chapter 2 and Chapter 3, presents a controller class with two request-handling methods.

The main difference between **app04a** and the previous applications is the controller class in **app04a** is annotated with **@Controller**. In addition, the Spring configuration file also includes additional elements. Various parts of the application are given in the following subsections.

Directory Structure

Figure 4.1 shows the directory structure of **app04a**. Note that there is only one controller class instead of two. An HTML file, **index.html**, has been added to the application directory to show how static resources can still be accessed when the URL pattern of the Spring MVC servlet is set to /.

Configuration Files

There are two configuration files in **app04a**. The first, the deployment descriptor (**web.xml** file), registers the Spring MVC dispatcher servlet. The second configuration file, **springmvc-config.xml**, is a Spring MVC configuration file.

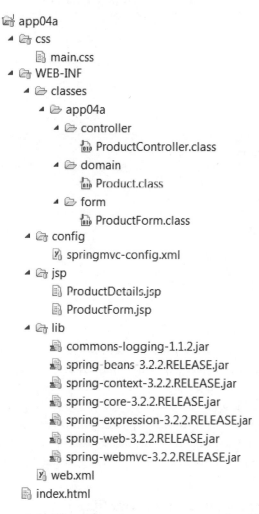

Figure 4.1: The directory structure of app04a

Listing 4.1 shows the deployment descriptor and Listing 4.2 the Spring MVC configuration file.

Listing 4.1: The deployment descriptor for app04a (web.xml)

```
<?xml version="1.0" encoding="UTF-8"?>
<web-app version="3.0"
```

```
    xmlns="http://java.sun.com/xml/ns/javaee"
    xmlns:xsi="http://www.w3.org/2001/XMLSchema-instance"
    xsi:schemaLocation="http://java.sun.com/xml/ns/javaee
➡http://java.sun.com/xml/ns/javaee/web-app_3_0.xsd">

    <servlet>
        <servlet-name>springmvc</servlet-name>
        <servlet-class>
            org.springframework.web.servlet.DispatcherServlet
        </servlet-class>
        <init-param>
            <param-name>contextConfigLocation</param-name>
            <param-value>
                /WEB-INF/config/springmvc-config.xml
            </param-value>
        </init-param>
        <load-on-startup>1</load-on-startup>
    </servlet>

    <servlet-mapping>
        <servlet-name>springmvc</servlet-name>
        <url-pattern>/</url-pattern>
    </servlet-mapping>
</web-app>
```

Note that in the **<servlet-mapping/>** element in the deployment descriptor, the URL pattern for the Spring MVC dispatcher servlet is set to / as opposed to **.action** as in Chapter 3. This is to show that you do not have to map actions with a certain URL extension. However, setting the URL pattern to / means that all requests, including those for static resources, are directed to the dispatcher servlet. In order for static resources to be handled properly, you need to add some **<resources/>** elements in the Spring MVC configuration file.

Listing 4.2: The springmvc-config.xml file

```
<?xml version="1.0" encoding="UTF-8"?>
<beans xmlns="http://www.springframework.org/schema/beans"
    xmlns:xsi="http://www.w3.org/2001/XMLSchema-instance"
    xmlns:p="http://www.springframework.org/schema/p"
    xmlns:mvc="http://www.springframework.org/schema/mvc"
    xmlns:context="http://www.springframework.org/schema/context"
    xsi:schemaLocation="
        http://www.springframework.org/schema/beans
        http://www.springframework.org/schema/beans/spring-beans.xsd
```

```
        http://www.springframework.org/schema/mvc
        http://www.springframework.org/schema/mvc/spring-mvc.xsd
        http://www.springframework.org/schema/context
        http://www.springframework.org/schema/context/spring-
      context.xsd">
    <context:component-scan base-package="app04a.controller"/>
    <mvc:annotation-driven/>
    <mvc:resources mapping="/css/**" location="/css/"/>
    <mvc:resources mapping="/*.html" location="/"/>

    <bean id="viewResolver"
        class="org.springframework.web.servlet.view.
➡ InternalResourceViewResolver">
        <property name="prefix" value="/WEB-INF/jsp/"/>
        <property name="suffix" value=".jsp"/>
    </bean>
</beans>
```

The main thing in the Spring MVC configuration file in Listing 4.2 is the presence of a **<component-scan/>** element. It is to tell Spring MVC to scan classes under a certain package, in this case the **app04a.controller** package. On top of that, there are also an **<annotation-driven/>** element and two **<resources/>** elements. The **<annotation-driven/>** element does several things, including registering beans to support request processing with annotated controller methods. The **<resources/>** element tells Spring MVC which static resources need to be served independently from the dispatcher servlet.

In the configuration file in Listing 4.2 there are two **<resources/>** elements. The first makes sure that all files in the **/css** directory will be visible. The second allows displaying of all **.html** files in the application directory.

Note
Without **<annotation-driven/>**, the **<resources/>** elements will prevent any controller from being invoked. You don't need an **<annotation-driven/>** element if you are not using **resources** elements.

The Controller Class

One of the advantages of using the **Controller** annotation type is that a controller class can contain multiple request-handling methods. As can be seen in the **ProductController** class in Listing 4.3, there are two methods in it, **inputProduct** and **saveProduct**.

Listing 4.3: The ProductController class in app04a

```
package app04a.controller;
import org.apache.commons.logging.Log;
import org.apache.commons.logging.LogFactory;
import org.springframework.stereotype.Controller;
import org.springframework.ui.Model;
import org.springframework.web.bind.annotation.RequestMapping;

import app04a.domain.Product;
import app04a.form.ProductForm;

@Controller
public class ProductController {

    private static final Log logger =
       LogFactory.getLog(ProductController.class);

    @RequestMapping(value="/product_input")
    public String inputProduct() {
        logger.info("inputProduct called");
        return "ProductForm";
    }

    @RequestMapping(value="/product_save")
    public String saveProduct(ProductForm productForm, Model model)
       {
        logger.info("saveProduct called");
        // no need to create and instantiate a ProductForm
        // create Product
        Product product = new Product();
        product.setName(productForm.getName());
        product.setDescription(productForm.getDescription());
        try {
            product.setPrice(Float.parseFloat(
                    productForm.getPrice()));
```

```
        } catch (NumberFormatException e) {
        }

        // add product

        model.addAttribute("product", product);
        return "ProductDetails";
    }
}
```

Note that the second argument to **saveProduct** in the **ProductController** class is of type **org.springframework.ui.Model**. Spring MVC creates a **Model** instance every time a request-handling method is invoked, whether or not you'll use the instance in your method. The main purpose of having a **Model** is for adding attributes that will be displayed in the view. In this example, you added a **Product** instance by calling **model.addAttribute**:

```
model.addAttribute("product", product);
```

The **Product** instance can then be accessed as if you had added it to the **HttpServletRequest**.

The View

In **app04a** there are two views similar to the ones in previous sample applications, the **ProductForm.jsp** page (given in Listing 4.4) and the **ProductDetails.jsp** page (shown in Listing 4.5).

Listing 4.4: The ProductForm.jsp page

```
<!DOCTYPE HTML>
<html>
<head>
<title>Add Product Form</title>
<style type="text/css">@import url(css/main.css);</style>
</head>
<body>

<div id="global">
<form action="product_save" method="post">
    <fieldset>
        <legend>Add a product</legend>
        <p>
            <label for="name">Product Name: </label>
```

```
        <input type="text" id="name" name="name"
            tabindex="1">
    </p>
    <p>
        <label for="description">Description: </label>
        <input type="text" id="description"
            name="description" tabindex="2">
    </p>
    <p>
        <label for="price">Price: </label>
        <input type="text" id="price" name="price"
            tabindex="3">
    </p>
    <p id="buttons">
        <input id="reset" type="reset" tabindex="4">
        <input id="submit" type="submit" tabindex="5"
            value="Add Product">
    </p>
    </fieldset>
</form>
</div>
</body>
</html>
```

Listing 4.5: The ProductDetails.jsp page

```
<!DOCTYPE HTML>
<html>
<head>
<title>Save Product</title>
<style type="text/css">@import url(css/main.css);</style>
</head>
<body>
<div id="global">
    <h4>The product has been saved.</h4>
    <p>
        <h5>Details:</h5>
        Product Name: ${product.name}<br/>
        Description: ${product.description}<br/>
        Price: $${product.price}
    </p>
</div>
</body>
</html>
```

Testing the Application

To test **app04a**, direct your browser to this URL:

`http://localhost:8080/app04a/product_input`

You'll see the Product Form in your browser, like the one in Figure 4.2.

Figure 4.2: The Product form

Pressing the Add Product button will invoke the **saveProduct** method in the controller.

Dependency Injection with @Autowired and @Service

One of the benefits of using the Spring Framework is that you get dependency injection for free. After all, Spring started as a dependency injection container. The easiest way to get a dependency injected to a Spring MVC controller is by annotating a field or a method with **@Autowired**. The **Autowired** annotation type belongs to the **org.springframework.beans.factory.annotation** package.

In order for a dependency to be found, its class must be annotated with **@Service**. A member of the **org.springframework.stereotype** package, the **Service** annotation type indicates that the annotated class is a service. In addition, in your configuration file you need to add a **<component-scan/>** element to scan the base package for your dependencies.

```
<context:component-scan base-package="dependencyPackage"/>
```

As an example of dependency injection in a Spring MVC application, consider another example, the **app04b** application. The **ProductController** class in the **app04b** application (See Listing 4.6) has been modified from the identically named class in **app04a**.

Listing 4.6: The ProductController class in app04b

```
package app04b.controller;
import org.apache.commons.logging.Log;
import org.apache.commons.logging.LogFactory;
import org.springframework.beans.factory.annotation.Autowired;
import org.springframework.stereotype.Controller;
import org.springframework.ui.Model;
import org.springframework.web.bind.annotation.PathVariable;
import org.springframework.web.bind.annotation.RequestMapping;
import org.springframework.web.bind.annotation.RequestMethod;
import org.springframework.web.servlet.mvc.support.
➡RedirectAttributes;
import app04b.domain.Product;
import app04b.form.ProductForm;
import app04b.service.ProductService;

@Controller
public class ProductController {
```

```java
    private static final Log logger = LogFactory
            .getLog(ProductController.class);

    @Autowired
    private ProductService productService;

    @RequestMapping(value = "/product_input")
    public String inputProduct() {
        logger.info("inputProduct called");
        return "ProductForm";
    }

    @RequestMapping(value = "/product_save", method =
RequestMethod.POST)
    public String saveProduct(ProductForm productForm,
            RedirectAttributes redirectAttributes) {
        logger.info("saveProduct called");
        // no need to create and instantiate a ProductForm
        // create Product
        Product product = new Product();
        product.setName(productForm.getName());
        product.setDescription(productForm.getDescription());
        try {
            product.setPrice(Float.parseFloat(
                    productForm.getPrice()));
        } catch (NumberFormatException e) {
        }

        // add product
        Product savedProduct = productService.add(product);

        redirectAttributes.addFlashAttribute("message",
                "The product was successfully added.");
        return "redirect:/product_view/" + savedProduct.getId();
    }

    @RequestMapping(value = "/product_view/{id}")
    public String viewProduct(@PathVariable Long id, Model model) {
        Product product = productService.get(id);
        model.addAttribute("product", product);
        return "ProductView";
    }
}
```

A couple of things make the **ProductController** class in **app04b** different from its counterpart in **app04a**. The first thing is the addition of the following private field that is annotated with **@Autowired**:

```
@Autowired
private ProductService productService
```

Here, **ProductService** is an interface that provides various methods for handling products. Annotating **productService** with **@Autowired** causes an instance of **ProductService** to be injected to the **ProductController** instance.

Listing 4.7 shows the **ProductService** interface and Listing 4.8 its implementation **ProductServiceImpl**. Note that for the implementation to be scannable, you must annotate its class definition with **@Service**.

Listing 4.7: The ProductService interface

```
package app04b.service
import app04b.domain.Product;
public interface ProductService {
    Product add(Product product);
    Product get(long id);
}
```

Listing 4.8: The ProductServiceImpl class

```
package app04b.service;
import java.util.HashMap;
import java.util.Map;
import java.util.concurrent.atomic.AtomicLong;
import org.springframework.stereotype.Service;
import app04b.domain.Product;

@Service
public class ProductServiceImpl implements ProductService {

    private Map<Long, Product> products =
            new HashMap<Long, Product>();
    private AtomicLong generator = new AtomicLong();

    public ProductServiceImpl() {
        Product product = new Product();
        product.setName("JX1 Power Drill");
        product.setDescription(
                "Powerful hand drill, made to perfection");
```

```
            product.setPrice(129.99F);
            add(product);
        }

        @Override
        public Product add(Product product) {
            long newId = generator.incrementAndGet();
            product.setId(newId);
            products.put(newId, product);
            return product;
        }

        @Override
        public Product get(long id) {
            return products.get(id);
        }
    }
}
```

As you can see in Listing 4.9, the Spring MVC configuration file for
app04b has two **<component-scan/>** elements, one for scanning controller
classes and one for scanning service classes.

Listing 4.9: The Spring MVC configuration file for app04b

```xml
<?xml version="1.0" encoding="UTF-8"?>
<beans xmlns="http://www.springframework.org/schema/beans"
    xmlns:xsi="http://www.w3.org/2001/XMLSchema-instance"
    xmlns:p="http://www.springframework.org/schema/p"
    xmlns:mvc="http://www.springframework.org/schema/mvc"
    xmlns:context="http://www.springframework.org/schema/context"
    xsi:schemaLocation="
        http://www.springframework.org/schema/beans
        http://www.springframework.org/schema/beans/spring-beans.xsd
        http://www.springframework.org/schema/mvc
        http://www.springframework.org/schema/mvc/spring-mvc.xsd
        http://www.springframework.org/schema/context
        http://www.springframework.org/schema/context/spring-
context.xsd">
    <context:component-scan base-package="app04b.controller"/>
    <context:component-scan base-package="app04b.service"/>
    <mvc:annotation-driven/>
    <mvc:resources mapping="/css/**" location="/css/"/>
    <mvc:resources mapping="/*.html" location="/"/>
```

```
    <bean id="viewResolver"
      class="org.springframework.web.servlet.view.InternalResourceV
      iewResolver">
       <property name="prefix" value="/WEB-INF/jsp/"/>
       <property name="suffix" value=".jsp"/>
    </bean>
</beans>
```

Redirect and Flash Attributes

As a seasoned servlet/JSP programmer, you must know the difference between and a forward and a redirect. A forward is faster than a redirect because a redirect requires a round-trip to the server and a forward does not. However, there are circumstances where a redirect is preferred. One of such events is when you need to redirect to an external site, like a different web site. You cannot use a forward to target an external site so a redirect is your only choice.

Another scenario where you want to use a redirect instead of a forward is when you want to avoid the same action from being invoked again when the user reloads the page. For example, in **app04a** when you submit the Product form, the **saveProduct** method will be invoked and this method will do what it's supposed to do. In a real-world application, this might include adding the product to the database. However, if you reload the page after you submits the form, **saveProduct** will be called again and the same product would potentially be added the second time. To avoid this, after a form submit, you may prefer to redirect the user to a different page. This page should have no side-effect when called repeatedly. For instance, in **app04a**, you could redirect the user to a **ViewProduct** page after a form submit.

In **app04b** you probably noticed that the **saveProduct** method in the **ProductController** class ends with this line:

```
return "redirect:/product_view/" + savedProduct.getId();
```

Here, you use a redirect instead of a forward to prevent the **saveProduct** method being called twice if the user reloads the page.

The trade-off when using a redirect is you cannot easily pass a value to the target page. With a forward, you can simply add attributes to the **Model** object and the attributes will be accessible to the view. Since a redirect is a round trip to the server, everything in the **Model** is lost when you redirect. Fortunately, Spring version 3.1 and later provide a way of preserving values in a redirect by using flash attributes.

To use flash attributes you must have an **<annotation-driven/>** element in your Spring MVC configuration file. And then, you must also add a new argument of type **org.springframework.web.servlet.mvc.support.RedirectAttributes** in your method. The **saveProduct** method in **ProductController** in **app04b** is reprinted in Listing 4.10.

Listing 4.10: Using flash attributes

```
@RequestMapping(value = "product_save", method = RequestMethod.POST)
public String saveProduct(ProductForm productForm,
        RedirectAttributes redirectAttributes) {
    logger.info("saveProduct called");
    // no need to create and instantiate a ProductForm
    // create Product
    Product product = new Product();
    product.setName(productForm.getName());
    product.setDescription(productForm.getDescription());
    try {
        product.setPrice(Float.parseFloat(productForm.getPrice()));
    } catch (NumberFormatException e) {
    }

    // add product
    Product savedProduct = productService.add(product);

    redirectAttributes.addFlashAttribute("message",
            "The product was successfully added.");

    return "redirect:/product_view/" + savedProduct.getId();
}
```

Request Parameters and Path Variables

Both request parameters and path variables are used to send values to the server. Both are also part of a URL. The request parameter takes the form of key=value pairs separated by an ampersand. For instance, this URL carries a **productId** request parameter with a value of 3.

```
http://localhost:8080/app04b/product_retrieve?productId=3
```

In servlet programming, you can retrieve a request parameter value by using the **getParameter** method on the **HttpServletRequest**:

```
String productId = httpServletRequest.getParameter("productId");
```

In Spring MVC there is an easier way to retrieve a request parameter value: by using the **org.springframework.web.bind.annotation.RequestParam** annotation type to annotate an argument to which the value of the request parameter will be copied. For example, the following method contains an argument that captures request parameter **productId**.

```
public void sendProduct(@RequestParam int productId)
```

As you can see, the type of argument annotated with **@RequestParam** does not need to be String.

A path variable is similar to a request parameter, except that there is no key part, just a value. For example, the **product_view** action in **app04b** is mapped to a URL with this format.

```
/product_view/productId
```

where *productId* is an integer representing a product identifier. In Spring MVC parlance, *productId* is called a path variable. It is used to send a value to the server.

Consider the **viewProduct** method in Listing 4.11 that demonstrates the use of a path variable.

Listing 4.11: Using path variables

```
@RequestMapping(value = "/product_view/{id}")
public String viewProduct(@PathVariable Long id, Model model) {
    Product product = productService.get(id);
    model.addAttribute("product", product);
```

```
    return "ProductView";
}
```

To use a path variable, first you need to add a variable that is the value attribute of your **RequestMapping** annotation. The variable must be put between curly brackets. For example, the following **RequestMapping** annotation defines a path variable called id:

```
@RequestMapping(value = "/product_view/{id}")
```

Then, in your method signature, add an identically named variable annotated with **@PathVariable**. Take a look at the signature of **viewProduct** in Listing 4.11. When the method is invoked, the **id** value in the request URL will be copied to the path variable and can be used in the method. The type of a path variable does not need to be **String**. Spring MVC will try its best to convert a non-string value. This great feature of Spring MVC's will be discussed in detail in Chapter 5, "Data Binding and the Form Tags."

You can use multiple path variables in your request mapping. For example, the following defines two path variables, **userId** and **orderId**.

```
@RequestMapping(value = "/product_view/{userId}/{orderId}")
```

To test the path variable in the **viewProduct** method, direct your browser to this URL.

```
http://localhost:8080/app04b/product_view/1
```

There is a slight problem when employing path variables: in some cases it may be confusing to the browser. Consider the following URL.

```
http://example.com/context/abc
```

The browser will think (correctly) that **abc** is the action. Any relative reference to a static file, such as a CSS file, will be resolved using http://example.com/context as the base. This is to say, if the page sent by the server contains this **img** element

```
<img src="logo.png"/>
```

The browser will look for **logo.png** in http://example.com/context/logo.png.

However, note that if the same application is deployed as the default context (where the path to the default context is an empty string), the URL for the same target would be this:

```
http://example.com/abc
```

Now, consider the following URL that carries a path variable in an application deployed as the default context:

```
http://example.com/abc/1
```

In ths case, the browser will think **abc** is the context, not the action. If you refer to **<img src="logo.png"/>** in your page, the browser will look for the image in http://example.com/abc/logo.png and it won't find the image.

Lucky for us there is an easy solution, i.e. by using the JSTL **url** tag. (JSTL is discussed in Chapter 8, "JSTL.") The tag fixes the issue by correctly resolving the URL. For example, all CSS imports in the JSP pages in **app04b** have been changed from

```
<style type="text/css">@import url(css/main.css);</style>
```

to

```
<style type="text/css">
@import url("<c:url value="/css/main.css"/>");
</style>
```

Thanks to the **url** tag, the URL will be translated into this if it is in the default context.

```
<style type="text/css">@import url("/css/main.css");</style>
```

And it will be translated into this if it is not in the default context.

```
<style type="text/css">@import url("/app04b/css/main.css");</style>
```

@ModelAttribute

In the previous section I talked about the **Model** type that Spring MVC creates an instance of every time a request-handling method is invoked. You can add a **Model** as an argument for your method if you intend to use it in your method. The **ModelAttribute** annotation type can be used to decorate a **Model** instance in a method. This annotation type is also part of the **org.springframework.web.bind.annotation** package.

@ModelAttribute can be used to annotate a method argument or a method. A method argument annotated with **@ModelAttribute** will have an instance of it retrieved or created and added to the **Model** object if the method body does not do it explicitly. For example, Spring MVC will create an instance of **Order** every time this **submitOrder** method is invoked.

```
@RequestMapping(method = RequestMethod.POST)
public String submitOrder(@ModelAttribute("newOrder") Order order,
    Model model) {

    ...
}
```

The **Order** instance retrieved or created will be added to the **Model** object with attribute key **newOrder**. If no key name is defined, then the name will be derived from the name of the type to be added to the **Model**. For instance, every time the following method is invoked, an instance of **Order** will be retrieved or created and added to the **Model** using attribute key **order**.

```
public String submitOrder(@ModelAttribute Order order, Model model)
```

The second use of **@ModelAttribute** is to annotate a non-request-handling method. Methods annotated with **@ModelAttribute** will be invoked every time a request-handling method in the same controller class is invoked. This means, if a controller class has two request-handling methods and another method annotated with **@ModelAttribute** method, the annotated method will likely be invoked more often than each of the request-handling methods.

A method annotated with **@ModelAttribute** will be invoked right before a request-handling method. Such a method may return an object or have a void return type. If it returns an object, the object is automatically added to the **Model** that was created for the request-handling method. For example, the return value of this method will be added to the **Model**.

```
@ModelAttribute
public Product addProduct(@RequestParam String productId) {
    return productService.get(productId);
}
```

If your annotated method returns void, then you must also add a **Model** argument type and add the instance yourself. Here is an example.

```
@ModelAttribute
public void populateModel(@RequestParam String id, Model model) er);
    model.addAttribute(new Account(id));
}
```

Summary

In this chapter you learned how to write Spring MVC applications that use annotation-based controllers. You have also learned various annotation types to annotate your classes, methods, or method arguments.

Chapter 5
Data Binding and
the Form Tag Library

Data binding is a feature that binds user input to the domain model. Thanks to data binding, HTTP request parameters, which are always of type **String**, can be used to populate object properties of various types. Data binding also makes form beans (e.g. instances of **ProductForm** in the previous chapters) redundant.

To use data binding effectively, you need the Spring form tag library. This chapter explains data binding and the form tag library and provides examples that highlight the use of the tags in the form tag library.

Data Binding Overview

Due to the nature of HTTP, all HTTP request parameters are strings. Recall that in the previous chapters you had to parse a string to a float in order to get the correct product price. To refresh your memory, here is some code from the **ProductController** class's **saveProduct** method in **app04a**.

```
@RequestMapping(value="product_save")
public String saveProduct(ProductForm productForm,
        Model model) {
    logger.info("saveProduct called");
    // no need to create and instantiate a ProductForm
    // create Product
    Product product = new Product();
    product.setName(productForm.getName());
    product.setDescription(productForm.getDescription());
    try {
        product.setPrice(Float.parseFloat(
```

```
                    productForm.getPrice()));
    } catch (NumberFormatException e) {
    }
```

You had to parse the **price** property in the **ProductForm** because it was a String and you needed a float to populate the **Product**'s **price** property. With data binding you can replace the **saveProduct** method fragment above with this.

```
@RequestMapping(value="product_save")
public String saveProduct(Product product, Model model)
```

Thanks to data binding, you don't need the **ProductForm** class anymore and no parsing is necessary for the price property of the Product object.

Another benefit of data binding is for repopulating an HTML form when input validation fails. With manual HTML coding, you have to worry about repopulating the input fields with the values the user previously entered. With Spring data binding and the form tag library, this is taken care of for you.

The Form Tag Library

The form tag library contains tags you can use to render HTML elements in your JSP pages. To use the tags, declare this **taglib** directive at the top of your JSP pages.

```
<%@taglib prefix="form"
    uri="http://www.springframework.org/tags/form" %>
```

Table 5.1 shows the tags in the form tag library.

Each of the tags will be explained in the following subsections. A sample application presented in the section, "Data Binding Example" demonstrates the use of data binding with the form tag library.

Tag	Description
form	Renders a form element.
input	Renders an <input type="text"/> element
password	Renders an <input type="password"/> element
hidden	Renders an <input type="hidden"/> element
textarea	Renders a textarea element
checkbox	Renders an <input type="checkbox"/> element
checkboxes	Renders multiple <input type="checkbox"/> elements
radiobutton	Renders an <input type="radio"/> element
radiobuttons	Renders multiple <input type="checkbox"/> elements
select	Renders a select element
option	Renders an option element.
options	Renders a list of option elements.
errors	Renders field errors in a span element.

Table 5.1: The Form tags

The form Tag

The **form** tag renders an HTML form. You must have a **form** tag to use any of the other tags that render a form input field. The attributes of the **form** tag are given in Table 5.2.

All attributes in Table 5.2 are optional. The table does not include HTML attributes, such as **method** and **action**.

The **commandName** attribute is probably the most important attribute as it specifies the name of the model attribute that contains a backing object whose properties will be used to populate the generated form. If this attribute is present, you must add the corresponding model attribute in the request-handling method that returns the view containing this form. For instance, in the **app05** application that accompanies this chapter, the following **form** tag is specified in the **BookAddForm.jsp**.

```
<form:form commandName="book" action="book_save" method="post">
    ...
</form:form>
```

Attribute	Description
acceptCharset	Specifies the list of character encodings accepted by the server.
commandName	The name of the model attribute under which the form object is exposed. The default is 'command.'
cssClass	Specifies the CSS class to be applied to the rendered form element.
cssStyle	Specifies the CSS style to be applied to the rendered form element
htmlEscape	Accepts true or false indicating whether or not the rendered value(s) should be HTML-escaped.
modelAttribute	The name of the model attribute under which the form-backing object is exposed. The default is 'command'.

Table 5.2: The form tag's attributes

The **inputBook** method in the **BookController** class is the request-handling method that returns **BookAddForm.jsp**. Here is the **inputBook** method.

```
@RequestMapping(value = "/book_input")
public String inputBook(Model model) {
    ...
    model.addAttribute("book", new Book());
    return "BookAddForm";
}
```

As you can see, a **Book** object is created and added to the **Model** with attribute name **book**. Without the model attribute, the **BookAddForm.jsp** page will throw an exception because the **form** tag cannot find a form-backing object specified in its **commandName** attribute.

In addition, you will still normally use the **action** and **method** attributes. Both are HTML attributes and therefore not included in Table 5.2.

The input Tag

The **input** tag renders an **<input type="text"/>** element. The most important attribute of this tag, the **path** attribute, binds this input field to a property of the form-backing object. For example, if the **commandName** attribute of the enclosing **<form/>** tag is assigned **book** and the **path** attribute of the **input** tag is given the value **isbn**, the **input** tag will be bound to the **isbn** property of the **Book** object.

Table 5.3 shows all the attributes in the **input** tag. All attributes in Table 5.3 are optional and the table does not include HTML attributes.

Attribute	Description
cssClass	Specifies the CSS class to be applied to the rendered input element.
cssStyle	Specifies the CSS style to be applied to the rendered input element
CssErrorClass	Specifies the CSS class to be applied to the rendered input element if the bound property contains errors, overriding the value of the cssClass attribute.
htmlEscape	Accepts true or false indicating whether or not the rendered value(s) should be HTML-escaped.
path	The path to the property to bind.

Table 5.3: The input tag's attributes

As an example, this **input** tag is bound to the **isbn** property of the form-backing object.

```
<form:input id="isbn" path="isbn" cssErrorClass="errorBox"/>
```

This will be rendered as the following **<input/>** element:

```
<input type="text" id="isbn" name="isbn"/>
```

The **cssErrorClass** attribute has no effect unless there is an input validation error in the **isbn** property and the same form is used to redisplay the user input, in which case the **input** tag will be rendered as this **input** element.

```
<input type="text" id="isbn" name="isbn" class="errorBox"/>
```

The **input** tag can also be bound to a property in a nested object. For example, the following **input** tag is bound to the **id** property of the **category** property of the form-backing object.

```
<form:input path="category.id"/>
```

The password Tag

The **password** tag renders an **<input type="password"/>** element and its attributes are given in Table 5.4. The **password** tag is similar to the **input** tag except that it has a **showPassword** attribute.

Attribute	Description
cssClass	Specifies the CSS class to be applied to the rendered input element.
cssStyle	Specifies the CSS style to be applied to the rendered input element
cssErrorClass	Specifies the CSS class to be applied to the rendered input element if the bound property contains errors, overriding the value of the cssClass attribute.
htmlEscape	Accepts true or false indicating whether or not the rendered value(s) should be HTML-escaped.
path	The path to the property to bind.
showPassword	Indicates whether the password should be shown rather than masked. The default is false.

Table 5.4: The password tag's attributes

All attributes in Table 5.4 are optional and the table does not include HTML attributes. Here is an example of the **password** tag.

```
<form:password id="pwd" path="password" cssClass="normal"/>
```

The hidden Tag

The **hidden** tag renders an **<input type="hidden"/>** element and its attributes are given in Table 5.5. The **hidden** tag is similar to the **input** tag except that it has no visual appearance and therefore does not support a **cssClass** or **cssStyle** attribute.

Attribute	Description
htmlEscape	Accepts true or false indicating whether or not the rendered value(s) should be HTML-escaped.
path	The path to the property to bind.

Table 5.5: The hidden tag's attributes

All attributes in Table 5.5 are optional and the table does not include HTML attributes.

The following is an example **hidden** tag.

```
<form:hidden path="productId"/>
```

The textarea Tag

The **textarea** tag renders an HTML **textarea** element. As you know, a **textarea** element is basically an **input** element that supports multiline input. The attributes of the textarea tag are presented in Table 5.6. All attributes in Table 5.6 are optional and the table does not include HTML attributes.

Attribute	Description
cssClass	Specifies the CSS class to be applied to the rendered input element.
cssStyle	Specifies the CSS style to be applied to the rendered input element
cssErrorClass	Specifies the CSS class to be applied to the rendered input element if the bound property contains errors, overriding the value of the cssClass attribute.
htmlEscape	Accepts true or false indicating whether or not the rendered value(s) should be HTML-escaped.
path	The path to the property to bind.

Table 5.6: The password tag's attributes

For example, the following **textarea** tag is bound to the **note** property of the form-backing object.

```
<form:textarea path="note" tabindex="4" rows="5" cols="80"/>
```

The checkbox Tag

The **checkbox** tag renders an **<input type="checkbox"/>** element. The attributes that can appear within the **checkbox** tag are listed in Table 5.7. All attributes are optional and this table does not include HTML attributes.

Attribute	Description
cssClass	Specifies the CSS class to be applied to the rendered input element.
cssStyle	Specifies the CSS style to be applied to the rendered input element
cssErrorClass	Specifies the CSS class to be applied to the rendered input element if the bound property contains errors, overriding the value of the cssClass attribute.
htmlEscape	Accepts true or false indicating whether or not the rendered value(s) should be HTML-escaped.
label	The value to be used as the label for the rendered checkbox.
path	The path to the property to bind.

Table 5.7: The checkbox tag's attributes

For example, the following **checkbox** tag is bound to the **outOfStock** property.

```
<form:checkbox path="outOfStock" value="Out of Stock"/>
```

The radiobutton Tag

The **radiobutton** tag renders an **<input type="radio"/>** element. The attributes for **radiobutton** are given in Table 5.8. All attributes in Table 5.8 are optional and the table does not include HTML attributes.

For instance, the following **radiobutton** tags are bound to a **newsletter** property.

```
Computing Now <form:radiobutton path="newsletter"
      value="Computing Now"/> <br/>
Modern Health <form:radiobutton path="newsletter"
      value="Modern Health"/>
```

Attribute	Description
cssClass	Specifies the CSS class to be applied to the rendered input element.
cssStyle	Specifies the CSS style to be applied to the rendered input element
cssErrorClass	Specifies the CSS class to be applied to the rendered input element if the bound property contains errors, overriding the value of the cssClass attribute.
htmlEscape	Accepts true or false indicating whether or not the rendered value(s) should be HTML-escaped.
label	The value to be used as the label for the rendered radio button.
path	The path to the property to bind.

Table 5.8: The radiobutton tag's attributes

The checkboxes Tag

The **checkboxes** tag renders multiple **<input type="checkbox"/>** elements. The attributes that may appear within **checkboxes** are given in Table 5.9. All attributes are optional and the table does not include HTML attributes.

For example, the following **checkboxes** tag renders the content of model attribute **categoryList** as check boxes. The **checkboxes** tag allows multiple selections.

```
<form:checkboxes path="category" items="${categoryList}"/>
```

Attribute	Description
cssClass	Specifies the CSS class to be applied to the rendered input element.
cssStyle	Specifies the CSS style to be applied to the rendered input element
cssErrorClass	Specifies the CSS class to be applied to the rendered input element if the bound property contains errors, overriding the value of the cssClass attribute.
delimiter	Specifies a delimiter between two input elements. By default, there is no delimiter.
element	Specifies an HTML element to enclosed each rendered input element. The default is 'span'.
htmlEscape	Accepts true or false indicating whether or not the rendered value(s) should be HTML-escaped.
items	The Collection, Map, or array of objects used to generate the input elements.
itemLabel	The property of the objects in the collection/Map/array specified in the items attribute that is to supply the label for each input element.
itemValue	The property of the objects in the collection/Map/array specified in the items attribute that is to supply the value for each input element.
path	The path to the property to bind.

Table 5.9: The checkboxes tag's attributes

The radiobuttons Tag

The **radiobuttons** tag renders multiple **<input type="radio"/>** elements. The attributes for **radiobuttons** tag are presented in Table 5.10.

For example, the following **radiobuttons** tag renders the content of model attribute **categoryList** as radio buttons. Only one radio button can be selected at a time.

```
<form:radiobuttons path="category" items="${categoryList}"/>
```

Attribute	Description
cssClass	Specifies the CSS class to be applied to the rendered input element.
cssStyle	Specifies the CSS style to be applied to the rendered input element
cssErrorClass	Specifies the CSS class to be applied to the rendered input element if the bound property contains errors, overriding the value of the cssClass attribute.
delimiter	Specifies a delimiter between two input elements. By default, there is no delimiter.
element	Specifies an HTML element to enclosed each rendered input element. The default is 'span'.
htmlEscape	Accepts true or false indicating whether or not the rendered value(s) should be HTML-escaped.
items	The Collection, Map, or array of objects used to generate the input elements.
itemLabel	The property of the objects in the collection/Map/array specified in the items attribute that is to supply the label for each input element.
itemValue	The property of the objects in the collection/Map/array specified in the items attribute that is to supply the value for each input element.
path	The path to the property to bind.

Table 5.10: The radiobuttons tag's attributes

The select Tag

The **select** tag renders a HTML select element. The options for the rendered element may come from a collection or a map or an array assigned to its **items** attribute or from a nested **option** or **options** tag. The properties of the **select** tag are given in Table 5.11. All attributes are optional and none of the HTML attributes is included in the table.

The **items** attribute is particularly useful as it may be bound to a collection, a map, or an array of objects to generate the options for the **select** element.

For example, the following **select** tag is bound to the **id** property of the **category** property of the form-backing object. Its options come from a

categories model attribute. The value for each option comes from the **id** property of the objects in the **categories** collection/map/array, and its label comes from the **name** property.

```
<form:select id="category" path="category.id"
    items="${categories}" itemLabel="name"
    itemValue="id"/>
```

Attribute	Description
cssClass	Specifies the CSS class to be applied to the rendered input element.
cssStyle	Specifies the CSS style to be applied to the rendered input element
cssErrorClass	Specifies the CSS class to be applied to the rendered input element if the bound property contains errors, overriding the value of the cssClass attribute.
htmlEscape	Accepts true or false indicating whether or not the rendered value(s) should be HTML-escaped.
items	The Collection, Map, or array of objects used to generate the input elements.
itemLabel	The property of the objects in the collection/Map/array specified in the items attribute that is to supply the label for each input element.
itemValue	The property of the objects in the collection/Map/array specified in the items attribute that is to supply the value for each input element.
path	The path to the property to bind.

Table 5.11: The select tag's attributes

The option Tag

The **option** tag renders an HTML **option** element to be used within a **select** element. Its attributes are given in Table 5.12. All attributes are optional and the table does not include HTML attributes.

For example, here is an example **option** tag.

Attribute	Description
cssClass	Specifies the CSS class to be applied to the rendered input element.
cssStyle	Specifies the CSS style to be applied to the rendered input element
cssErrorClass	Specifies the CSS class to be applied to the rendered input element if the bound property contains errors, overriding the value of the cssClass attribute.
htmlEscape	Accepts true or false indicating whether or not the rendered value(s) should be HTML-escaped.

Table 5.12: The option tag's attributes

```
<form:select id="category" path="category.id"
      items="${categories}" itemLabel="name"
      itemValue="id">
    <option value="0">-- Please select --</option>
</form:select>
```

This code snippet renders a **select** element whose options come from a **categories** model attribute as well as from the **option** tag.

The options Tag

The **options** tag generates a list of HTML option elements. Table 5.13 shows the attributes that may appear in the options tag. It does not include HTML attributes.

The **app05a** application provides an example of the **options** tag.

Attribute	Description
cssClass	Specifies the CSS class to be applied to the rendered input element.
cssStyle	Specifies the CSS style to be applied to the rendered input element
cssErrorClass	Specifies the CSS class to be applied to the rendered input element if the bound property contains errors, overriding the value of the cssClass attribute.
htmlEscape	Accepts true or false indicating whether or not the rendered value(s) should be HTML-escaped.
items	The Collection, Map, or array of objects used to generate the input elements.
itemLabel	The property of the objects in the collection/Map/array specified in the items attribute that is to supply the label for each input element.
itemValue	The property of the objects in the collection/Map/array specified in the items attribute that is to supply the value for each input element.

Table 5.13: The options tag's attributes

The errors Tag

The **errors** tag renders one or more HTML **span** element that each contains a field error message. This tag can be used to display a specific field error or all field errors.

The attributes of the **errors** tag are listed in Table 5.14. All attributes are optional and the table does not include HTML attributes that may appear in the HTML **span** elements.

For example, this **errors** tag displays all field errors.

```
<form:errors path="*"/>
```

The following **errors** tag displays a field error associated with the **author** property of the form-backing object.

```
<form:errors path="author"/>
```

Attribute	Description
cssClass	Specifies the CSS class to be applied to the rendered input element.
cssStyle	Specifies the CSS style to be applied to the rendered input element
delimiter	Delimiter for separating multiple error messages.
element	Specifies an HTML element to enclose the error messages.
htmlEscape	Accepts true or false indicating whether or not the rendered value(s) should be HTML-escaped.
path	The path to the errors object to bind.

Table 5.14: The errors tag's attributes

Data Binding Example

As an example of using the tags in the form tag library to take advantage of data binding, consider the **app05a** application. This example centers around the **Book** domain class. The class has several properties, including a **category** property of type **Category**. **Category** has two properties, **id** and **name**.

The application allows you to list books, add a new book, and edit a book.

The Directory Structure

Figure 5.1 shows the directory structure of **app05a**.

The Domain Classes

The **Book** class and the **Category** class are the domain classes in this application. They are given in Listing 5.1 and Listing 5.2, respectively.

```
📁 app05a
 ▲ 📁 css
      📄 main.css
 ▲ 📁 WEB-INF
      ▲ 📂 classes
          ▲ 📂 app05a
              ▲ 📂 controller
                   📄 BookController.class
              ▲ 📂 domain
                   📄 Book.class
                   📄 Category.class
              ▲ 📂 service
                   📄 BookService.class
                   📄 BookServiceImpl.class
      ▲ 📁 config
           📄 springmvc-config.xml
      ▲ 📁 jsp
           📄 BookAddForm.jsp
           📄 BookEditForm.jsp
           📄 BookList.jsp
      ▲ 📁 lib
           📄 commons-logging-1.1.2.jar
           📄 javax.servlet.jsp.jstl-1.2.1.jar
           📄 javax.servlet.jsp.jstl-api-1.2.1.jar
           📄 spring-beans-3.2.2.RELEASE.jar
           📄 spring-context-3.2.2.RELEASE.jar
           📄 spring-core-3.2.2.RELEASE.jar
           📄 spring-expression-3.2.2.RELEASE.jar
           📄 spring-web-3.2.2.RELEASE.jar
           📄 spring-webmvc-3.2.2.RELEASE.jar
      📄 web.xml
```

Figure 5.1: The directory structure of app05a

Listing 5.1: The Book class

```
package app05a.domain;
import java.io.Serializable;

public class Book implements Serializable {
```

```
    private static final long serialVersionUID =
            1520961851058396786L;
    private long id;
    private String isbn;
    private String title;
    private Category category;
    private String author;

    public Book() {
    }

    public Book(long id, String isbn, String title,
            Category category, String author) {
        this.id = id;
        this.isbn = isbn;
        this.title = title;
        this.category = category;
        this.author = author;
    }

    // get and set methods not shown

}
```

Listing 5.2: The Category class

```
package app05a.domain;

import java.io.Serializable;

public class Category implements Serializable {
    private static final long serialVersionUID =
            5658716793957904104L;
    private int id;
    private String name;

    public Category() {
    }

    public Category(int id, String name) {
        this.id = id;
        this.name = name;
    }

    // get and set methods not shown
```

```
}
```

The Controller Class

The example provides a controller for **Book**, the **BookController** class. It allows the user to create a new book, update a book's details, and list all books in the system. Listing 5.3 shows the **BookController** class.

Listing 5.2: The BookController class

```java
package app05a.controller;

import java.util.List;
import org.apache.commons.logging.Log;
import org.apache.commons.logging.LogFactory;
import org.springframework.beans.factory.annotation.Autowired;
import org.springframework.stereotype.Controller;
import org.springframework.ui.Model;
import org.springframework.web.bind.annotation.ModelAttribute;
import org.springframework.web.bind.annotation.PathVariable;
import org.springframework.web.bind.annotation.RequestMapping;
import app05a.domain.Book;
import app05a.domain.Category;
import app05a.service.BookService;

@Controller
public class BookController {

    @Autowired
    private BookService bookService;

    private static final Log logger =
        LogFactory.getLog(BookController.class);

    @RequestMapping(value = "/book_input")
    public String inputBook(Model model) {
        List<Category> categories = bookService.getAllCategories();
        model.addAttribute("categories", categories);
        model.addAttribute("book", new Book());
        return "BookAddForm";
    }

    @RequestMapping(value = "/book_edit/{id}")
    public String editBook(Model model, @PathVariable long id) {
        List<Category> categories = bookService.getAllCategories();
```

```
        model.addAttribute("categories", categories);
        Book book = bookService.get(id);
        model.addAttribute("book", book);
        return "BookEditForm";
    }

    @RequestMapping(value = "/book_save")
    public String saveBook(@ModelAttribute Book book) {
        Category category =
      bookService.getCategory(book.getCategory().getId());
        book.setCategory(category);
        bookService.save(book);
        return "redirect:/book_list";
    }

    @RequestMapping(value = "/book_update")
    public String updateBook(@ModelAttribute Book book) {
        Category category =
      bookService.getCategory(book.getCategory().getId());
        book.setCategory(category);
        bookService.update(book);
        return "redirect:/book_list";
    }

    @RequestMapping(value = "/book_list")
    public String listBooks(Model model) {
        logger.info("book_list");
        List<Book> books = bookService.getAllBooks();
        model.addAttribute("books", books);
        return "BookList";
    }
}
}
```

BookController is dependent on a **BookService** for some back-end
processing. The **@Autowired** annotation is used to inject an instance of
BookService implementation to the **BookController**.

```
@Autowired
private BookService bookService;
```

The Service Class

Finally, Listing 5.4 and Listing 5.5 show the **BookService** interface and the **BookServiceImpl** class, respectively. As the name implies, **BookServiceImpl** implements **BookService**.

Listing 5.4: The BookService interface

```
package app05a.service;

import java.util.List;
import app05a.domain.Book;
import app05a.domain.Category;

public interface BookService {

    List<Category> getAllCategories();
    Category getCategory(int id);
    List<Book> getAllBooks();
    Book save(Book book);
    Book update(Book book);
    Book get(long id);
    long getNextId();

}
```

Listing 5.5: The BookServiceImpl class

```
package app05a.service;

import java.util.ArrayList;
import java.util.List;

import org.springframework.stereotype.Service;
import app05a.domain.Book;
import app05a.domain.Category;

@Service
public class BookServiceImpl implements BookService {

    /*
     * this implementation is not thread-safe
     */
    private List<Category> categories;
```

```java
    private List<Book> books;

    public BookServiceImpl() {
        categories = new ArrayList<Category>();
        Category category1 = new Category(1, "Computing");
        Category category2 = new Category(2, "Travel");
        Category category3 = new Category(3, "Health");
        categories.add(category1);
        categories.add(category2);
        categories.add(category3);

        books = new ArrayList<Book>();
        books.add(new Book(1L, "9780980839623",
                "Servlet & JSP: A Tutorial",
                category1, "Budi Kurniawan"));
        books.add(new Book(2L, "9780980839630",
                "C#: A Beginner's Tutorial",
                category1, "Jayden Ky"));
    }

    @Override
    public List<Category> getAllCategories() {
        return categories;
    }

    @Override
    public Category getCategory(int id) {
        for (Category category : categories) {
            if (id == category.getId()) {
                return category;
            }
        }
        return null;
    }

    @Override
    public List<Book> getAllBooks() {
        return books;
    }

    @Override
    public Book save(Book book) {
        book.setId(getNextId());
        books.add(book);
        return book;
    }
```

```java
    @Override
    public Book get(long id) {
        for (Book book : books) {
            if (id == book.getId()) {
                return book;
            }
        }
        return null;
    }

    @Override
    public Book update(Book book) {
        int bookCount = books.size();
        for (int i = 0; i < bookCount; i++) {
            Book savedBook = books.get(i);
            if (savedBook.getId() == book.getId()) {
                books.set(i, book);
                return book;
            }
        }
        return book;
    }

    @Override
    public long getNextId() {
        // needs to be locked
        long id = 0L;
        for (Book book : books) {
            long bookId = book.getId();
            if (bookId > id) {
                id = bookId;
            }
        }
        return id + 1;
    }
}
```

The **BookServiceImpl** class contains a **List** of **Book** objects and a **List** of **Category** object. Both lists are populated when the class is instantiated. The class also contains methods for retrieving all books, retrieve a single book, and add and update a book.

The Configuration File

Listing 5.6 presents the Spring MVC configuration file for **app05a**.

Listing 5.6: The Spring MVC configuration file

```
<?xml version="1.0" encoding="UTF-8"?>
<beans xmlns="http://www.springframework.org/schema/beans"
    xmlns:xsi="http://www.w3.org/2001/XMLSchema-instance"
    xmlns:p="http://www.springframework.org/schema/p"
    xmlns:mvc="http://www.springframework.org/schema/mvc"
    xmlns:context="http://www.springframework.org/schema/context"
    xsi:schemaLocation="
        http://www.springframework.org/schema/beans
        http://www.springframework.org/schema/beans/spring-beans.xsd
        http://www.springframework.org/schema/mvc
        http://www.springframework.org/schema/mvc/spring-mvc.xsd
        http://www.springframework.org/schema/context
        http://www.springframework.org/schema/context/spring-
    context.xsd">

    <context:component-scan base-package="app05a.controller"/>
    <context:component-scan base-package="app05a.service"/>

    ... <!-- other elements are not shown -->

</beans>
```

The **component-scan** beans causes the **app05a.controller** and **app05a.service** packages to be scanned.

The View

The three JSP pages used in **app05a** are given in Listings 5.7, 5.8, and 5.9. In the **BookAddForm.jsp** and **BookEditForm.jsp** pages, the tags from the form tag library are used.

Listing 5.7: The BookList.jsp page

```
<%@ taglib uri="http://java.sun.com/jsp/jstl/core" prefix="c" %>
<!DOCTYPE HTML>
<html>
<head>
```

```
<title>Book List</title>
<style type="text/css">@import url("<c:url
     value="/css/main.css"/>");</style>
</head>
<body>

<div id="global">
<h1>Book List</h1>
<a href="<c:url value="/book_input"/>">Add Book</a>
<table>
<tr>
    <th>Category</th>
    <th>Title</th>
    <th>ISBN</th>
    <th>Author</th>
    <th> </th>
</tr>
<c:forEach items="${books}" var="book">
    <tr>
        <td>${book.category.name}</td>
        <td>${book.title}</td>
        <td>${book.isbn}</td>
        <td>${book.author}</td>
        <td><a href="book_edit/${book.id}">Edit</a></td>
    </tr>
</c:forEach>
</table>
</div>
</body>
</html>
```

Listing 5.8: The BookAddForm.jsp page

```
<%@ taglib prefix="form"
       uri="http://www.springframework.org/tags/form" %>
<%@ taglib uri="http://java.sun.com/jsp/jstl/core" prefix="c" %>
<!DOCTYPE HTML>
<html>
<head>
<title>Add Book Form</title>
<style type="text/css">@import url("<c:url
     value="/css/main.css"/>");</style>
</head>
<body>

<div id="global">
```

```
<form:form commandName="book" action="book_save" method="post">
    <fieldset>
        <legend>Add a book</legend>
        <p>
            <label for="category">Category: </label>
             <form:select id="category" path="category.id"
                items="${categories}" itemLabel="name"
                itemValue="id"/>
        </p>
        <p>
            <label for="title">Title: </label>
            <form:input id="title" path="title"/>
        </p>
        <p>
            <label for="author">Author: </label>
            <form:input id="author" path="author"/>
        </p>
        <p>
            <label for="isbn">ISBN: </label>
            <form:input id="isbn" path="isbn"/>
        </p>

        <p id="buttons">
            <input id="reset" type="reset" tabindex="4">
            <input id="submit" type="submit" tabindex="5"
                value="Add Book">
        </p>
    </fieldset>
</form:form>
</div>
</body>
</html>
```

Listing 5.9: The BookEditForm.jsp page

```
<%@ taglib prefix="form"
     uri="http://www.springframework.org/tags/form" %>
<%@ taglib uri="http://java.sun.com/jsp/jstl/core" prefix="c" %>
<!DOCTYPE HTML>
<html>
<head>
<title>Edit Book Form</title>
<style type="text/css">@import url("<c:url
     value="/css/main.css"/>");</style>
</head>
<body>
```

```
<div id="global">
<form:form commandName="book" action="/book_update" method="post">
    <fieldset>
        <legend>Edit a book</legend>
        <form:hidden path="id"/>
        <p>
            <label for="category">Category: </label>
             <form:select id="category" path="category.id" items="$
    {categories}"
                itemLabel="name" itemValue="id"/>
        </p>
        <p>
            <label for="title">Title: </label>
            <form:input id="title" path="title"/>
        </p>
        <p>
            <label for="author">Author: </label>
            <form:input id="author" path="author"/>
        </p>
        <p>
            <label for="isbn">ISBN: </label>
            <form:input id="isbn" path="isbn"/>
        </p>

        <p id="buttons">
            <input id="reset" type="reset" tabindex="4">
            <input id="submit" type="submit" tabindex="5"
                value="Update Book">
        </p>
    </fieldset>
</form:form>
</div>
</body>
</html>
```

Testing the Application

To test the application, go to this page.

```
http://localhost:8080/app05a/book_list
```

Figure 5.2 shows the list of books when the application is first started.

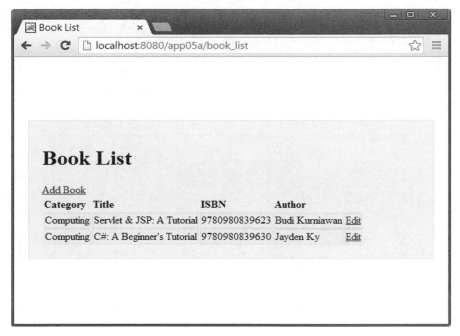

Figure 5.2: The book list

You can click the Add Book link to add a book or an Edit link to the right of a book's details to edit the book.

Figure 5.3 shows the Add Book form and Figure 5.4 the Edit Book form.

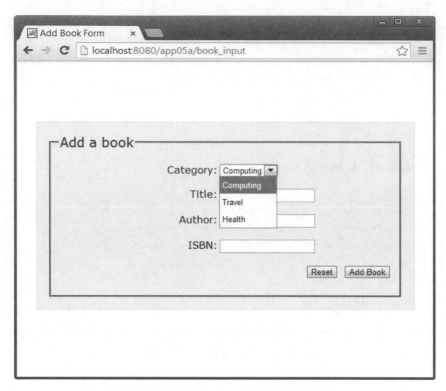

Figure 5.3: The Add Book form

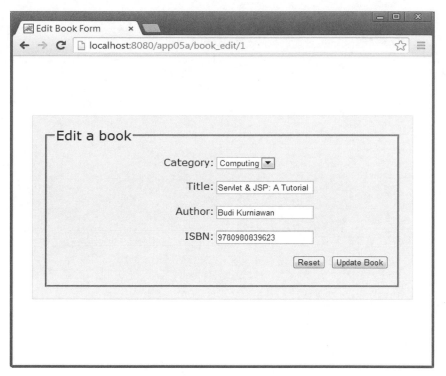

Figure 5.4: The Edit Book form

Summary

In this chapter you learned about data binding and the tags in the form tag library. The next two chapters discuss how you can further take advantage of data binding with converters, formatters, and validators.

Chapter 6
Converters and Formatters

In Chapter 5, "Data Binding and the Form Tag Library" you witnessed the power of data binding and learned to harness it using the tags in the form tag library. However, Spring data binding is not without limit. There are cases where Spring is clueless on how to bind data correctly. For example, Spring will always try to bind a date input to a **java.util.Date** using the default locale. If you want Spring to use a different date pattern, for example, you need to use a converter or a formatter to help Spring.

This chapter discusses the converter and the formatter. Both are used to convert one type of object to another. Converters are generic components that can be used in any tier of the application. Formatters, on the other hand, are specifically designed for the web tier.

Converters

A Spring converter is an object that converts a type to another type. For example, user input for a date can be in many forms. "December 25, 2014," 12/25/2014," "2014-12-25" can all represent the same date. By default, Spring expects the input to be in the same pattern as the current locale, which is probably in MM/dd/yyyy format if you live in the United States. If you want Spring to use a different date pattern when binding an input string to a **Date**, you need to write a string-to-date converter.

To create a converter, you must write a Java class that implement the **org.springframework.core.convert.converter.Converter** interface. The declaration of this interface is parameterized:

```
public interface Converter<S, T>
```

Here, *S* represents the source type and *T* the target type. For instance, to create a converter that can convert a **Long** to a **Date**, you would declare your converter class like so.

```
public class MyConverter implements Converter<Long, Date> {

}
```

In your class body, you need to write an implementation of the **convert** method from the **Converter** interface. The signature of this method is as follows.

```
T convert(S source)
```

For example, Listing 6.1 shows a converter that can work with any date pattern.

Listing 6.1: The StringToDate converter

```
package app06a.converter;

import java.text.ParseException;
import java.text.SimpleDateFormat;
import java.util.Date;

import org.springframework.core.convert.converter.Converter;

public class StringToDateConverter implements Converter<String,
        Date> {

    private String datePattern;

    public StringToDateConverter(String datePattern) {
        this.datePattern = datePattern;
        System.out.println("instantiating .... converter with
    pattern:*"
                + datePattern);
    }

    @Override
    public Date convert(String s) {
        try {
            SimpleDateFormat dateFormat =
                    new SimpleDateFormat(datePattern);
            dateFormat.setLenient(false);
            return dateFormat.parse(s);
```

```
        } catch (ParseException e) {
            // the error message will be displayed when using
            // <form:errors>
            throw new IllegalArgumentException(
                    "invalid date format. Please use this pattern\""
                            + datePattern + "\"");
        }
    }
}
```

Note that the **convert** method in Listing 6.1 converts a **String** to a **Date** using the date pattern passed to the constructor.

To use custom converters in a Spring MVC application, you need to write a **conversionService** bean in your Spring MVC configuration file. The class name for the bean must be **org.springframework.context.support.ConversionServiceFactoryBean**. The bean must contain a **converters** property that lists all custom converters to be used in the application. For example, the following bean declaration registers the **StringToDateConverter** in Listing 6.1.

```
<bean id="conversionService"
        class="org.springframework.context.support.
➡ConversionServiceFactoryBean">
    <property name="converters">
        <list>
            <bean class="app06a.converter.StringToDateConverter">
                <constructor-arg type="java.lang.String"
                        value="MM-dd-yyyy"/>
            </bean>
        </list>
    </property>
</bean>
```

After that, you need to assign the bean name (in this case, **conversionService**) to the **conversion-service** attribute of the **annotation-driven** element, like so

```
<mvc:annotation-driven
        conversion-service="conversionService"/>
```

As an example, the **app06a** is a sample application that uses the **StringToDateConverter** to convert a **String** to the **birthDate** property of the **Employee** object. The **Employee** class is given in Listing 6.2.

Listing 6.2: The Employee class

```
package app06a.domain;

import java.io.Serializable;
import java.util.Date;

public class Employee implements Serializable {
    private static final long serialVersionUID = -908L;

    private long id;
    private String firstName;
    private String lastName;
    private Date birthDate;
    private int salaryLevel;

    // getters and setters not shown

}
```

The **EmployeeController** class in Listing 6.3 is the controller for the **Employee** domain object.

Listing 6.3: The EmployeeController class in app06a

```
package app06a.controller;

import org.apache.commons.logging.Log;
import org.apache.commons.logging.LogFactory;
import org.springframework.ui.Model;
import org.springframework.validation.BindingResult;
import org.springframework.validation.FieldError;
import org.springframework.web.bind.annotation.ModelAttribute;
import org.springframework.web.bind.annotation.RequestMapping;
import app06a.domain.Employee;

@org.springframework.stereotype.Controller

public class EmployeeController {

    private static final Log logger =
        LogFactory.getLog(ProductController.class);

    @RequestMapping(value="employee_input")
    public String inputEmployee(Model model) {
        model.addAttribute(new Employee());
```

```
        return "EmployeeForm";
    }

    @RequestMapping(value="employee_save")
    public String saveEmployee(@ModelAttribute Employee employee,
            BindingResult bindingResult, Model model) {
        if (bindingResult.hasErrors()) {
            FieldError fieldError = bindingResult.getFieldError();
            logger.info("Code:" + fieldError.getCode()
                    + ", field:" + fieldError.getField());
            return "EmployeeForm";
        }

        // save employee here

        model.addAttribute("employee", employee);
        return "EmployeeDetails";
    }
}
```

The **EmployeeController** class has two request-handling methods, **inputEmployee** and **saveEmployee**. The **inputEmployee** method returns the **EmployeeForm.jsp** page in Listing 6.4. The **saveEmployee** method takes an **Employee** object that gets created when the Employee form is submitted. Thanks to the **StringToDateConverter** converter, you do not need to do parsing in your controller class to convert a string to a **Date**.

The **BindingResult** argument of the **saveEmployee** method is populated with all binding errors by Spring. The method uses the **BindingResult** to log any binding error. Binding errors can also be displayed in a form using the **errors** tag, as you can see in the **EmployeeForm.jsp** page.

Listing 6.4: The EmployeeForm.jsp page

```
<%@ taglib prefix="form"
        uri="http://www.springframework.org/tags/form" %>
<%@ taglib uri="http://java.sun.com/jsp/jstl/core" prefix="c" %>
<!DOCTYPE HTML>
<html>
<head>
<title>Add Employee Form</title>
<style type="text/css">@import url("<c:url
        value="/css/main.css"/>");</style>
</head>
```

```
<body>

<div id="global">
<form:form commandName="employee" action="employee_save"
      method="post">
    <fieldset>
        <legend>Add an employee</legend>
        <p>
            <label for="firstName">First Name: </label>
            <form:input path="firstName" tabindex="1"/>
        </p>
        <p>
            <label for="lastName">First Name: </label>
            <form:input path="lastName" tabindex="2"/>
        </p>
        <p>
            <form:errors path="birthDate" cssClass="error"/>
        </p>
        <p>
            <label for="birthDate">Date Of Birth: </label>
            <form:input path="birthDate" tabindex="3" />
        </p>
        <p id="buttons">
            <input id="reset" type="reset" tabindex="4">
            <input id="submit" type="submit" tabindex="5"
                value="Add Employee">
        </p>
    </fieldset>
</form:form>
</div>
</body>
</html>
```

You can test the converter by directing your browser to this URL:

```
http://localhost:8080/app06a/employee_input
```

Type in an invalid date and you'll be redirected to the same Employee form and see an error message in the form.

Figure 6.1: Conversion error in the Employee form

Formatters

A formatter is like a converter, it also converts a type to another type. However, the source type for a formatter must be a **String** whereas a converter can work with any source type. Formatters are more suitable for the web-tier whereas converters can be used in any tier. For converting user input in a form in a Spring MVC application, you should always choose a formatter over a converter.

To create a formatter, write a Java class that implements the **org.springframework.format.Formatter** interface. Here is the declaration of the interface.

```
public interface Formatter<T>
```

Here, *T* represents the type to which the input string should be converted. The interface has two methods that all implementations must override, **parse** and **print**.

```
T parse(String text, java.util.Locale locale)

String print(T object, java.util.Locale locale)
```

The **parse** method parses a **String** to the target type using the specified **Locale**. The **print** method does the reverse, it returns the string representation of the target object.

As an example, the **app06b** application employs a **DateFormatter** for converting a **String** to a **Date**. It does the same job as the **StringToDateConverter** converter in **app06a**.

The **DateFormatter** class is given in Listing 6.5.

Listing 6.5: The DateFormatter class

```
package app06b.formatter;

import java.text.ParseException;
import java.text.SimpleDateFormat;
import java.util.Date;
import java.util.Locale;

import org.springframework.format.Formatter;

public class DateFormatter implements Formatter<Date> {

    private String datePattern;
    private SimpleDateFormat dateFormat;

    public DateFormatter(String datePattern) {
        this.datePattern = datePattern;
        dateFormat = new SimpleDateFormat(datePattern);
        dateFormat.setLenient(false);
    }
```

```
    @Override
    public String print(Date date, Locale locale) {
        return dateFormat.format(date);
    }

    @Override
    public Date parse(String s, Locale locale) throws ParseException
        {
        try {
            return dateFormat.parse(s);
        } catch (ParseException e) {
            // the error message will be displayed when using
            // <form:errors>
            throw new IllegalArgumentException(
                    "invalid date format. Please use this pattern\""
                            + datePattern + "\"");
        }
    }
}
```

To use a formatter in a Spring MVC application, you need to register it using the **conversionService** bean. The class name for the bean must be **org.springframework.format.support.FormattingConversion-ServiceFactoryBean**. This is a different class than the one used in **app06a** for registering the converter. The bean can have a **formatters** property for registering formatters and a **converters** property for registering converters. Listing 6.6 shows the Spring configuration file for **app06b**.

Listing 6.6: The Spring configuration file for app06b

```xml
<?xml version="1.0" encoding="UTF-8"?>
<beans xmlns="http://www.springframework.org/schema/beans"
    xmlns:xsi="http://www.w3.org/2001/XMLSchema-instance"
    xmlns:p="http://www.springframework.org/schema/p"
    xmlns:mvc="http://www.springframework.org/schema/mvc"
    xmlns:context="http://www.springframework.org/schema/context"
    xsi:schemaLocation="
        http://www.springframework.org/schema/beans
        http://www.springframework.org/schema/beans/spring-beans.xsd
        http://www.springframework.org/schema/mvc
        http://www.springframework.org/schema/mvc/spring-mvc.xsd
        http://www.springframework.org/schema/context
        http://www.springframework.org/schema/context/spring-
context.xsd">
```

```
    <context:component-scan base-package="app06b.controller"/>
    <context:component-scan base-package="app06b.formatter"/>

    <mvc:annotation-driven conversion-service="conversionService"/>

    <mvc:resources mapping="/css/**" location="/css/"/>
    <mvc:resources mapping="/*.html" location="/"/>

    <bean id="viewResolver"
          class="org.springframework.web.servlet.view.
➡InternalResourceViewResolver">
        <property name="prefix" value="/WEB-INF/jsp/" />
        <property name="suffix" value=".jsp" />
    </bean>

    <bean id="conversionService"
          class="org.springframework.format.support.
➡FormattingConversionServiceFactoryBean">
        <property name="formatters">
            <set>
                <bean class="app06b.formatter.DateFormatter">
                    <constructor-arg type="java.lang.String"
                        value="MM-dd-yyyy" />
                </bean>
            </set>
        </property>
    </bean>
</beans>
```

Note that you also need to add a **component-scan** element for the formatter.

To test the formatter in **app06b**, direct your browser to this URL:

```
http://localhost:8080/app06b/employee_input
```

Using a Registrar to Register A Formatter

Another way of registering a formatter is by using a Registrar. For example, the code in Listing 6.7 is an example of a registrar that registers the **DateFormatter**.

Listing 6.7: The MyFormatterRegistrar class

```
package app06b.formatter;
```

```java
import org.springframework.format.FormatterRegistrar;
import org.springframework.format.FormatterRegistry;

public class MyFormatterRegistrar implements FormatterRegistrar {

    private String datePattern;
    public MyFormatterRegistrar(String datePattern) {
        this.datePattern = datePattern;
    }

    @Override
    public void registerFormatters(FormatterRegistry registry) {
        registry.addFormatter(new DateFormatter(datePattern));
        // register more formatters here
    }

}
```

With a registrar, you don't need to register any formatter in your spring
MVC config file. Instead, you register the registrar in the Spring
configuration file, as shown in Listing 6.8.

Listing 6.8: Registering a registrar in the springmvc-config.xml file

```xml
<?xml version="1.0" encoding="UTF-8"?>
<beans xmlns="http://www.springframework.org/schema/beans"
    xmlns:xsi="http://www.w3.org/2001/XMLSchema-instance"
    xmlns:p="http://www.springframework.org/schema/p"
    xmlns:mvc="http://www.springframework.org/schema/mvc"
    xmlns:context="http://www.springframework.org/schema/context"
    xsi:schemaLocation="
        http://www.springframework.org/schema/beans
        http://www.springframework.org/schema/beans/spring-beans.xsd
        http://www.springframework.org/schema/mvc
        http://www.springframework.org/schema/mvc/spring-mvc.xsd
        http://www.springframework.org/schema/context
        http://www.springframework.org/schema/context/spring-
context.xsd">

    <context:component-scan base-package="app06b.controller" />
    <context:component-scan base-package="app06b.service" />

    <mvc:annotation-driven conversion-service="conversionService" />

    <mvc:resources mapping="/css/**" location="/css/" />
    <mvc:resources mapping="/*.html" location="/" />
```

```
    <bean id="viewResolver"
            class="org.springframework.web.servlet.view.
➡InternalResourceViewResolver">
        <property name="prefix" value="/WEB-INF/jsp/" />
        <property name="suffix" value=".jsp" />
    </bean>

    <bean id="conversionService"
            class="org.springframework.format.support.
➡FormattingConversionServiceFactoryBean">

        <property name="formatterRegistrars">
            <set>
                <bean class="app06b.formatter.MyFormatterRegistrar">
                    <constructor-arg type="java.lang.String"
                            value="MM-dd-yyyy" />
                </bean>
            </set>
        </property>
    </bean>
</beans>
```

Choosing Between Converters and Formatters

A converter is used as a general purpose utility to convert one type to another, such as a **String** to a **Date** or a **Long** to a **Date**. A converter can be used not only in the web tier, but also in other tiers.

On the other hand, a formatter can only convert a **String** to another Java type, such as a **String** to a **Date**. It cannot be used to convert a **Long** to a **Date**, for instance. Therefore, a formatter is suitable for the web tier and as such, in a Spring MVC application, a formatter is more appropriate than a converter.

Summary

In this chapter you learned about converters and formatter, which you can use to direct data binding in a Spring MVC application. Converters are a general-purpose tool for converting any type to another type whereas formatters are for converting **String** to another Java type. Formatters are more suitable to be used in the web-tier.

Chapter 7
Validators

Input validation is one of the most important web development tasks that Spring handles extremely well. There are two ways you can validate input in Spring MVC, by using Spring's own validation framework or by utilizing a JSR 303 implementation. This chapter covers both methods of input validation.

Validation Overview

Converters and formatters work on the field level. In an MVC application, they convert or format a **String** to another Java type, such as a **java.util.Date**. A validator, on the other hand, works on the object level. It determines whether or not all fields in an object are valid and some rules are followed.

The sequence of events in an application that employs both formatters and validators goes like this. During the invocation of a controller, one or more formatter will try to convert input strings to field values in the domain object. Once formatting is successful, the validators step in.

For example, an **Order** object may have a **shippingDate** property (of type **Date**, obviously) whose value cannot be earlier than today's date. When the **OrderController** is invoked, a **DateFormatter** would convert a string to a **Date** and assign it to the **shippingDate** property of the **Order** object. If the conversion failed, the user will be redirected to the previous form. If the conversion was successful, a validator will be invoked to check if **shippingDate** is earlier than today.

Now, you may ask if it is wise to move the validation logic to the **DateFormatter**. After all, it is not hard to compare dates. The answer is no.

First, the **DateFormatter** may be used for formatting other strings to dates, such as **birthDate** or **purchaseDate**. Both dates have different rules than **shippingDate**. In fact, a date of birth for an employee, for example, cannot be a future date. Second, a validator may work by inspecting the relationship between two or more fields, each of which is supported by a different formatter. For example, given an **Employee** object with a **birthDate** property and a **startDate** property, a validator may rule that there is no way someone starts working in the company before he or she was born. Therefore, a valid **Employee** object must have its **birthDate** property value that is earlier than its **startDate** value. That's the job of a validator.

Spring Validators

Right from the start, Spring has been designed with input validation in mind. This was even before JSR 303 (Java validation specification) was conceived. As such, the Spring Validation framework was commonplace even today, although JSR 303 validators are generally recommended for new projects.

To create a Spring validator, implement the **org.springframework.validation.Validator** interface. This interface is given in Listing 7.1 and has two methods, **supports** and **validate**.

Listing 7.1: The Spring Validator interface

```
package org.springframework.validation;
public interface Validator {
    boolean supports(Class<?> clazz);
    void validate(Object target, Errors errors);
}
```

The **supports** method returns **true** if the validator can handle the specified **Class**. The **validate** method validates the target object and populate the **Errors** object with validation errors.

An **Errors** object is an instance of the **org.springframework.validation.Errors** interface. An **Errors** object contains a list of **FieldError** and **ObjectError** objects. A **FieldError** represents an error that is related to one of the properties in the validated object. For example, if the **price** property of a product must not be negative and the price of a **Product** object being validated is negative, then a **FieldError** needs to be created. An **ObjectError** is any error that is not a **FieldError**. For example, if a **Book** that is for sale in Europe is being purchased on an American online branch, then an **ObjectError** should be raised.

When writing a validator, you don't need to create an error object directly as instantiating **ObjectError** or **FieldError** takes a lot of programming effort. This is because the **ObjectError** class's constructor expects four arguments and the **FieldError** class's constructor takes seven, as you can see in the constructor signatures below.

```
ObjectError(String objectName, String[] codes, Object[] arguments,
        String defaultMessage)

FieldError(String objectName, String field, Object rejectedValue,
        boolean bindingFailure, String[] codes, Object[] arguments,
        String defaultMessage)
```

The easier way to add an error to the **Errors** object is by calling one of the **reject** or **rejectValue** methods on the **Errors** object. You call **reject** to add an **ObjectError** and **rejectValue** to add a **FieldError**.

Here are some of the method overloads of **reject** and **rejectValue**.

```
void reject(String errorCode)

void reject(String errorCode, String defaultMessage)

void rejectValue(String field, String errorCode)

void rejectValue(String field, String errorCode,
        String defaultMessage)
```

Most of the time, you just need to pass an error code to the **reject** or **rejectValue** method. Spring can then look up the error code against a properties file to obtain the corresponding error message. You can also pass a default message that will be used if the error code is not found.

The error messages in an **Errors** object can be displayed on an HTML page by using the **errors** tag of the form tag library. Error messages can be localized through the internationalization feature that Spring supports. More about internationalization can be found in Chapter 10, "Internationalization."

The ValidationUtils Class

The **org.springframework.validation.ValidationUtils** class is a utility that can help you write a Spring validator. Instead of writing this.

```
if (firstName == null || firstName.isEmpty()) {
    errors.rejectValue("price");
}
```

you can use the **ValidationUtils** class's **rejectIfEmpty** method like this.

```
ValidationUtils.rejectIfEmpty("price");
```

Or instead of this.

```
if (firstName == null || firstName.trim().isEmpty()) {
    errors.rejectValue("price");
}
```

you can write this.

```
ValidationUtils.rejectIfEmptyOrWhitespace("price");
```

Here are the complete method overloads of **rejectIfEmpty** and **rejectIfEmptyOrWhitespace** methods in **ValidationUtils**.

```
public static void rejectIfEmpty(Errors errors, String field,
        String errorCode)

public static void rejectIfEmpty(Errors errors, String field,
        String errorCode, Object[] errorArgs)

public static void rejectIfEmpty(Errors errors, String field,
        String errorCode, Object[] errorArgs, String defaultMessage)

public static void rejectIfEmpty(Errors errors, String field,
        String errorCode, String defaultMessage)

public static void rejectIfEmptyOrWhitespace(Errors errors,
        String field, String errorCode)

public static void rejectIfEmptyOrWhitespace(Errors errors,
        String field, String errorCode, Object[] errorArgs)

public static void rejectIfEmptyOrWhitespace(Errors errors,
        String field, String errorCode, Object[] errorArgs,
        String defaultMessage)

public static void rejectIfEmptyOrWhitespace(Errors errors,
```

```
        String field, String errorCode, String defaultMessage)
```

In addition, **ValidationUtils** also has an **invokeValidator** method for invoking a validator.

```
public static void invokeValidator(Validator validator,
        Object obj, Errors errors)
```

You learn how to use this useful tool in the example in the next section.

A Spring Validator Example

The **app07a** application contains a validator named **ProductValidator** for validating **Product** objects. The **Product** class for **app07a** is given in Listing 7.2 and the **ProductValidator** class in Listing 7.3.

Listing 7.2: The Product class

```
package app07a.domain;
import java.io.Serializable;
import java.util.Date;

public class Product implements Serializable {
    private static final long serialVersionUID = 748392348L;
    private String name;
    private String description;
    private Float price;
    private Date productionDate;

    // getters and setters not shown
}
```

Listing 7.3: The ProductValidator class

```
package app07a.validator;

import java.util.Date;
import org.springframework.validation.Errors;
import org.springframework.validation.ValidationUtils;
import org.springframework.validation.Validator;
import app07a.domain.Product;

public class ProductValidator implements Validator {
```

```
@Override
public boolean supports(Class<?> klass) {
    return Product.class.isAssignableFrom(klass);
}

@Override
public void validate(Object target, Errors errors) {
    Product product = (Product) target;
    ValidationUtils.rejectIfEmpty(errors, "name",
            "productname.required");
    ValidationUtils.rejectIfEmpty(errors, "price",
            "price.required");
    ValidationUtils.rejectIfEmpty(errors, "productionDate",
            "productiondate.required");
    Float price = product.getPrice();
    if (price != null && price < 0) {
        errors.rejectValue("price", "price.negative");
    }
    Date productionDate = product.getProductionDate();
    if (productionDate != null) {
        // The hour,minute,second components of productionDate
        // are 0
        if (productionDate.after(new Date())) {
            System.out.println("salah lagi");
            errors.rejectValue("productionDate",
                    "productiondate.invalid");
        }
    }
}
}
```

The **ProductValidator** validator is a very simple validator. Its **validate** method checks if a **Product** has a name and a price and the price is not negative. It also makes sure the production date is not later than today.

The Resource File

You don't need to explicitly register a validator. However, if you want the error messages to be taken from a properties file, you need to tell Spring where to find the file by declaring a **messageSource** bean. Here is the messageSource bean declaration in **app07a**.

```
<bean id="messageSource" class="org.springframework.context.support.
➥ReloadableResourceBundleMessageSource">
```

```
        <property name="basename" value="/WEB-INF/resource/messages"/>
</bean>
```

The bean essentially says that error codes and error messages can be found in the **messages.properties** file under **/WEB-INF/resource**.

Listing 7.4 shows the content of the **messages.properties** file.

Listing 7.4: The messages.properties file

```
productname.required.product.name=Please enter a product name
price.required=Please enter a price
productiondate.required=Please enter a production date
productiondate.invalid=Invalid production date. Please ensure the
production date is not later than today.
```

The Controller class

You can use a Spring validator in a controller class by directly instantiating the validator class. The **saveProduct** method in the **ProductController** class in Listing 7.5 creates a **ProductValidator** and calls its **validate** method. To check if the validator generated an error message, call the **hasErrors** method on the **BindingResult**.

Listing 7.5: The ProductController class

```
package app07a.controller;

import org.apache.commons.logging.Log;
import org.apache.commons.logging.LogFactory;
import org.springframework.stereotype.Controller;
import org.springframework.ui.Model;
import org.springframework.validation.BindingResult;
import org.springframework.validation.FieldError;
import org.springframework.web.bind.annotation.ModelAttribute;
import org.springframework.web.bind.annotation.RequestMapping;

import app07a.domain.Product;
import app07a.validator.ProductValidator;

@Controller
public class ProductController {

    private static final Log logger = LogFactory
```

```
                    .getLog(ProductController.class);

    @RequestMapping(value = "/product_input")
    public String inputProduct(Model model) {
        model.addAttribute("product", new Product());
        return "ProductForm";
    }

    @RequestMapping(value = "/product_save")
    public String saveProduct(@ModelAttribute Product product,
            BindingResult bindingResult, Model model) {

        ProductValidator productValidator = new ProductValidator();
        productValidator.validate(product, bindingResult);

        if (bindingResult.hasErrors()) {
            FieldError fieldError = bindingResult.getFieldError();
            logger.info("Code:" + fieldError.getCode() + ", field:"
                    + fieldError.getField());

            return "ProductForm";
        }

        // save product here

        model.addAttribute("product", product);
        return "ProductDetails";
    }
}
```

Another way of using a Spring validator is by writing an **initBinder** method in your controller, and passing the validator to the **WebDataBinder** and calling its **validate** method.

```
@org.springframework.web.bind.annotation.InitBinder
public void initBinder(WebDataBinder binder) {
    // this will apply the validator to all request-handling methods
    binder.setValidator(new ProductValidator());
    binder.validate();
}
```

Passing a validator to the **WebDataBinder** will apply the validator to all request-handling methods in the controller class.

Alternatively, you can annotate the object argument to be validated with **@javax.validation.Valid**. For example,

```
public String saveProduct(@ModelAttribute Product product,
        BindingResult bindingResult, Model model) {
```

The **Valid** annotation type is defined in JSR 303 and I will defer any discussion of JSR 303 until the next section.

Testing the Validator

To test the validator in **app07a**, direct your browser to this URL.

```
http://localhost:8080/app07a/product_input
```

You will see a blank Product form. If you click the Add Product button without entering any value, you will be redirected back to the Product form and this time there will be error messages from the validator, as shown in Figure 7.1.

Figure 7.1: The ProductValidator in action

JSR 303 Validation

JSR 303, "Bean Validation" (published in November 2009) and JSR 349, "Bean Validation 1.1" (published in May 2013) specify a set of API's for applying constraints on object properties through annotations. JSR 303 and JSR 349 can be downloaded from these URLs, respectively.

```
http://jcp.org/en/jsr/detail?id=303
```

```
http://jcp.org/en/jsr/detail?id=349
```

Of course, a JSR is just a specification document and of little use until someone writes an implementation of it. In the case of bean validation

JSR's, there are currently two implementations. The first is Hibernate Validator, which is currently at version 5 and implement both JSR 303 and JSR 349. It can be downloaded from this site.

`http://sourceforge.net/projects/hibernate/files/hibernate-validator/`

The second implementation is Apache BVal, which implements JSR 303 only and can be downloaded from this site.

`http://bval.apache.org/downloads.html`

Apache BVal 0.5 was the latest version at the time of writing and did not seem stable enough. For this apparent reason, I am using Hibernate Validator for the accompanying application (**app07b**).

As a side note, the following is an important website for everything related to Java bean validation.

`http://beanvalidation.org`

With JSR 303, there is no validator to write. Instead, you embed constraints in the domain class by using JSR 303 annotation types. The list of constraints is given in Table 7.1.

Once you understand how it works, JSR 303 validation is easier to use than Spring validators. As with Spring validators, you can overwrite error messages from a JSR 303 validator by using property keys in this format in your properties file.

constraint.object.property

For example, to overwrite a message from **@Size** constraining the **name** property of a **Product** object, use this key in your properties file.

`Size.product.name`

To overwrite a message from **@Past** constraining the **productionDate** property of a **Product** object, use this key.

`Past.product.productionDate`

Constraint	Description	Example
@AssertFalse	Applied to a boolean property. The value of the property must be false.	@AssertFalse boolean hasChildren;
@AssertTrue	Applied to a boolean property. The value of the property must be true.	@AssertTrue boolean isEmpty;
@DecimalMax	The value of the property must be a decimal value lower than or equal to the specified value.	@DecimalMax("1.1") BigDecimal price;
@DecimalMin	The value of the property must be a decimal value greater than or equal to the specified value.	@DecimalMin("0.04") BigDecimal price;
@Digits	The value of the property must be within the specified range. The integer attribute specifies the maximum integral digits for the number and the fraction attribute the maximum fractional digits for the number.	@Digits(integer=5, fraction=2) BigDecimal price;
@Future	The value of the property must be a date in the future.	@Future Date shippingDate;
@Max	The value of the property must be an integer lower than or equal to the specified value	@Max(150) int age;
@Min	The value of the property must be an integer greater than or equal to the specified value	@Min(0) int age;
@NotNull	The property must not be null	@NotNull String firstName;
@Null	The property must be null	@Null String testString;
@Past	The value of the property must be a date in the past.	@Past Date birthDate;
@Pattern	The value of the property must match the specified regular expression	@Pattern(regext="\\d{3}") String areaCode;
@Size	The size of the property must be within the specified range.	Size(min=2, max=140) String description;

Table 7.1: JSR 303 Constraints

A JSR 303 Validator Example

The **app07b** application shows JSR 303 input validation in action. The application is a modified version of **app07a** with a few differences. First, there is no **ProductValidator** class. Second, the jar files from the Hibernate Validator library have been added to **WEB-INF/lib**.

Listing 7.6 shows the **Product** class whose **name** and **productionDate** fields have been annotated with JSR 303 annotation types.

Listing 7.6: The Product class in app07b

```
package app07b.domain;
import java.io.Serializable;
import java.util.Date;

import javax.validation.constraints.Past;
import javax.validation.constraints.Size;

public class Product implements Serializable {
    private static final long serialVersionUID = 78L;

    @Size(min=1, max=10)
    private String name;

    private String description;
    private Float price;

    @Past
    private Date productionDate;

    // getters and setters not shown

}
```

In the **ProductController** class's **saveProduct** method, you must annotate the **Product** argument with **@Valid**, as shown in Listing 7.7.

Listing 7.7: The ProductController class in app07b

```
package app07b.controller;

import javax.validation.Valid;

import org.apache.commons.logging.Log;
```

```
import org.apache.commons.logging.LogFactory;
import org.springframework.stereotype.Controller;
import org.springframework.ui.Model;
import org.springframework.validation.BindingResult;
import org.springframework.validation.FieldError;
import org.springframework.web.bind.annotation.ModelAttribute;
import org.springframework.web.bind.annotation.RequestMapping;

import app07b.domain.Product;

@Controller
public class ProductController {

    private static final Log logger = LogFactory
            .getLog(ProductController.class);

    @RequestMapping(value = "/product_input")
    public String inputProduct(Model model) {
        model.addAttribute("product", new Product());
        return "ProductForm";
    }

    @RequestMapping(value = "/product_save")
    public String saveProduct(@Valid @ModelAttribute Product
      product,
            BindingResult bindingResult, Model model) {

        if (bindingResult.hasErrors()) {
            FieldError fieldError = bindingResult.getFieldError();
            logger.info("Code:" + fieldError.getCode() + ", object:"
                    + fieldError.getObjectName() + ", field:"
                    + fieldError.getField());
            return "ProductForm";
        }

        // save product here

        model.addAttribute("product", product);
        return "ProductDetails";
    }
}
```

To customize error messages from the validator, two keys are used in the messages.properties file. This file is printed in Listing 7.8.

Listing 7.8: The messages.properties file in app07b

```
Size.product.name = Product name must be 1 to 10 characters long
Past.product.productionDate=Production date must a past date
```

To test the validator in **app07b**, direct your browser to this URL.

```
http://localhost:8080/app07b/product_input
```

Summary

In this chapter you learned the two types of validators you can use in your Spring MVC applications, Spring MVC validators and JSR 303 validators. JSR 303 validators are the recommended validation method for new projects as JSR 303 is a formal Java specification.

Chapter 8
The Expression Language

One of the most important features in JSP 2.0 was the Expression Language (EL), which JSP authors can use to access application data. Inspired by both the ECMAScript and the XPath expression languages, the EL is designed to make it possible and easy to author script-free JSP pages, that is, pages that do not use JSP declarations, expressions, or scriptlets.

The EL that was adopted into JSP 2.0 first appeared in the JSP Standard Tag Library (JSTL) 1.0 specification. JSP 1.2 programmers could use the language by importing the standard libraries into their applications. JSP 2.0 and later developers can use the EL without JSTL, even though JSTL is still needed in many applications as it also contains other tags not related to the EL.

The EL in JSP 2.1 and JSP 2.2 is an attempt to unify the EL in JSP 2.0 and the expression language defined in JavaServer Faces (JSF) 1.0. JSF is a framework for rapidly building web applications in Java and was built on top of JSP 1.2. Because JSP 1.2 lacked an integrated expression language and the JSP 2.0 EL did not meet all the requirements of JSF, a variant of the EL was developed for JSF 1.0. The two language variants were later unified. This chapter is only concerned with the EL for non-JSF developers.

The Expression Language Syntax

An EL expression starts with **${** and ends with **}**. The construct of an EL expression is as follows:

```
${expression}
```

For example, to write the expression **x+y**, you use the following construct:

```
${x+y}
```

It is also common to concatenate two expressions. A sequence of expressions will be evaluated from left to right, coerced to **String**s, and concatenated. If **a+b** equals **8** and **c+d** equals **10**, the following two expressions produce **810**:

```
${a+b}${c+d}
```

And **${a+b}and${c+d}** results in **8and10**.

If an EL expression is used in an attribute value of a custom tag, the expression will be evaluated and the resulting string coerced to the attribute's expected type:

```
<my:tag someAttribute="${expression}"/>
```

The **${** sequence of characters denotes the beginning of an EL expression. If you want to send the literal **${** instead, you need to escape the first character: **\${**.

Reserved Words

The following words are reserved and must not be used as identifiers:

and	**eq**	**gt**	**true**	**instanceof**
or	**ne**	**le**	**false**	**empty**
not	**lt**	**ge**	**null**	**div** **mod**

The [ ] and . Operators

An EL expression can return any type. If an EL expression results in an object that has a property, you can use the **[]** or **.** operators to access the property. The **[]** and **.** operators function similarly; **[]** is a more generalized form, but **.** provides a nice shortcut.

To access an object's property, you use one of the following forms.

```
${object["propertyName"]}
${object.propertyName}
```

However, you can only use the **[]** operator] if *propertyName* is not a valid Java variable name. For instance, the following two EL expressions can be used to access the HTTP header **host** in the implicit object header.

```
${header["host"]}
${header.host}
```

However, to access the **accept-language** header, you can only use the **[]** operator because **accept-language** is not a legal Java variable name. Using the **.** operator to access it will cause an exception to be thrown.

If an object's property happens to return another object that in turn has a property, you can use either **[]** or **.** to access the property of the second object. For example, the **pageContext** implicit object represents the **PageContext** object of the current JSP. It has the **request** property, which represents the **HttpServletRequest**. The **HttpServletRequest** has the **servletPath** property. The following expressions are equivalent and result in the value of the **servletPath** property of the **HttpServletRequest** in **pageContext**:

```
${pageContext["request"]["servletPath"]}
${pageContext.request["servletPath"]}
${pageContext.request.servletPath}
${pageContext["request"].servletPath}
```

To access the **HttpSession**, use this syntax:

```
${pageContext.session}
```

For example, this expression prints the session identifier.

```
${pageContext.session.id}
```

The Evaluation Rule

An EL expression is evaluated from left to right. For an expression of the form *expr-a[expr-b]*, here is how the EL expression is evaluated:

1. Evaluate *expr-a* to get *value-a*.
2. If *value-a* is **null**, return **null**.
3. Evaluate *expr-b* to get *value-b*.
4. If *value-b* is **null**, return **null**.

5. If the type of *value-a* is **java.util.Map**, check whether *value-b* is a key in the **Map**. If it is, return *value-a*.**get(***value-b***)**. If it is not, return **null**.
6. If the type of *value-a* is **java.util.List** or if it is an array, do the following:
   a. Coerce *value-b* to **int**. If coercion fails, throw an exception.
   b. If *value-a*.**get(***value-b***)** throws an **IndexOutOfBoundsException** or if **Array.get(***value-a, value-b***)** throws an **ArrayIndexOutOfBoundsException**, return **null**.
   c. Otherwise, return *value-a*.**get(***value-b***)** if *value-a* is a **List**, or return **Array.get(***value-a, value-b***)** if *value-a* is an array.
7. If *value-a* is not a **Map**, a **List**, or an array, *value-a* must be a JavaBean. In this case, coerce *value-b* to **String**. If *value-b* is a readable property of *value-a*, call the getter of the property and return the value from the getter method. If the getter method throws an exception, the expression is invalid. Otherwise, the expression is invalid.

Accessing JavaBeans

You can use either the **.** operator or the **[]** operator to access a bean's property. Here are the constructs:

```
${beanName["propertyName"]}
${beanName.propertyName}
```

For example, to access the property **secret** on a bean named **myBean**, use the following expression:

```
${myBean.secret}
```

If the property is an object that in turn has a property, you can access the property of the second object too, again using the **.** or **[]** operator. Or, if the property is a **Map**, a **List**, or an array, you can use the same rule explained in the preceding section to access the **Map**'s values or the members of the **List** or the element of the array.

EL Implicit Objects

From a JSP page you can use JSP scripts to access JSP implicit objects. However, from a script-free JSP page, it is impossible to access these implicit objects. The EL allows you to access various objects by providing a set of its own implicit objects.

Object	Description
pageContext	The **javax.servlet.jsp.PageContext** for the current JSP.
initParam	A **Map** containing all context initialization parameters with the parameter names as the keys.
param	A **Map** containing all request parameters with the parameters names as the keys. The value for each key is the first parameter value of the specified name. Therefore, if there are two request parameters with the same name, only the first can be retrieved using the **param** object. For accessing all parameter values that share the same name, use the **params** object instead.
paramValues	A **Map** containing all request parameters with the parameter names as the keys. The value for each key is an array of strings containing all the values for the specified parameter name. If the parameter has only one value, it still returns an array having one element.
header	A **Map** containing the request headers with the header names as the keys. The value for each key is the first header of the specified header name. In other words, if a header has more than one value, only the first value is returned. To obtain multi-value headers, use the **headerValues** object instead.
headerValues	A **Map** containing all request headers with the header names as the keys. The value for each key is an array of strings containing all the values for the specified header name. If the header has only one value, it returns a one-element array.
cookie	A **Map** containing all **Cookie** objects in the current request object. The cookies' names are the **Map**'s keys, and each key is mapped to a **Cookie** object.
applicationScope	A **Map** that contains all attributes in the **ServletContext** object with the attribute names as the keys.
sessionScope	A **Map** that contains all the attributes in the **HttpSession** object in which the attribute names are the keys.
requestScope	A **Map** that contains all the attributes in the current **HttpServletRequest** object with the attribute names as the keys.
pageScope	A **Map** that contains all attributes with the page scope. The attributes' names are the keys of the **Map**.

Table 8.1: The EL Implicit Objects

The EL implicit objects are listed in Table 8.1. Each of the implicit objects is given in the following subsections.

pageContext

The **pageContext** object represents the **javax.servlet.jsp.PageContext** of the current JSP page. It contains all the other JSP implicit objects, which are given in Table 8.2.

Object	Type From the EL
request	javax.servlet.http.HttpServletRequest
response	javax.servlet.http.HttpServletResponse
out	javax.servlet.jsp.JspWriter
session	javax.servlet.http.HttpSession
application	javax.servlet.ServletContext
config	javax.servlet.ServletConfig
pageContext	javax.servlet.jsp.PageContext
page	javax.servlet.jsp.HttpJspPage
exception	java.lang.Throwable

Table 8.2: JSP Implicit Objects

For example, you can obtain the current **ServletRequest** using one of the following expressions:

```
${pageContext.request}
${pageContext["request"]
```

And, the request method can be obtained using any of the following expressions:

```
${pageContext["request"]["method"]}
${pageContext["request"].method}
${pageContext.request["method"]}
${pageContext.request.method}
```

Request parameters are accessed more frequently than other implicit objects; therefore, two implicit objects, **param** and **paramValues**, are provided. The **param** and **paramValues** implicit objects are discussed in the sections "param" and "paramValues."

initParam

The **initParam** implicit object is used to retrieve the value of a context parameter. For example, to access the context parameter named password, you use the following expression:

```
${initParam.password}
```

or

```
${initParam["password"]
```

param

The **param** implicit object is used to retrieve a request parameter. This object represents a **Map** containing all the request parameters. For example, to retrieve the parameter called **userName**, use one of the following:

```
${param.userName}
${param["userName"]}
```

paramValues

You use the **paramValues** implicit object to retrieve the values of a request parameter. This object represents a **Map** containing all request parameters with the parameter names as the keys. The value for each key is an array of strings containing all the values for the specified parameter name. If the parameter has only one value, it still returns an array having one element. For example, to obtain the first and second values of the **selectedOptions** parameter, you use the following expressions:

```
${paramValues.selectedOptions[0]}
${paramValues.selectedOptions[1]}
```

header

The **header** implicit object represents a **Map** that contains all request headers. To retrieve a header value, use the header name as the key. For example, to retrieve the value of the **accept-language** header, use the following expression:

```
${header["accept-language"]}
```

If the header name is a valid Java variable name, such as **connection**, you can also use the . operator:

```
${header.connection}
```

headerValues

The **headerValues** implicit object represents a **Map** containing all request headers with the header names as keys. Unlike **header**, however, the **Map** returned by the **headerValues** implicit object returns an array of strings. For example, to obtain the first value of the **accept-language** header, use this expression:

```
${headerValues["accept-language"][0]}
```

cookie

You use the **cookie** implicit object to retrieve a cookie. This object represents a **Map** containing all cookies in the current **HttpServletRequest**. For example, to retrieve the value of a cookie named **jsessionid**, use the following expression:

```
${cookie.jsessionid.value}
```

To obtain the path value of the **jsessionid** cookie, use this:

```
${cookie.jsessionid.path}
```

applicationScope, sessionScope, requestScope, and pageScope

You use the **applicationScope** implicit object to obtain the value of an application-scoped variable. For example, if you have an application-scoped variable called **myVar**, you may use this expression to access the attribute:

```
${applicationScope.myVar}
```

Note that in servlet/JSP programming a scoped object is an object placed as an attribute in any of the following objects: **PageContext**, **ServletRequest**,

HttpSession, or **ServletContext**. The **sessionScope**, **requestScope**, and **pageScope** implicit objects are similar to **applicationScope**. However, the scopes are session, request, and page, respectively.

A scoped object can also be accessed in an EL expression without the scope. In this case, the JSP container will return the first identically named object in the **PageContext**, **ServletRequest**, **HttpSession**, or **ServletContext**. Searches are conducted starting from the narrowest scope (**PageContext**) to the widest (**ServletContext**). For example, the following expression will return the object referenced by **today** in any scope.

```
${today}
```

Using Other EL Operators

In addition to the **.** and **[]** operators, the EL also provides several other operators: arithmetic operators, relational operators, logical operators, the conditional operator, and the **empty** operator. Using these operators, you can perform various operations. However, because the aim of the EL is to facilitate the authoring of script-free JSP pages, these EL operators are of limited use, except for the conditional operator.

The EL operators are given in the following subsections.

Arithmetic Operators

There are five arithmetic operators:

- Addition (**+**)
- Subtraction (**-**)
- Multiplication (*****)
- Division (**/** and **div**)
- Remainder/modulo (**%** and **mod**)

The division and remainder operators have two forms, to be consistent with XPath and ECMAScript.

Note that an EL expression is evaluated from the highest to the lowest precedence, and then from left to right. The following are the arithmetic operators in the decreasing lower precedence:

* / div % mod
+ -

This means that *****, /, **div**, **%**, and **mod** operators have the same level of precedence, and + has the same precedence as **-** , but lower than the first group. Therefore, the expression

```
${1+2*3}
```

results in 7 and not 6.

Relational Operators

The following is the list of relational operators:

- equality (== and **eq**)
- non-equality (!= and **ne**)
- greater than (> and **gt**)
- greater than or equal to (>= and **ge**)
- less than (< and **lt**)
- less than or equal to (<= and **le**)

For instance, the expression **${3==4}** returns **false**, and **${"b"<"d"}** returns **true**.

Logical Operators

Here is the list of logical operators:

- AND (**&&** and **and**)
- OR (‖ and **or**)
- NOT (**!** and **not**)

The Conditional Operator

The EL conditional operator has the following syntax:

```
${statement? A:B}
```

If *statement* evaluates to **true**, the output of the expression is *A*. Otherwise, the output is *B*.

For example, you can use the following EL expression to test whether the **HttpSession** contains the attribute called **loggedIn**. If the attribute is found, the string "You have logged in" is displayed. Otherwise, "You have not logged in" is displayed.

```
${(sessionScope.loggedIn==null)? "You have not logged in" :
      "You have logged in"}
```

The empty Operator

The **empty** operator is used to examine whether a value is **null** or empty. The following is an example of the use of the **empty** operator:

```
${empty X}
```

If *X* is **null** or if *X* is a zero-length string, the expression returns **true**. It also returns **true** if *X* is an empty **Map**, an empty array, or an empty collection. Otherwise, it returns **false**.

Configuring the EL in JSP 2.0 and Later Versions

With the EL, JavaBeans, and custom tags, it is now possible to write script-free JSP pages. JSP 2.0 and later versions even provide a switch to disable scripting in all JSP pages. Software architects can now enforce the writing of script-free JSP pages.

On the other hand, in some circumstances you'll probably want to disable the EL in your applications. For example, you'll want to do so if you are using a JSP 2.0-compliant container but are not ready yet to upgrade to JSP 2.0. In this case, you can disable the evaluation of EL expressions.

This section discusses how to enforce script-free JSP pages and how to disable the EL in JSP 2.0 and later.

Achieving Script-Free JSP Pages

To disable scripting elements in JSP pages, use the **jsp-property-group** element with two subelements: **url-pattern** and **scripting-invalid**. The **url-pattern** element defines the URL pattern to which scripting disablement will apply. Here is how you disable scripting in all JSP pages in an application:

```
<jsp-config>
    <jsp-property-group>
        <url-pattern>*.jsp</url-pattern>
        <scripting-invalid>true</scripting-invalid>
    </jsp-property-group>
</jsp-config>
```

Note
There can be only one **jsp-config** element in the deployment descriptor. If you have specified a **jsp-property-group** for deactivating the EL, you must write your **jsp-property-group** for disabling scripting under the same **jsp-config** element.

Deactivating EL Evaluation

In some circumstances, such as when you need to deploy JSP 1.2 applications in a JSP 2.0 or later container, you may want to deactivate EL evaluation in a JSP page. When you do so, an occurrence of the EL construct will not be evaluated as an EL expression. There are two ways to deactivate EL evaluation in a JSP.

First, you can set the **isELIgnored** attribute of the **page** directive to **true**, such as in the following:

```
<%@ page isELIgnored="true" %>
```

The default value of the **isELIgnored** attribute is **false**. Using the **isELIgnored** attribute is recommended if you want to deactivate EL evaluation in one or a few JSP pages.

Second, you can use the **jsp-property-group** element in the deployment descriptor. The **jsp-property-group** element is a subelement of the **jsp-config** element. You use **jsp-property-group** to apply certain settings to a set of JSP pages in the application.

To use the **jsp-property-group** element to deactivate EL evaluation, you must have two subelements: **url-pattern** and **el-ignored**. The **url-pattern** element specifies the URL pattern to which EL deactivation will apply. The **el-ignored** element must be set to **true**.

As an example, here is how to deactivate EL evaluation in a JSP page named **noEl.jsp**.

```
<jsp-config>
    <jsp-property-group>
        <url-pattern>/noEl.jsp</url-pattern>
        <el-ignored>true</el-ignored>
    </jsp-property-group>
</jsp-config>
```

You can also deactivate the EL evaluation in all the JSP pages in an application by assigning *****.jsp** to the **url-pattern** element, as in the following:

```
<jsp-config>
    <jsp-property-group>
        <url-pattern>*.jsp</url-pattern>
        <el-ignored>true</el-ignored>
    </jsp-property-group>
</jsp-config>
```

EL evaluation in a JSP page will be deactivated if either the **isELIgnored** attribute of its **page** directive is set to **true** or its URL matches the pattern in the **jsp-property-group** element whose **el-ignored** subelement is set to **true**. For example, if you set the **page** directive's **isELIgnored** attribute of a JSP page to **false** but its URL matches the pattern of JSP pages whose EL evaluation must be deactivated in the deployment descriptor, EL evaluation of that page will be deactivated.

In addition, if you use the deployment descriptor that is compliant to Servlet 2.3 or earlier, the EL evaluation is already disabled by default, even though you are using a JSP 2.0 or later container.

Summary

The EL is one of the most important features in JSP 2.0 and later. It can help you write shorter and more effective JSP pages, as well as helping you author script-free pages. In this chapter you have seen how to use the EL to access JavaBeans and implicit objects. Additionally, you have seen how to use EL operators. In the last section of this chapter, you learned how to use EL-related application settings related in a JSP 2.0 and later container.

Chapter 9
JSTL

The JavaServer Pages Standard Tag Library (JSTL) is a collection of custom tag libraries for solving common problems such as iterating over a map or collection, conditional testing, XML processing, and even database access and data manipulation.

This chapter discusses the most important tags in JSTL, especially those for accessing scoped objects, iterating over a collection, and formatting numbers and dates. If you are interested to know more, a complete discussion of all JSTL tags can be found in the JSTL Specification document.

Downloading JSTL

JSTL is currently at version 1.2 and defined by the JSR-52 expert group under the Java Community Process (www.jcp.org). The implementation is available for download from java.net:

```
http://jstl.java.net
```

There are two pieces of software you need to download, the JSTL API and the JSTL implementation. The JSTL API contains the **javax.servlet.jsp.jstl** package, which consists of types defined in the JSTL specification. The JSTL implementation contains the implementation classes. You must copy both jar files to the **WEB-INF/lib** directory of every application utilizing JSTL.

JSTL Libraries

JSTL is referred to as the standard tag library; however, it exposes its actions through multiple tag libraries. The tags in JSTL 1.2 can be categorized into five areas, which are summarized in Table 9.1.

Area	Subfunction	URI	Prefix
Core	Variable Support	http://java.sun.com/jsp/jstl/core	c
	Flow Control		
	URL Management		
	Miscellaneous		
XML	Core	http://java.sun.com/jsp/jstl/xml	x
	Flow Control		
	Transformation		
I18n	Locale	http://java.sun.com/jsp/jstl/fmt	fmt
	Message formatting		
	Number and date formatting		
Database	SQL	http://java.sun.com/jsp/jstl/sql	sql
Functions	Collection length	http://java.sun.com/jsp/jstl/functions	fn
	String manipulation		

Table 9.1: JSTL Tag Libraries

To use a JSTL library in a JSP page, use the **taglib** directive with the following format:

```
<%@ taglib uri="uri" prefix="prefix" %>
```

For instance, to use the Core library, declare this at the beginning of the JSP page:

```
<%@ taglib uri="http://java.sun.com/jsp/jstl/core" prefix="c" %>
```

The prefix can be anything. However, using the convention makes your code look more familiar to the other developers in your team and others who later join the project. It is therefore recommended to use the prescribed prefixes.

Note

Each of the tags discussed in this chapter is presented in its own section and the attributes for each tag are listed in a table. An asterisk (*) following an attribute name indicates that the attribute is required. A plus sign (+) indicates the value of the **rtexprvalue** element for that attribute is **true**, which means the attribute can be assigned a static string or a dynamic value (a Java expression, an Expression Language expression, or a value set by a **<jsp:attribute>**). A value of **false** for **rtexprvalue** means that the attribute can only be assigned a static string only.

Note

The body content of a JSTL tag can be empty, JSP, or tagdependent.

General-Purpose Actions

The following section discusses three general-purpose actions in the Core library used for manipulating scoped variables: **out**, **set**, **remove**.

The out Tag

The **out** tag evaluates an expression and outputs the result to the current **JspWriter**. The syntax for **out** has two forms, with and without a body content:

```
<c:out value="value" [escapeXml="{true|false}"]
       [default="defaultValue"]/>

<c:out value="value" [escapeXml="{true|false}"]>
    default value
</c:out>
```

Note

In a tag's syntax, [ ] indicates optional attributes. The underlined value, if any, indicates the default value.

The body content for **out** is JSP. The list of the tag's attributes is given in Table 9.2.

Attribute	Type	Description
value*+	Object	The expression to be evaluated.
escapeXml+	boolean	Indicates whether the characters <, >, &, ', and " in the result will be converted to the corresponding character entity codes, i.e. < to <, etc.
default+	Object	The default value

Table 9.2: The out tag's attributes

For example, the following **out** tag prints the value of the scoped variable **x**:

```
<c:out value="${x}"/>
```

By default, **out** encodes the special characters <, >, ', ", and & to their corresponding character entity codes **<**, **>**, **'**, **"**, and **&**, respectively.

Prior to JSP 2.0, the **out** tag was the easiest way to print the value of a scoped object. In JSP 2.0 or later, unless you need to XML-escape a value, you can safely use an EL expression:

```
${x}
```

Warning

If a string containing one or more special characters is not XML escaped, its value may not be rendered correctly in the browser. On top of that, unescaped special characters will make your web site susceptible to cross-site scripting attacks, i.e. someone can post a JavaScript function/expression that will be automatically executed.

The **default** attribute in **out** lets you assign a default value that will be displayed if the EL expression assigned to its **value** attribute returns **null**. The **default** attribute may be assigned a dynamic value. If this dynamic value returns **null**, the **out** tag will display an empty string.

For example, in the following **out** tag, if the variable **myVar** is not found in the **HttpSession**, the value of the application-scoped variable **myVar** is displayed. If the latter is also not found, an empty string is sent to the output.

```
<c:out value="${sessionScope.myVar}"
       default="${applicationScope.myVar"/>
```

The set Tag

You can use the **set** tag to do the following.

1. Create a string and a scoped variable that references the string.
2. Create a scoped variable that references an existing scoped object.
3. Set the property of a scoped object.

If **set** is used to create a scoped variable, the variable can be used throughout the same JSP page after the occurrence of the tag.

The **set** tag's syntax has four forms. The first form is used to create a scoped variable in which the **value** attribute specifies the string to be created or an existing scoped object.

```
<c:set value="value" var="varName"
       [scope="{page|request|session|application}"]/>
```

where the **scope** attribute specifies the scope of the scoped variable.

For instance, the following **set** tag creates the string "The wisest fool" and assigns it to the newly created page-scoped variable **foo**.

```
<c:set var="foo" value="The wisest fool"/>
```

The following **set** tag creates a scoped variable named **job** that references the request-scoped object **position**. The variable **job** has a **page** scope.

```
<c:set var="job" value="${requestScope.position}" scope="page"/>
```

Note
The last example might be a bit confusing because it created a page-scoped variable that references a request-scoped object. This should not be so if you bear in mind that the scoped object itself is not really "inside" the **HttpServletRequest**. Instead, a reference (named **position**) exists that references the object. With the **set** tag in the last example, you were simply creating another scoped variable (**job**) that referenced the same object.

The second form is similar to the first form, except that the string to be created or the scoped object to be referenced is passed as the body content.

```
<c:set var="varName" [scope="{page|request|session|application}"]>
    body content
</c:set>
```

The second form allows you to have JSP code in the body content.

The third form sets the value of a scoped object's property. The **target** attribute specifies the scoped object and the **property** attribute the scoped object's property. The value to assign to the property is specified by the **value** attribute.

```
<c:set target="target" property="propertyName" value="value"/>
```

For example, the following **set** tag assigns the string "Tokyo" to the **city** property of the scoped object **address**.

```
<c:set target="${address}" property="city" value="Tokyo"/>
```

Note that you must use an EL expression in the **target** attribute to reference the scoped object.

The fourth form is similar to the third form, but the value to assign is passed as body content.

```
<c:set target="target" property="propertyName">
    body content
</c:set>
```

For example, the following **set** tag assigns the string "Beijing" to the **city** property of the scoped object **address**.

```
<c:set target="${address}" property="city">Beijing</c:set>
```

The list of the **set** tag's attributes is given in Table 9.3.

Attribute	Type	Description
value+	Object	The string to be created, or the scoped object to reference, or the new property value.
var	String	The scoped variable to be created.
scope	String	The scope of the newly created scoped variable.
target+	Object	The scoped object whose property will be assigned a new value; this must be a JavaBeans instance or a **java.util.Map** object.
property+	String	The name of the property to be assigned a new value.

Table 9.3: The set tag's attributes

The remove Tag

You use the **remove** tag to remove a scoped variable. The syntax is as follows:

```
<c:remove var="varName"
        [scope="{page|request|session|application}"]/>
```

Note that the object referenced by the scoped variable is not removed. Therefore, if another scoped variable is also referencing the same object, you can still access the object through the other scoped variable.

The list of the **remove** tag's attributes is given in Table 9.4.

Attribute	Type	Description
var	String	The name of the scoped variable to remove.
scope	String	The scope of the scoped variable to be removed

Table 9.4: The remove tag's attributes

As an example, the following **remove** tag removes the page-scoped variable **job**.

```
<c:remove var="job" scope="page"/>
```

Conditional Actions

Conditional actions are used to deal with situations in which the output of a page depends on the value of certain input, which in Java are solved using **if**, **if ... else**, and **switch** statements.

There are four tags that perform conditional actions in JSTL: **if**, **choose**, **when**, and **otherwise**. Each will be discussed in a section below.

The if Tag

The **if** tag tests a condition and processes its body content if the condition evaluates to **true**. The test result is stored in a **Boolean** object, and a scoped variable is created to reference the **Boolean** object. You specify the name of the scoped variable using the **var** attribute and the scope in the **scope** attribute.

The syntax of **if** has two forms. The first form has no body content:

```
<c:if test="testCondition" var="varName"
        [scope="{page|request|session|application}"]/>
```

In this case, normally the scoped object specified by **var** will be tested by some other tag at a later stage in the same JSP.

The second form is used with a body content:

```
<c:if test="testCondition [var="varName"]
        [scope="{page|request|session|application}"]>
    body content
</c:if>
```

The body content is JSP and will be processed if the test condition evaluates to **true**. The list of the **if** tag's attributes is given in Table 9.5.

Attribute	Type	Description
test+	Boolean	The test condition that determines whether any existing body content should be processed
var	String	The name of the scoped variable that references the value of the test condition; the type of **var** is **Boolean**
scope	String	The scope of the scoped variable specified by **var**.

Table 9.5: The if tag's attributes

For example, the following **if** tag displays "You logged in successfully" if there exists a request parameter named **user** and its value is **ken** and there exists a request parameter named **password** and its value is **blackcomb**:

```
<c:if test="${param.user=='ken' && param.password=='blackcomb'}">
    You logged in successfully.
</c:if>
```

To simulate an **else**, use two **if** tags with conditions that are opposite. For instance, the following snippet displays "You logged in successfully" if the **user** and **password** parameters are **ken** and **blackcomb**, respectively. Otherwise, it displays "Login failed".

```
<c:if test="${param.user=='ken' && param.password=='blackcomb'}">
    You logged in successfully.
</c:if>
<c:if test="${!(param.user=='ken' && param.password=='blackcomb')}">
    Login failed.
</c:if>
```

The following **if** tag tests whether the **user** and **password** parameters are **ken** and **blackcomb**, respectively, and stores the result in the page-scoped variable **loggedIn**. You then use an EL expression to display "You logged in successfully" if the **loggedIn** variable is **true** or "Login failed" if the **loggedIn** variable is **false**.

```
<c:if var="loggedIn"
        test="${param.user=='ken' && param.password=='blackcomb'}"/>
    ...
${(loggedIn)? "You logged in successfully" : "Login failed"}
```

The choose, when and otherwise Tags

The **choose** and **when** tags act similarly to the **switch** and **case** keywords in Java, that is, they are used to provide the context for mutually exclusive conditional execution. The **choose** tag must have one or more **when** tags nested inside it, and each **when** tag represents a case that can be evaluated and processed. The **otherwise** tag is used for a default conditional block that will be processed if none of the **when** tags' test conditions evaluates to **true**. If present, **otherwise** must appear after the last **when**.

    choose and **otherwise** do not have attributes. **when** must have the **test** attribute specifying the test condition that determines whether the body content should be processed.

    As an example, the following code tests the value of a parameter called **status**. If the value of **status** is **full**, it displays "You are a full member". If the value is **student**, it displays "You are a student member". If the parameter **status** does not exist or if its value is neither **full** nor **student**, the code displays nothing.

```
<c:choose>
    <c:when test="${param.status=='full'}">
        You are a full member
    </c:when>
    <c:when test="${param.status=='student'}">
        You are a student member
    </c:when>
</c:choose>
```

The following example is similar to the preceding one, but it uses the **otherwise** tag to display "Please register" if the **status** parameter does not exist or if its value is not **full** or **student**:

```
<c:choose>
    <c:when test="${param.status=='full'}">
        You are a full member
    </c:when>
    <c:when test="${param.status=='student'}">
        You are a student member
    </c:when>
    <c:otherwise>
        Please register
```

```
    </c:otherwise>
</c:choose>
```

Iterator Actions

Iterator actions are useful when you need to iterate a number of times or over a collection of objects. JSTL provides two tags that perform iterator actions, **forEach** and **forTokens**, both of which are discussed in the following sections.

The forEach Tag

forEach iterates a body content a number of times or iterates over a collection of objects. Objects that can be iterated over include all implementations of **java.util.Collection** and **java.util.Map**, and arrays of objects or primitive types. You can also iterate over a **java.util.Iterator** and **java.util.Enumeration**, but you should not use **Iterator** or **Enumeration** in more than one action because neither **Iterator** nor **Enumeration** will be reset.

The syntax for **forEach** has two forms. The first form is for repeating the body content a fixed number of times:

```
<c:forEach [var="varName"] begin="begin" end="end" step="step">
    body content
</c:forEach>
```

The second form is used to iterate over a collection of objects:

```
<c:forEach items="collection" [var="varName"]
        [varStatus="varStatusName"] [begin="begin"] [end="end"]
        [step="step"]>
    body content
</c:forEach>
```

The body content is JSP. The **forEach** tag's attributes are given in Table 9.6.

Attribute	Type	Description
var	String	The name of the scoped variable that references the current item of the iteration.
items+	Any of the supported type.	Collections of objects to iterate over.
varStatus	String	The name of the scoped variable that holds the status of the iteration. The value is of type **javax.servlet.jsp.jstl.core.LoopTagStatus**.
begin+	int	If **items** is specified, iteration begins at the item located at the specified index, in which the first item of the collection has an index of 0. If **items** is not specified, iteration begins with the index set at the value specified. If specified, the value of **begin** must be equal to or greater than zero.
end+	int	If **items** is specified, iteration ends at the item located at the specified index (inclusive). If **items** is not specified, iteration ends when index reaches the value specified.
step+	int	Iteration will process only every **step** items of the collection, starting with the first one. If present, the value of step must be equal to or greater than 1.

Table 9.6: The forEach Tag's attributes

For example, the following **forEach** tag displays "1, 2, 3, 4, 5".

```
<c:forEach var="x" begin="1" end="5">
    <c:out value="${x}"/>,
</c:forEach>
```

And, the following **forEach** tag iterates over the **phones** property of an **address** scoped variable.

```
<c:forEach var="phone" items="${address.phones}">
    ${phone}"<br/>
</c:forEach>
```

For each iteration, the **forEach** tag creates a scoped variable whose name is specified by the **var** attribute. In this case, the scoped variable is named **phone**. The EL expression within the **forEach** tag is used to display the value of **phone**. The scoped variable is only available from within the beginning and closing **forEach** tags, and will be removed right before the closing **forEach** tag.

The **forEach** tag has a **varStatus** variable of type **javax.servlet.jsp.jstl.core.LoopTagStatus**. The **LoopTagStatus** interface has the **count** property that returns the "count" of the current round of iteration. The value of **status.count** is 1 for the first iteration, 2 for the second iteration, and so on. By testing the remainder of **status.count%2**, you know whether the tag is processing an even-numbered or odd-numbered element.

As an example, consider the **BookController** class and **BookList.jsp** page in the **app09a** application. The **BookController** class, presented in Listing 9.1, calls a service method that returns a **List** of **Book** objects. The **Book** class is given in Listing 9.2.

Listing 9.1: The BookController class

```
package app09a.controller;

import java.util.List;
import org.springframework.beans.factory.annotation.Autowired;
import org.springframework.stereotype.Controller;
import org.springframework.ui.Model;
import org.springframework.web.bind.annotation.RequestMapping;
import app09a.domain.Book;
import app09a.service.BookService;

@Controller
public class BookController {

    @Autowired
    private BookService bookService;
    @RequestMapping(value = "/book_list")
    public String listBooks(Model model) {
        List<Book> books = bookService.getAllBooks();
        model.addAttribute("books", books);
        return "BookList";
    }
}
```

Listing 9.2: The Book class

```
package app09a.domain;
```

```java
import java.io.Serializable;

public class Book implements Serializable {

    private static final long serialVersionUID =
        1520961851058396786L;
    private long id;
    private String isbn;
    private String title;
    private Category category;
    private String author;

    public Book() {
    }

    public Book(long id, String isbn, String title,
            Category category, String author) {
        this.id = id;
        this.isbn = isbn;
        this.title = title;
        this.category = category;
        this.author = author;
    }

    // getters and setters not shown

}
```

Listing 9.3: The BookList.jsp page

```jsp
<%@ taglib uri="http://java.sun.com/jsp/jstl/core" prefix="c" %>
<!DOCTYPE HTML>
<html>
<head>
<title>Book List</title>
</head>
<body>

<div id="global">
<h1>Book List</h1>
<table>
<tr>
    <th>Category</th>
    <th>Title</th>
    <th>ISBN</th>
    <th>Author</th>
```

```
    </tr>
    <c:forEach items="${books}" var="book">
        <tr>
            <td>${book.category.name}</td>
            <td>${book.title}</td>
            <td>${book.isbn}</td>
            <td>${book.author}</td>
        </tr>
    </c:forEach>
    </table>
    <br/>
    <table>
        <tr style="background:#ababff">
            <th>Category</th>
            <th>Title</th>
            <th>ISBN</th>
            <th>Author</th>
        </tr>
        <c:forEach items="${books}" var="book"
              varStatus="status">
            <c:if test="${status.count%2 == 0}">
                <tr style="background:#eeeeff">
            </c:if>
            <c:if test="${status.count%2 != 0}">
                <tr style="background:#dedeff">
            </c:if>
            <td>${book.category.name}</td>
            <td>${book.title}</td>
            <td>${book.isbn}</td>
            <td>${book.author}</td>
        </tr>
        </c:forEach>
    </table>
    </div>
    </body>
    </html>
```

Note that the **Books.jsp** page displays the books twice, the first one using **forEach** without the **varStatus** attribute.

```
<table>
<tr>
    <th>Category</th>
    <th>Title</th>
    <th>ISBN</th>
    <th>Author</th>
```

```
</tr>
<c:forEach items="${books}" var="book">
    <tr>
        <td>${book.category.name}</td>
        <td>${book.title}</td>
        <td>${book.isbn}</td>
        <td>${book.author}</td>
    </tr>
</c:forEach>
</table>
```

The second time the books are displayed using **forEach** with the **varStatus** attribute in order to give the table rows different colors depending whether a row is an even-numbered row or an odd-numbered row.

```
<table>
    <tr style="background:#ababff">
        <th>Category</th>
        <th>Title</th>
        <th>ISBN</th>
        <th>Author</th>
    </tr>
    <c:forEach items="${books}" var="book"
            varStatus="status">
        <c:if test="${status.count%2 == 0}">
            <tr style="background:#eeeeff">
        </c:if>
        <c:if test="${status.count%2 != 0}">
            <tr style="background:#dedeff">
        </c:if>
        <td>${book.category.name}</td>
        <td>${book.title}</td>
        <td>${book.isbn}</td>
        <td>${book.author}</td>
    </tr>
    </c:forEach>
</table>
```

You can test the example by using this URL:

```
http://localhost:8080/app09a/book_list
```

The output should be similar to the screen shot in Figure 9.1.

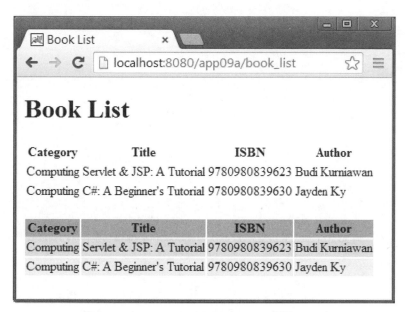

Figure 9.1: Using forEach with a List

You can also use **forEach** to iterate over a map. You refer to a map key and a map value using the **key** and **value** properties, respectively. The pseudocode for iterating over a map is as follows.

```
<c:forEach var="mapItem" items="map">
    ${mapItem.key} : ${mapItem.value}
</c:forEach>
```

The next example illustrates the use of **forEach** with a **Map**. The **CityController** class in Listing 9.4 instantiates two **Map**s and populates them with key/value pairs. Each element in the first **Map** is a **String/String** pair and each element in the second **Map** a **String/String[]** pair.

Listing 9.4: The CityController class

```
package app09a.controller;

import java.util.HashMap;
import java.util.Map;
import org.springframework.stereotype.Controller;
import org.springframework.ui.Model;
import org.springframework.web.bind.annotation.RequestMapping;

@Controller
```

```
public class CityController {

    @RequestMapping(value = "/cities")
    public String listCities(Model model) {
        Map<String, String> capitals =
                new HashMap<String, String>();
        capitals.put("Indonesia", "Jakarta");
        capitals.put("Malaysia", "Kuala Lumpur");
        capitals.put("Thailand", "Bangkok");
        model.addAttribute("capitals", capitals);


        Map<String, String[]> bigCities =
                new HashMap<String, String[]>();
        bigCities.put("Australia", new String[] {"Sydney",
                "Melbourne", "Perth"});
        bigCities.put("New Zealand", new String[] {"Auckland",
                "Christchurch", "Wellington"});
        bigCities.put("Indonesia", new String[] {"Jakarta",
                "Surabaya", "Medan"});
        model.addAttribute("bigCities", bigCities);
        return "Cities";
    }
}
```

At the end of the **listCities** method, the controller forwards to the **Cities.jsp** page, which uses **forEach** to iterate over the **Map**s. The **Cities.jsp** is given in Listing 9.5.

Listing 9.5: The Cities.jsp page

```
<%@ taglib uri="http://java.sun.com/jsp/jstl/core" prefix="c" %>
<!DOCTYPE HTML>
<html>
<head>
<title>Big Cities</title>
<style>
table, tr, td {
    border: 1px solid #aaee77;
    padding: 3px;
}
</style>
</head>
<body>
Capitals
<table>
```

```
    <tr style="background:#448755;color:white;font-weight:bold">
        <td>Country</td>
        <td>Capital</td>
    </tr>
    <c:forEach items="${requestScope.capitals}" var="mapItem">
    <tr>
        <td>${mapItem.key}</td>
        <td>${mapItem.value}</td>
    </tr>
    </c:forEach>
</table>
<br/>
Big Cities
<table>
    <tr style="background:#448755;color:white;font-weight:bold">
        <td>Country</td>
        <td>Cities</td>
    </tr>
    <c:forEach items="${requestScope.bigCities}" var="mapItem">
    <tr>
        <td>${mapItem.key}</td>
        <td>
            <c:forEach items="${mapItem.value}" var="city"
                    varStatus="status">
                ${city}<c:if test="${!status.last}">,</c:if>
            </c:forEach>
        </td>
    </tr>
    </c:forEach>
</table>
</body>
</html>
```

Of special importance is the second **forEach** that nests another **forEach**:

```
<c:forEach items="${requestScope.bigCities}" var="mapItem">
        <c:forEach items="${mapItem.value}" var="city"
                    varStatus="status">
            ${city}<c:if test="${!status.last}">,</c:if>
        </c:forEach>
</c:forEach>
```

Here the second **forEach** iterates over the **Map**'s element value, which is a **String** array.

You can test the example by directing your browser here:

```
http://localhost:8080/app09a/cities
```

Your browser should display several capitals and big cities in HTML tables like the ones in Figure 9.2.

Figure 9.2: forEach with Map

The forTokens Tag

You use the **forTokens** tag to iterate over tokens that are separated by the specified delimiters. The syntax for this action is as follows:

```
<c:forTokens items="stringOfTokens" delims="delimiters"
        [var="varName"] [varStatus="varStatusName"]
        [begin="begin"] [end="end"] [step="step"]
>
    body content
</c:forTokens>
```

The body content is JSP. The list of the **forTokens** tag's attributes is given in Table 9.7.

Attribute	Type	Description
var	String	The name of the scoped variable that references the current item of the iteration.
items+	String	The string of tokens to iterate over.
varStatus	String	The name of the scoped variable that holds the status of the iteration. The value is of type **javax.servlet.jsp.jstl.core.LoopTagStatus**.
begin+	int	The start index of the iteration, where index is zero-based. If specified, **begin** must be 0 or greater.
end+	int	The end index of the iteration, where index is zero-based.
step+	int	Iteration will process only every **step** tokens of the string, starting with the first one. If specified, **step** must be 1 or greater.
delims+	String	The set of delimiters.

Table 9.7: The forTokens tag's attributes

Here is an example of **forTokens**:

```
<c:forTokens var="item" items="Argentina,Brazil,Chile" delims=",">
    <c:out value="${item}"/><br/>
</c:forTokens>
```

When pasted in a JSP, the preceding **forTokens** will result in the following:

```
Argentina
Brazil
Chile
```

URL Related Actions

This section discusses two of three URL-related tags, **url** and **redirect**.

The url Tag

The url tag is used to compose the correct URL of a resource by taking account whether or not the application context is the default context. To understand why the **url** tag is very important, consider the following URL.

```
http://example.com/myapp/abc
```

The browser will think (correctly) that **myapp** is the context and **abc** is the action. Any relative reference to a static file, such as a CSS file, will be resolved using http://example.com/myapp as the base. This is to say, if the page sent by the server contains this **img** element

```
<img src="logo.png"/>
```

The browser will look for **logo.png** in http://example.com/myapp/logo.png.

However, note that if the same application is deployed as the default context (where the path to the default context is an empty string), the URL for the same action would be

```
http://example.com/abc
```

Now, consider the following URL that carries a path variable in an application deployed as the default context:

```
http://example.com/abc/1
```

In this case, the browser will think **abc** is the context, not the action. If you refer to **<img src="logo.png"/>** in your page, the browser will look for the image in http://example.com/abc/logo.png and it won't find the image.

Lucky for us the **url** tag provides a solution. It fixes the issue by correctly resolving the URL. For example, a CSS import in a JSP page like this is sensitive to whether or not the context is the default context.

```
<style type="text/css">@import url(css/main.css);</style>
```

If you use the url tag like this

```
<style type="text/css">
@import url("<c:url value="/css/main.css"/>");
</style>
```

the URL will be translated into this if it is in the default context.

```
<style type="text/css">@import url("/css/main.css");</style>
```

And it will be translated into this if it is not in the default context.

```
<style type="text/css">@import url("/myapp/css/main.css");</style>
```

The **url** tag can be used without body content with the following syntax

```
<c:url value="value" [context="context"] [var="varName"]
    [scope="{page|request|session|application}"]/>
```

or with body content with this syntax.

```
<c:url value="value" [context="context"] [var="varName"]
    [scope="{page|request|session|application}"]/>
    <c:param> subtags
</c:url>
```

The attributes for the **url** tag are given in Table 9.8.

Attribute	Type	Description
value	String	The URL to be processed.
context	String	The name of the context when specifying a relative URL resource that belongs to a foreign context.
var	String	The scoped variable to be created for the processed URL.
scope	String	The scope of the newly created scoped variable.

Table 9.8: The url tag's attributes

The redirect Tag

The **redirect** tag sends an HTTP redirect to the client. Attributes that may appear within this tag are presented in Table 9.9.

Attribute	Type	Description
url	String	The URL to redirect to.
context	String	The name of the context when redirecting to a relative URL resource that belongs to a foreign context.

Table 9.9: The redirect tag's attributes

Formatting Actions

JSTL provides tags for formatting and parsing numbers and dates. The tags are **formatNumber**, **formatDate**, **timeZone**, **setTimeZone**, **parseNumber**, and **parseDate**. These tags are discussed in the sections to follow.

The formatNumber Tag

You use **formatNumber** to format numbers. This tag gives you the flexibility of using its various attributes to get a format that suits your need. The syntax of **formatNumber** has two forms. The first is used without a body content:

```
<fmt:formatNumber value="numericValue"
        [type="{number|currency|percent}"]
        [pattern="customPattern"]
        [currencyCode="currencyCode"]
        [currencySymbol="currencySymbol"]
        [groupingUsed="{true|false}"]
        [maxIntegerDigits="maxIntegerDigits"]
        [minIntegerDigits="minIntegerDigits"]
        [maxFractionDigits="maxFractionDigits"]
        [minFractionDigits="minFractionDigits"]
        [var="varName"]
        [scope="{page|request|session|application}"]
/>
```

The second form is used with a body content:

```
<fmt:formatNumber [type="{number|currency|percent}"]
        [pattern="customPattern"]
        [currencyCode="currencyCode"]
        [currencySymbol="currencySymbol"]
        [groupingUsed="{true|false}"]
        [maxIntegerDigits="maxIntegerDigits"]
        [minIntegerDigits="minIntegerDigits"]
        [maxFractionDigits="maxFractionDigits"]
        [minFractionDigits="minFractionDigits"]
        [var="varName"]
        [scope="{page|request|session|application}"]>
    numeric value to be formatted
</fmt:formatNumber>
```

The body content is JSP. The **formatNumber** tag's attributes are given in Table 9.10.

Attribute	Type	Description
value+	String or Number	Numeric value to be formatted.
type+	String	Indicates whether the value is to be formatted as number, currency, or percentage. The value of this attribute is one of the following: **number, currency, percent**.
pattern+	String	Custom formatting pattern.
currencyCode+	String	ISO 4217 code. See Table 9.9.
currencySymbol+	String	Currency symbol.
groupingUsed+	Boolean	Indicates whether the output will contain grouping separators.
maxIntegerDigits+	int	The maximum number of digits in the integer portion of the output.
minIntegerDigits+	int	The minimum number of digits in the integer portion of the output.
maxFractionDigits+	int	The maximum number of digits in the fractional portion of the output.
minFractionDigits+	int	The minimum number of digits in the fractional portion of the output.
var	String	The name of the scoped variable to store the output as a String.
scope	String	The scope of **var**. If the **scope** attribute is present, the **var** attribute must be specified.

Table 9.10: The formatNumber tag's attributes

One of the uses of **formatNumber** is to format numbers as currencies. For this, you can use the **currencyCode** attribute to specify an ISO 4217 currency code. Some of the codes are given in Table 9.11.

Currency	ISO 4217 Code	Major Unit Name	Minor Unit Name
Canadian Dollar	CAD	dollar	cent
Chinese Yuan	CNY	yuan	jiao
Euro	EUR	euro	euro-cent
Japanese Yen	JPY	yen	sen
Sterling	GBP	pound	pence
US Dollar	USD	dollar	cent

Table 9.11: ISO 4217 Currency Codes

The examples of how to use **formatNumber** are given in Table 9.12.

Action	Result
<fmt:formatNumber value="12" type="number"/>	12
<fmt:formatNumber value="12" type="number" minIntegerDigits="3"/>	012
<fmt:formatNumber value="12" type="number" minFractionDigits="2"/>	12.00
<fmt:formatNumber value="123456.78" pattern=".000"/>	123456.780
<fmt:formatNumber value="123456.78" pattern="#,#00.0#"/>	123,456.78
<fmt:formatNumber value="12" type="currency"/>	$12.00
<fmt:formatNumber value="12" type="currency" currencyCode="GBP"/>	GBP 12.00
<fmt:formatNumber value="0.12" type="percent"/>	12%
<fmt:formatNumber value="0.125" type="percent" minFractionDigits="2"/>	12.50%

Table 9.12: Using the formatNumber tag

Note that when formatting currencies, if the **currencyCode** attribute is not specified, the browser's locale is used.

The formatDate Tag

You use the **formatDate** tag to format dates. The syntax is as follows:

```
<fmt:formatDate value="date"
       [type="{time|date|both}"]
       [dateStyle="{default|short|medium|long|full}"]
       [timeStyle="{default|short|medium|long|full}"]
       [pattern="customPattern"]
```

```
[timeZone="timeZone"]
[var="varName"]
[scope="{page|request|session|application}"]
/>
```

The body content is JSP. The **formatDate** tag's attributes are given in Table 9.13.

Attribute	Type	Description
value+	java.util.Date	Date and/or time to be formatted
type+	String	Indicates whether the time, the date, or both the time and the date components are to be formatted
dateStyle+	String	Predefined formatting style for dates that follows the semantics defined in **java.text.DateFormat**.
timeStyle+	String	Predefined formatting style for times that follows the semantics defined in **java.text.DateFormat**.
pattern+	String	The custom pattern for formatting
timezone+	String or **java.util.TimeZone**	The time in which to represent the time
var	String	The name of the scoped variable to store the result as a string
scope	String	Scope of **var**.

Table 9.13: The formatDate tag's attributes

For possible values of the **timeZone** attribute, see the section, "The timeZone Tag".

The following code uses the **formatDate** tag to format the **java.util.Date** object referenced by the scoped variable **now**.

```
Default: <fmt:formatDate value="${now}"/>
Short: <fmt:formatDate value="${now}" dateStyle="short"/>
Medium: <fmt:formatDate value="${now}" dateStyle="medium"/>
Long: <fmt:formatDate value="${now}" dateStyle="long"/>
Full: <fmt:formatDate value="${now}" dateStyle="full"/>
```

The following **formatDate** tags are used to format times.

```
Default: <fmt:formatDate type="time" value="${now}"/>
Short: <fmt:formatDate type="time" value="${now}"
```

```
        timeStyle="short"/>
Medium: <fmt:formatDate type="time" value="${now}"
        timeStyle="medium"/>
Long: <fmt:formatDate type="time" value="${now}" timeStyle="long"/>
Full: <fmt:formatDate type="time" value="${now}" timeStyle="full"/>
```

The following **formatDate** tags format both dates and times.

```
Default: <fmt:formatDate type="both" value="${now}"/>
Short date short time: <fmt:formatDate type="both"
  value="${now}" dateStyle="short" timeStyle="short"/>
Long date long time format: <fmt:formatDate type="both"
  value="${now}" dateStyle="long" timeStyle="long"/>
```

The following **formatDate** tags are used to format times with time zones.

```
Time zone CT: <fmt:formatDate type="time" value="${now}"
        timeZone="CT"/><br/>
Time zone HST: <fmt:formatDate type="time" value="${now}"
        timeZone="HST"/><br/>
```

The following **formatDate** tags are used to format dates and times using custom patterns.

```
<fmt:formatDate type="both" value="${now}" pattern="dd.MM.yy"/>
<fmt:formatDate type="both" value="${now}" pattern="dd.MM.yyyy"/>
```

The timeZone Tag

The **timeZone** tag is used to specify the time zone in which time information is to be formatted or parsed in its body content. The syntax is as follows:

```
<fmt:timeZone value="timeZone">
    body content
</fmt:timeZone>
```

The body content is JSP. The attribute value can be passed a dynamic value of type **String** or **java.util.TimeZone**. The values for US and Canada time zones are given in Table 9.14.

If the **value** attribute is **null** or empty, the GMT time zone is used.

The following example uses the **timeZone** tag to format dates with time zones.

```
<fmt:timeZone value="GMT+1:00">
    <fmt:formatDate value="${now}" type="both"
            dateStyle="full" timeStyle="full"/>
</fmt:timeZone>
<fmt:timeZone value="HST">
    <fmt:formatDate value="${now}" type="both"
            dateStyle="full" timeStyle="full"/>
</fmt:timeZone>
<fmt:timeZone value="CST">
    <fmt:formatDate value="${now}" type="both"
            dateStyle="full" timeStyle="full"/>
</fmt:timeZone>
```

Abbreviation	Full Name	Time Zone
NST	Newfoundland Standard Time	UTC-3:30 hours
NDT	Newfoundland Daylight Time	UTC-2:30 hours
AST	Atlantic Standard Time	UTC-4 hours
ADT	Atlantic Daylight Time	UTC-3 hours
EST	Eastern Standard Time	UTC-5 hours
EDT	Eastern Daylight Saving Time	UTC-4 hours
ET	Eastern Time, as EST or EDT	*
CST	Central Standard Time	UTC-6 hours
CDT	Central Daylight Saving Time	UTC-5 hours
CT	Central Time, as either CST or CDT	*
MST	Mountain Standard Time	UTC-7 hours
MDT	Mountain Daylight Saving Time	UTC-6 hours
MT	Mountain Time, as either MST or MDT	*
PST	Pacific Standard Time	UTC-8 hours
PDT	Pacific Daylight Saving Time	UTC-7 hours
PT	Pacific Time, as either PST or PDT	*
AKST	Alaska Standard Time	UTC-9 hours
AKDT	Alaska Standard Daylight Saving Time	UTC-8 hours
HST	Hawaiian Standard Time	UTC-10 hours

Table 9.14: US and Canada Time Zones

The setTimeZone Tag

You use the **setTimeZone** tag to store the specified time zone in a scoped variable or the time configuration variable. The syntax of **setTimeZone** is as follows:

```
<fmt:setTimeZone value="timeZone" [var="varName"]
        [scope="{page|request|session|application}"]
/>
```

Table 9.15 presents the **setTimeZone** tag's attributes.

Attribute	Type	Description
value+	**String** or **java.util.TimeZone**	The time zone
var	String	The name of the scoped variable to hold the time zone of type **java.util.TimeZone**
scope	String	The scope of **var** or the time zone configuration variable

Table 9.15: The setTimeZone tag's attributes

The parseNumber Tag

You use **parseNumber** to parse a string representation of a number, a currency, or a percentage in a locale-sensitive format into a number. The syntax has two forms. The first form is used without body content:

```
<fmt:parseNumber value="numericValue"
        [type="{number|currency|percent}"]
        [pattern="customPattern"]
        [parseLocale="parseLocale"]
        [integerOnly="{true|false}"]
        [var="varName"]
        [scope="{page|request|session|application}"]
/>
```

The second form is used with body content:

```
<fmt:parseNumber [type="{number|currency|percent}"]
        [pattern="customPattern"]
        [parseLocale="parseLocale"]
        [integerOnly="{true|false}"]
        [var="varName"]
        [scope="{page|request|session|application}"]>
    numeric value to be parsed
</fmt:parseNumber>
```

The body content is JSP. The **parseNumber** tag's attributes are given in Table 9.16.

As an example, the following **parseNumber** tag parses the value referenced by the scoped variable **quantity** and stores the result in the **formattedNumber** scoped variable.

```
<fmt:parseNumber var="formattedNumber" type="number"
        value="${quantity}"/>
```

Attribute	Type	Description
value+	**String**	String to be parsed
type+	**String**	Indicates whether the string to be parsed is to be parsed as a number, currency, or percentage
pattern+	**String**	Custom formatting pattern that determines how the string in the **value** attribute is to be parsed
parseLocale+	**String** or **java.util.Locale**	Locale whose default formatting pattern is to be used during the parse operation, or to which the pattern specified via the **pattern** attribute is applied
integerOnly+	**Boolean**	Indicates whether only the integer portion of the given value should be parsed
var	**String**	The name of the scoped variable to hold the result
scope	**String**	The scope of **var**

Table 9.16: The parseNumber tag's attributes

The parseDate Tag

parseDate parses the string representation of a date and time in locale-sensitive format. The syntax has two forms. The first form is used without a body content:

```
<fmt:parseDate value="dateString"
        [type="{time|date|both}"]
        [dateStyle="{default|short|medium|long|full}"]
        [timeStyle="{default|short|medium|long|full}"]
        [pattern="customPattern"]
        [timeZone="timeZone"]
```

```
            [parseLocale="parseLocale"]
            [var="varName"]
            [scope="{page|request|session|application}"]
/>
```

The second form is used with a body content:

```
<fmt:parseDate [type="{time|date|both}"]
        [dateStyle="{default|short|medium|long|full}"]
        [timeStyle="{default|short|medium|long|full}"]
        [pattern="customPattern"]
        [timeZone="timeZone"]
        [parseLocale="parseLocale"]
        [var="varName"]
        [scope="{page|request|session|application}"]>
    date value to be parsed
</fmt:parseDate>
```

The body content is JSP. Table 9.17 lists the **parseDate** tag's attributes.

Attribute	Type	Description
value+	**String**	String to be parsed
type+	**String**	Indicates whether the string to be parsed contains a date, a time, or both
dateStyle+	**String**	The formatting style of the date
timeStyle+	**String**	The formatting style of the time
pattern+	**String**	Custom formatting pattern that determines how the string is to be parsed
timeZone+	**String** or **java.util.TimeZone**	Time zone in which to interpret any time information in the date string
parseLocale+	**String** or **java.util.Locale**	Locale whose default formatting pattern is to be used during the parse operation, or to which the pattern specified via the pattern attribute is applied
var	**String**	The name of the scoped variable to hold the result
scope	**String**	The scope of **var**

Table 9.17: The parseDate tag's attributes

As an example, the following **parseDate** tag parses a date referenced by the scoped variable **myDate** and stores the resulting **java.util.Date** in a page-scoped variable **formattedDate**.

```
<c:set var="myDate" value="12/12/2005"/>
<fmt:parseDate var="formattedDate" type="date"
        dateStyle="short" value="${myDate}"/>
```

Functions

In addition to custom actions, JSTL 1.1 and 1.2 define a set of standard functions you can use in EL expressions. These functions are grouped in the function tag library. To use the functions, you must use the following **taglib** directive on top of your JSP.

```
<%@ taglib uri="http://java.sun.com/jsp/jstl/functions"
        prefix="fn" %>
```

To invoke a function, you use an EL in this format.

```
${fn:functionName}
```

where *functionName* is the name of the function.

Most of the functions are for string manipulation. For instance, the **length** function works for both strings and collections, returning the number of items in a collection or array or the number of characters in a string.

All these functions are described in the sections to follow.

The contains Function

The **contains** function tests whether a string contains the specified substring. The return value is **true** if the string contains the substring, and **false** otherwise. Its syntax is as follows:

```
contains(string, substring).
```

For example, both of these EL expressions return **true**:

```
<c:set var="myString" value="Hello World"/>
${fn:contains(myString, "Hello")}

${fn:contains("Stella Cadente", "Cadente")}
```

The containsIgnoreCase Function

The **containsIgnoreCase** function is similar to the **contains** function, but testing is performed in a case-insensitive way. The syntax is as follows:

```
containsIgnoreCase(string, substring)
```

For instance, the following EL expression returns **true**:

```
${fn:containsIgnoreCase("Stella Cadente", "CADENTE")}
```

The endsWith Function

The **endsWith** function tests whether a string ends with the specified suffix. The return value is a **Boolean**. Its syntax is as follows:

```
endsWith(string, suffix)
```

For example, the following EL expression returns **true**:

```
${fn:endsWith("Hello World", "World")}
```

The escapeXml Function

This function is useful for encoding a **String**. The conversion is the same as the **out** tag with its **escapeXml** attribute set to **true**. The syntax of **escapeXml** is as follows:

```
escapeXml(string)
```

For example, the EL expression

```
${fn:escapeXml("Use <br/> to change lines")}
```

is rendered as the following:

```
Use &lt;br/&gt; to change lines
```

The indexOf Function

The **indexOf** function returns the index within a string of the first occurrence of the specified substring. If the substring is not found, it returns -1. Its syntax is as follows:

```
indexOf(string, substring)
```

For instance, the following EL expression returns 7:

```
${fn:indexOf("Stella Cadente", "Cadente")}
```

The join Function

The **join** function joins all elements of a **String** array into a string, separated by the specified separator. The syntax is as follows:

```
join(array, separator)
```

If the array is **null**, an empty string is returned.

For example, if **myArray** is a **String** array having the two elements "my" and "world", the EL expression

```
${fn:join(myArray,",")}
```

returns "my,world".

The length Function

The **length** function returns the number of items in a collection, or the number of characters in a string. Its syntax is as follows:

```
length{input}
```

As an example, the following EL expression returns 14:

```
${fn:length("Stella Cadente", "Cadente")}
```

The replace Function

The **replace** function replaces all occurrences of *beforeString* with *afterString* in a string and returns the result. Its syntax is as follows:

```
replace(string, beforeSubstring, afterSubstring)
```

For example, the EL expression

```
${fn:replace("Stella Cadente", "e", "E")}
```

returns "StElla CadEntE".

The split Function

The **split** function splits a string into an array of substrings. It does the opposite of the join function. For example, the following code splits the string "my,world" and stores the result in the scoped variable **split**. It then formats split into an HTML table using the **forEach** tag.

```
<c:set var="split" value='${fn:split("my,world",",")}'/>
<table>
<c:forEach var="substring" items="${split}">
    <tr><td>${substring}</td></tr>
</c:forEach>
</table>
```

The result is this:

```
<table>
    <tr><td>my</td></tr>
    <tr><td>world</td></tr>
</table>
```

The startsWith Function

The **startsWith** function tests whether a string starts with the specified prefix. The syntax is as follows:

```
startsWith(string, prefix)
```

For instance, the following EL expression returns **true**:

```
${fn:startsWith("Stella Cadente", "St")}
```

The substring Function

The **substring** function returns a substring from the specified zero-based begin index (inclusive) to the specified zero-based end index. The syntax is as follows:

```
substring(string, beginIndex, endIndex)
```

For example, the following EL expression returns "Stel".

```
${fn:substring("Stella Cadente", 0, 4)}
```

The substringAfter Function

The **substringAfter** function returns the portion of a string after the first occurrence of the specified substring. Its syntax is as follows:

```
substringAfter(string, substring)
```

For example, the EL expression

```
${fn:substringAfter("Stella Cadente", "e")}
```

returns "lla Cadente".

The substringBefore Function

The **substringBefore** function returns the portion of a string before the first occurrence of the specified substring. Its syntax is as follows:

```
substringBefore(string, substring)
```

For instance, the following EL expression returns "St".

```
${fn:substringBefore("Stella Cadente", "e")}
```

The toLowerCase Function

The **toLowerCase** function converts a string into its lowercase version. Its syntax is as follows:

```
toLowerCase(string)
```

For example, the following EL expression returns "stella cadente".

```
${fn:toLowerCase("Stella Cadente")}
```

The toUpperCase Function

The **toUpperCase** function converts a string into its uppercase version. Its syntax is as follows:

```
toUpperCase(string)
```

For instance, the following EL expression returns "STELLA CADENTE".

```
${fn:toUpperCase("Stella Cadente")}
```

The trim Function

The **trim** function removes the leading and trailing whitespaces of a string. Its syntax is as follows:

```
trim(string)
```

For example, the following EL expression returns "Stella Cadente".

```
${fn:trim("            Stella Cadente   ")}
```

Summary

You can use JSTL for common tasks (such as iteration, collection, and conditionals), for processing XML documents, formatting text, accessing databases and manipulating data, etc. This chapter discussed the more important tags such as the tags for manipulating scoped objects (**out**, **set**, **remove**), for performing conditional tests (**if**, **choose**, **when**, **otherwise**), for iterating over a collection or token (**forEach**, **forTokens**), for parsing and formatting dates and numbers (**parseNumber**, **formatNumber**, **parseDate**,

formatDate, etc), and JSTL 1.2 functions that can be used from EL expressions.

Chapter 10
Internationalization

In this era of globalization, it is now more compelling than ever to be able to write applications that can be deployed in different countries and regions that speak different languages. There are two terms you need to be familiar with in this regard. The first is internationalization, often abbreviated to i18n because the word starts with an I and ends with an n, and there are 18 characters between the first I and the last n. Internationalization is the technique for developing applications that support multiple languages and data formats without rewriting the programming logic.

The second term in localization, which is the technique for adapting an internationalized application to support a specific locale. A locale is a specific geographical, political, or cultural region. An operation that takes a locale into consideration is said to be locale-sensitive. For example, displaying a date is locale-sensitive because the date must be in the format used by the country or region of the user. The fifteenth day of November 2014 is written 11/15/2014 in the US, but printed as 15/11/2014 in Australia. For the same reason internationalization is abbreviated i18n, localization is abbreviated l10n.

Java was designed with internationalization in mind, employing Unicode for characters and strings. Making internationalized applications in Java is therefore easy. How you internationalize your applications depends on how much static data needs to be presented in different languages. There are two approaches.

1. If a large amount of data is static, create a separate version of the resource for each locale. This approach normally applies to web application with lots of static HTML pages. It is straightforward and will not be discussed in this chapter.
2. If the amount of static data that needs to be internationalized is limited, isolate textual elements such as component labels and error

messages into text files. Each text file stores the translations of all textual elements for a locale. The application then retrieves each element dynamically. The advantage is clear. Each textual element can be edited easily without recompiling the application. This is the technique that will discussed in this chapter.

This chapter starts by explaining what a locale is. Next comes the technique for internationalizing your applications, followed by a Spring MVC example.

Locales

The **java.util.Locale** class represents a locale. There are three main components of a **Locale** object: language, country, and variant. The language is obviously the most important part; however, sometimes the language itself is not sufficient to differentiate a locale. For example, the English language is spoken in countries such as the US and England. However, the English language spoken in the US is not exactly the same as the one used in the UK. Therefore, it is necessary to specify the country of the language. As another example, the Chinese language used in China is not exactly the same as the one used in Taiwan.

The variant argument is a vendor- or browser-specific code. For example, you use WIN for Windows, MAC for Macintosh, and POSIX for POSIX. Where there are two variants, separate them with an underscore, and put the most important one first. For example, a Traditional Spanish collation might construct a locale with parameters for language, country, and variant as es, ES, Traditional_WIN, respectively.

To construct a **Locale** object, use one of the **Locale** class's constructors.

```
public Locale(java.lang.String language)

public Locale(java.lang.String language, java.lang.String country)

public Locale(java.lang.String language, java.lang.String country,
        java.lang.String variant)
```

The language code is a valid ISO language code. Table 10.1 displays examples of language codes.

The country argument is a valid ISO country code, which is a two-letter, uppercase code specified in ISO 3166 (http://userpage.chemie.fu-berlin.de/diverse/doc/ISO_3166.html). Table 10.2 lists some of the country codes in ISO 3166.

Code	Language
de	German
el	Greek
en	English
es	Spanish
fr	French
hi	Hindi
it	Italian
ja	Japanese
nl	Dutch
pt	Portuguese
ru	Russian
zh	Chinese

Table 10.1: Examples of ISO 639 Language Codes

Country	Code
Australia	AU
Brazil	BR
Canada	CA
China	CN
Egypt	EG
France	FR
Germany	DE
India	IN
Mexico	MX
Switzerland	CH
Taiwan	TW
United Kingdom	GB
United States	US

Table 10.2: Examples of ISO 3166 Country Codes

For example, to construct a **Locale** object representing the English language used in Canada, write this.

```
Locale locale = new Locale("en", "CA");
```

In addition, the **Locale** class provides static final fields that return locales for specific countries or languages, such as **CANADA, CANADA_FRENCH, CHINA, CHINESE, ENGLISH, FRANCE, FRENCH, UK, US**, etc. Therefore, you can also construct a **Locale** object by calling its static field.

```
Locale locale = Locale.CANADA_FRENCH;
```

In addition, the static **getDefault** method returns the user computer's locale.

```
Locale locale = Locale.getDefault();
```

Internationalizing Spring MVC Applications

Internationalizing and localizing your application require you to

1. isolate textual components into properties files
2. be able to select and read the correct properties file This section elaborates the two steps and provides a simple example.

Isolating Textual Components into Properties Files

An internationalized application stores its textual elements in a separate properties file for each locale. Each file contains key/value pairs, and each key uniquely identifies a locale-specific object. Keys are always strings, and values can be strings or any other type of object. For example, to support American English, German, and Chinese you will have three properties files, all of which will have the same keys.

The following is the English version of the properties file. Note that it has two keys: **greetings** and **farewell**.

```
Greetings = Hello
farewell = Goodbye
```

The German version would be as follows:

```
greetings = Hallo
farewell = Tschüß
```

And the properties file for the Chinese language would be

```
greetings=\u4f60\u597d
farewell=\u518d\u89c1
```

Read the sidebar "Converting Chinese Characters to Unicode" on how I arrived at this properties file.

Converting Chinese Characters to Unicode

In the Chinese language, 你好 (meaning hello, represented by the Unicode codes 4f60 and 597d, respectively) and 再见 (meaning good bye and is represented by Unicode codes 518d and 89c1, respectively) are the most common expressions. Of course, no one remembers the Unicode code of each Chinese character. Therefore, you create the .properties file in two steps:

1. Using your favorite Chinese text editor, create a text file like this:

    ```
    greetings=你好
    farewell=再见
    ```

2. Convert the content of the text file into the Unicode representation. Normally, a Chinese text editor has the feature for converting Chinese characters into Unicode codes. You will get the end result:

    ```
    greetings=\u4f60\u597d
    farewell=\u518d\u89c1
    ```

Now, you need to master the **java.util.ResourceBundle** class. It enables you to easily choose and read the properties file specific to the user's locale and look up the values. **ResourceBundle** is an abstract class, but it provides static **getBundle** methods that return an instance of a concrete subclass.

A **ResourceBundle** has a base name, which can be any name. In order for a **ResourceBundle** to pick up a properties file, the filename must be composed of the **ResourceBundle** base name, followed by an underscore, followed by the language code, and optionally followed by another underscore and the country code. The format for the properties file name is as follows:

```
basename_languageCode_countryCode
```

For example, suppose the base name is **MyResources** and you define the following three locales:

- US-en
- DE-de
- CN-zh

Then you would have these three properties files:

- **MyResources_en_US.properties**
- **MyResources_de_DE.properties**
- **MyResources_zh_CN.properties**

Reading the Properties Files

As mentioned previously, **ResourceBundle** is an abstract class. Nonetheless, you can obtain an instance of **ResourceBundle** by calling its static **getBundle** method. The signatures of its overloads are

```
public static ResourceBundle getBundle(java.lang.String baseName)

public static ResourceBundle getBundle(java.lang.String baseName,
        Locale locale)
```

For example:

```
ResourceBundle rb =
        ResourceBundle.getBundle("MyResources", Locale.US);
```

This will load the **ResourceBundle** with the values in the corresponding properties file.

If a suitable properties file is not found, the **ResourceBundle** object will fall back to the default properties file. The name of the default properties file will be the base name with a **properties** extension. In this case, the default file would be **MyResources.properties**. If the default properties file is not found, a **java.util.MissingResourceException** will be thrown.

Then, to read a value, you use the **ResourceBundle** class's **getString** method, passing a key.

```
public java.lang.String getString(java.lang.String key)
```

If the entry with the specified key is not found, a
java.util.MissingResourceException will be thrown.

In Spring MVC, you don't work with **ResourceBundle** directly. Instead,
you use the **messageSource** bean to tell Spring MVC where you store
properties files. For example, the following **messageSource** bean reads two
properties files.

```
<bean id="messageSource" class="org.springframework.context.support.
ReloadableResourceBundleMessageSource">
    <property name="basenames" >
        <list>
            <value>resource/messages</value>
            <value>resource/labels</value>
        </list>
    </property>
</bean>
```

In the bean definition above, the
ReloadableResourceBundleMessageSource class is used as the
implementation. Another implementation includes
ResourceBundleMessageSource, which is not reloadable. This means, if
you change a property key or value in any properties file and you are using
ResourceBundelMessageSource, you have to restart the JVM before the
changes take effect. On the other hand, you can set
ReloadableResourceBundlemessageSource to be reloadable.

Another difference between the two implementations is that with
ReloadableResourceBundleMessageSource the properties files are
searched in the application directory. With
ResourceBundleMessagesource, the properties files must be located in the
class path, in other words under the **WEB-INF/classes** directory.

Note also, if you only have one set of properties files, you can use the
basename property instead of **basenames**. Here is an example.

```
<bean id="messageSource" class="org.springframework.context.support.
➡ResourceBundleMessageSource">
    <property name="basename" value="resource/messages"/>
</bean>
```

Telling Spring MVC What Locale to Use

The most common method for choosing a locale to use for a user is probably by reading the value of the **accept-language** header of the user browser. The **accept-language** header carries information about the user's language preferences.

Other methods for choosing a locale include reading a certain session attribute or a cookie.

To select a locale in Spring MVC, you use the locale resolver bean. There are several implementations, including the following.

- **AcceptHeaderLocaleResolver**
- **SessionLocaleResolver**
- **CookieLocaleResolver**

All these implementations are part of the **org.springframework.web.servlet.i18n** package. **AcceptHeaderLocaleResolver** is probably the easiest one to use. If you choose to use this locale resolver, Spring MVC will read the browser's **accept-language** header to determine the locale(s) that the browser will accept. If one of the browser's locales matches a locale supported by the Spring MVC application, that one will be used. If nothing matched, the default locale will be used.

Here is the definition of the **localeResolver** bean that uses **AcceptHeaderLocaleResolver**.

```
<bean id="localeResolver" class="org.springframework.web.servlet.
➡ i18n.AcceptHeaderLocaleResolver">
</bean>
```

Using the message Tag

The easiest way to display localized messages in Spring MVC is by using the Spring **message** tag. To use this tag, declare this **taglib** directive at the top of all JSP pages that use the tag.

```
<%@taglib prefix="spring"
    uri="http://www.springframework.org/tags"%>
```

The attributes that may appear in the tag are given in Table 10.3. All attributes are optional.

Attribute	Description
arguments	Arguments for this tag written as a delimited string, an object array, or a single object
argumentSeparator	The character used for separating arguments to this tag.
code	The key to retrieve the message.
htmlEscape	Accepts true or false indicating whether or not the rendered text should be HTML-escaped.
javaScriptEscape	Accepts true or false indicating whether or not the rendered text should be free from JavaScript
message	A MessageSourceResolvable argument.
scope	The scope to store the variable defined in the var attribute
text	The default text to render if the code attribute is not present or the given code failed to retrieve a message
var	A scoped variable for storing the message.

Table 10.3: The message tag's attributes

Example

For example, the **app10a** application illustrates the use of the **localeResolver** bean to localize messages in the JSP pages. The directory structure is shown in Figure 10.1 and the Spring MVC configuration file for **app10a** is given in Listing 10.1.

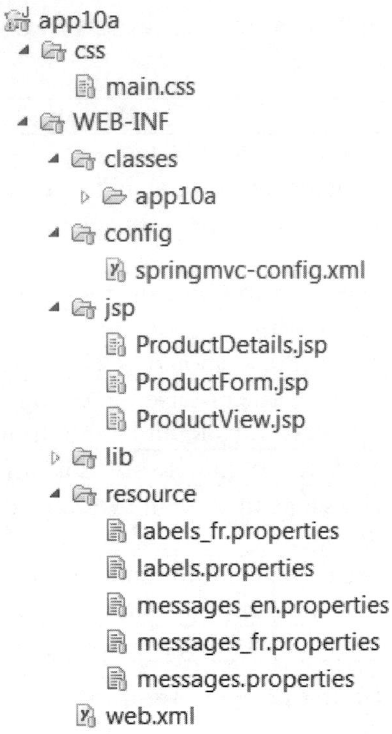

```
🖳 app10a
   ▲ 🗁 css
        📄 main.css
   ▲ 🗁 WEB-INF
      ▲ 🗁 classes
         ▷ 🗁 app10a
      ▲ 🗁 config
           📄 springmvc-config.xml
      ▲ 🗁 jsp
           📄 ProductDetails.jsp
           📄 ProductForm.jsp
           📄 ProductView.jsp
      ▷ 🗁 lib
      ▲ 🗁 resource
           📄 labels_fr.properties
           📄 labels.properties
           📄 messages_en.properties
           📄 messages_fr.properties
           📄 messages.properties
        📄 web.xml
```

Figure 10.1: The directory structure of app10a

Listing 10.1: The Spring MVC configuration file for app10a

```xml
<?xml version="1.0" encoding="UTF-8"?>
<beans xmlns="http://www.springframework.org/schema/beans"
    xmlns:xsi="http://www.w3.org/2001/XMLSchema-instance"
    xmlns:p="http://www.springframework.org/schema/p"
    xmlns:mvc="http://www.springframework.org/schema/mvc"
    xmlns:context="http://www.springframework.org/schema/context"
    xsi:schemaLocation="
        http://www.springframework.org/schema/beans
        http://www.springframework.org/schema/beans/spring-beans.xsd
        http://www.springframework.org/schema/mvc
        http://www.springframework.org/schema/mvc/spring-mvc.xsd
        http://www.springframework.org/schema/context
        http://www.springframework.org/schema/context/spring-
context.xsd">

    <context:component-scan base-package="app10a.controller" />
    <context:component-scan base-package="app10a.formatter" />
```

```xml
    <mvc:annotation-driven conversion-service="conversionService" />

    <mvc:resources mapping="/css/**" location="/css/" />
    <mvc:resources mapping="/*.html" location="/" />

    <bean id="viewResolver" class="org.springframework.web.servlet.
view.InternalResourceViewResolver">
        <property name="prefix" value="/WEB-INF/jsp/" />
        <property name="suffix" value=".jsp" />
    </bean>

    <bean id="conversionService"
        class="org.springframework.format.support.
FormattingConversionServiceFactoryBean">

        <property name="formatters">
            <set>
                <bean class="app10a.formatter.DateFormatter">
                    <constructor-arg type="java.lang.String"
                            value="MM-dd-yyyy" />
                </bean>
            </set>
        </property>
    </bean>

    <bean id="messageSource"
            class="org.springframework.context.support.
ReloadableResourceBundleMessageSource">
        <property name="basenames" >
            <list>
                <value>/WEB-INF/resource/messages</value>
                <value>/WEB-INF/resource/labels</value>
            </list>
        </property>
    </bean>

    <bean id="localeResolver"
            class="org.springframework.web.servlet.i18n.
AcceptHeaderLocaleResolver">
    </bean>
</beans>
```

Two beans are of interest here, the **messageSource** bean and the
localeResolver bean. The **mssageSource** bean declaration sets the

basenames property with two base names, **/WEB-INF/resource/messages** and **/WEB-INF/resource/labels**. The **localeResolver** bean enables message localization using the **AcceptHeaderLocaleResolver** class.

Two locales, **en** and **fr**, are supported, so each of the properties file comes in two versions. To enable localization, every piece of text in the JSP page is replaced with the **message** tag. Listing 10.2 shows the **ProductForm.jsp** page. Note that for debugging purpose, the current locale and **accept-language** header are shown at the top of the page.

Listing 10.2: The ProductForm.jsp page

```
<%@ taglib prefix="form"
    uri="http://www.springframework.org/tags/form"%>
<%@ taglib
    prefix="spring" uri="http://www.springframework.org/tags"%>
<%@ taglib uri="http://java.sun.com/jsp/jstl/core" prefix="c"%>
<!DOCTYPE HTML>
<html>
<head>
<title><spring:message code="page.productform.title"/></title>
<style type="text/css">@import url("<c:url
    value="/css/main.css"/>");</style>
</head>
<body>
<div id="global">
Current Locale : ${pageContext.response.locale}
<br/>
accept-language header: ${header["accept-language"]}

<form:form commandName="product" action="product_save"
    method="post">
    <fieldset>
        <legend><spring:message code="form.name"/></legend>
        <p>
            <label for="name"><spring:message
                code="label.productName" text="default text" />:
            </label>
            <form:input id="name" path="name"
                cssErrorClass="error"/>
            <form:errors path="name" cssClass="error"/>
        </p>
        <p>
            <label for="description"><spring:message
                code="label.description"/>:
```

```
        </label>
        <form:input id="description" path="description"/>
    </p>
    <p>
        <label for="price"><spring:message code="label.price"
            text="default text" />: </label>
        <form:input id="price" path="price"
            cssErrorClass="error"/>
    </p>
    <p id="buttons">
        <input id="reset" type="reset" tabindex="4"
            value="<spring:message code="button.reset"/>">
        <input id="submit" type="submit" tabindex="5"
            value="<spring:message code="button.submit"/>">
    </p>
    </fieldset>
</form:form>
</div>
</body>
</html>
```

To test the internationalization feature of **app10a**, change your browser's **accept-language** header. In Internet Explorer 7 onwards, go to **Tools** > **Internet Options** > **General** (tab) > **Languages** > **Language Preference**. In the Language Preference window, shown in Figure 10.2, click the **Add** button to add a language. To change the priority of a language when multiple languages are selected, use the **Move up** and **Move down** buttons.

Figure 10.2: The Language Preference window in IE 10

Instructions for changing the **accept-language** header in other browsers can be found here.

`http://www.w3.org/International/questions/qa-lang-priorities.en.php`

To test the application, direct your browser to this URL:

`http://localhost:8080/app10a/product_input`

You will see either the English or French version of the Product form, shown in Figure 10.3 and Figure 10.4, respectively.

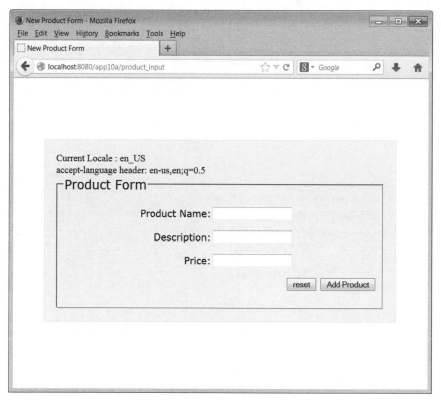

Figure 10.3: The Product form with en_US locale

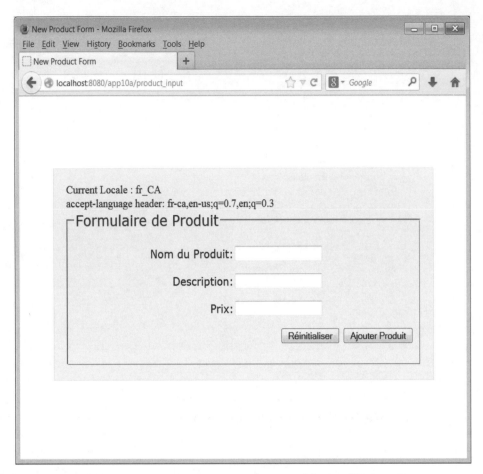

Figure 10.4: The Product form with fr_CA locale

Summary

This chapter explains how to develop an internationalized application. First it explained the **java.util.Locale** class and the **java.util.ResourceBundle** class. It then continued with an example of an internationalized application.

Chapter 11
File Upload

Once upon a time not long after Servlet technology had emerged, file upload programming was still a challenging task that involved parsing raw HTTP responses on the server side. To alleviate the pain, developers would resort to commercial file upload components, some of which cost an arm and a leg. Fortunately, in 2003 the Apache Software Foundation released its open source Commons FileUpload component, which soon became a hit with servlet/JSP programmers worldwide.

It took years before the designers of Servlet realized that file upload was essential, but file upload was finally a built-in feature in Servlet 3. Servlet 3 developers do not have to import the Commons FileUpload component into their projects anymore.

As such, there are two methods for handling file upload in Spring MVC:

1. By using Apache Commons FileUpload component.
2. By taking advantage of Servlet 3.0 or later built-in support. You can only use this approach if you will deploy your application to a container that supports Servlet 3.0 or later.

No matter which approach you choose, you'll be using the same API to handle the uploaded files. This chapter shows how to make use of the Commons FileUpload and Servlet 3 file upload feature in a Spring MVC application that need support for file upload. In addition, it also demonstrates how you can enhance user experience with HTML 5.

Client Side Programming

To upload a file, you must set the value of the **enctype** attribute of your HTML form with **multipart/form-data**, like this:

```
<form action="action" enctype="multipart/form-data" method="post">
    Select a file <input type="file" name="fieldName"/>
    <input type="submit" value="Upload"/>
</form>
```

The form must contain an **input** element of type **file**, which will be rendered as a button that, when clicked, opens a dialog to select a file. The form may also contain other field types such as a text area or a hidden field.

Prior to HTML 5, if you wanted to upload multiple files, you had to use multiple file **input** elements. HTML 5, however, makes multiple file uploads simpler by introducing the **multiple** attribute in the **input** element. You can write one of the following in HTML 5 to generate a button for selecting multiple files:

```
<input type="file" name="fieldName" multiple/>

<input type="file" name="fieldName" multiple="multiple"/>

<input type="file" name="fieldName" multiple=""/>
```

The MultipartFile Interface

Handling uploaded files is very easy in Spring MVC. A file uploaded to a Spring MVC application will be wrapped in a **MultipartFile** objcct. Your only responsibility is to write a domain class with a property of type **MultipartFile**.

The **org.springframework.web.multipart.MultipartFile** interface has the following methods.

```
byte[] getBytes()
```
Returns the contents of the file as an array of bytes.

```
String getContentType()
```
Returns the content type of the file.

```
InputStream getInputStream()
```
Returns an **InputStream** from which to read the content of the file.

```
String getName()
```
Returns the name of the parameter in the multipart form.

```
String getOriginalFilename()
```
Returns the original filename in the client's local drive.

```
long getSize()
```
Returns the size of the file in bytes.

```
boolean isEmpty()
```
Indicates whether or not the uploaded file is empty.

```
void transferTo(File destination)
```
Saves the uploaded file to *destination*.

The examples in the following sections show how you can retrieve an uploaded file in a controller.

File Upload with Commons FileUpload

Only servlet containers that implement Servlet 3.0 or later specification support file upload. For pre-Servlet 3.0 containers, you need the Apache Commons FileUpload component that you can download from this web page.

```
http://commons.apache.org/proper/commons-fileupload/
```

This is an open source project, so it is free and its source code is available. For Commons FileUpload to work successfully, it needs another Apache Commons component, Apache Commons IO. You can download Apache Commons IO from here.

```
http://commons.apache.org/proper/commons-io/
```

Therefore, two JARs need to be copied to the **WEB-INF/lib** directory of your application. The Commons FileUpload JAR will have a name that follows this pattern:

```
commons-fileupload-x.y.jar
```

where *x* is the major version and *y* the minor version of the software. For example, the one used in this chapter is **commons-fileupload-1.3.jar**.

The name of the Commons IO JAR follows this pattern.

```
commons-io-x.y.jar
```

Here, *x* is the major version and *y* the minor version of the software. For instance, the one used in this chapter is **commons-io-2.4.jar**.

In addition, you need to define this **multipartResolver** bean in your Spring MVC configuration file.

```
<bean id="multipartResolver"
        class="org.springframework.web.multipart.commons.
➡CommonsMultipartResolver">
    <property name="maxUploadSize" value="2000000"/>
</bean>
```

The **app11a** example shows how to use Apache Commons FileUpload to handle uploaded files. This example will also work in Servlet 3.0 containers. **app11a** has one domain class, the **Product** class, that contains a list of **MultipartFile** objects. You learn in this example how to write a controller that can handle uploaded product images.

The Domain Class

Listing 11.1 shows the **Product** domain class. It is similar to the **Product** classes in the previous examples, except that the one in Listing 11.1 has an **images** property of type **List<MultipartFile>**.

Listing 11.1: The Revised Product domain class

```
package app11a.domain;
import java.io.Serializable;
```

```java
import java.util.List;
import javax.validation.constraints.NotNull;
import javax.validation.constraints.Size;
import org.springframework.web.multipart.MultipartFile;

public class Product implements Serializable {
    private static final long serialVersionUID = 74458L;

    @NotNull
    @Size(min=1, max=10)
    private String name;

    private String description;
    private Float price;
    private List<MultipartFile> images;

    public String getName() {
        return name;
    }
    public void setName(String name) {
        this.name = name;
    }
    public String getDescription() {
        return description;
    }
    public void setDescription(String description) {
        this.description = description;
    }
    public Float getPrice() {
        return price;
    }
    public void setPrice(Float price) {
        this.price = price;
    }
    public List<MultipartFile> getImages() {
        return images;
    }
    public void setImages(List<MultipartFile> images) {
        this.images = images;
    }
}
```

The Controller

The controller for **app11a** is shows in Listing 11.2. There are two request-handling methods in this class, **inputProduct** and **saveProduct**. The **inputProduct** method sends a product form to the browser. The **saveProduct** method saves the uploaded image files in the **image** directory under the application directory.

Listing 11.2: The ProductController class

```
package app11a.controller;

import java.io.File;
import java.io.IOException;
import java.util.ArrayList;
import java.util.List;
import javax.servlet.http.HttpServletRequest;
import org.apache.commons.logging.Log;
import org.apache.commons.logging.LogFactory;
import org.springframework.stereotype.Controller;
import org.springframework.ui.Model;
import org.springframework.validation.BindingResult;
import org.springframework.web.bind.annotation.ModelAttribute;
import org.springframework.web.bind.annotation.RequestMapping;
import org.springframework.web.multipart.MultipartFile;
import app11a.domain.Product;

@Controller
public class ProductController {

    private static final Log logger =
        LogFactory.getLog(ProductController.class);

    @RequestMapping(value = "/product_input")
    public String inputProduct(Model model) {
        model.addAttribute("product", new Product());
        return "ProductForm";
    }

    @RequestMapping(value = "/product_save")
    public String saveProduct(HttpServletRequest servletRequest,
            @ModelAttribute Product product,
            BindingResult bindingResult, Model model) {
```

```
        List<MultipartFile> files = product.getImages();

        List<String> fileNames = new ArrayList<String>();

        if (null != files && files.size() > 0) {
            for (MultipartFile multipartFile : files) {

                String fileName =
                        multipartFile.getOriginalFilename();
                fileNames.add(fileName);

                File imageFile = new
                        File(servletRequest.getServletContext()
                        .getRealPath("/image"), fileName);
                try {
                    multipartFile.transferTo(imageFile);
                } catch (IOException e) {
                    e.printStackTrace();
                }
            }
        }

        // save product here
        model.addAttribute("product", product);
        return "ProductDetails";
    }
}
```

As you can see in the **saveProduct** method in Listing 11.2, saving an uploaded file is easy. You just need to call the **transferTo** method on the **MultipartFile**.

The Configuration File

Listing 11.3 shows the Spring MVC configuration file for **app11a**.

Listing 11.3: The Spring MVC configuration file for app11a

```
<?xml version="1.0" encoding="UTF-8"?>
<beans xmlns="http://www.springframework.org/schema/beans"
    xmlns:xsi="http://www.w3.org/2001/XMLSchema-instance"
```

```
    xmlns:p="http://www.springframework.org/schema/p"
    xmlns:mvc="http://www.springframework.org/schema/mvc"
    xmlns:context="http://www.springframework.org/schema/context"
    xsi:schemaLocation="
        http://www.springframework.org/schema/beans
        http://www.springframework.org/schema/beans/spring-beans.xsd
        http://www.springframework.org/schema/mvc
        http://www.springframework.org/schema/mvc/spring-mvc.xsd
        http://www.springframework.org/schema/context
        http://www.springframework.org/schema/context/spring-
context.xsd">

    <context:component-scan base-package="app11a.controller" />
    <context:component-scan base-package="app11a.formatter" />

    <mvc:annotation-driven conversion-service="conversionService" />

    <mvc:resources mapping="/css/**" location="/css/" />
    <mvc:resources mapping="/*.html" location="/" />
    <mvc:resources mapping="/image/**" location="/image/" />

    <bean id="viewResolver"
            class="org.springframework.web.servlet.view.
InternalResourceViewResolver">
        <property name="prefix" value="/WEB-INF/jsp/" />
        <property name="suffix" value=".jsp" />
    </bean>

    <bean id="messageSource"
            class="org.springframework.context.support.
ReloadableResourceBundleMessageSource">
        <property name="basename"
                value="/WEB-INF/resource/messages" />
    </bean>

    <bean id="conversionService"
        class="org.springframework.format.support.
FormattingConversionServiceFactoryBean">

        <property name="formatters">
            <set>
                <bean class="app11a.formatter.DateFormatter">
                    <constructor-arg type="java.lang.String"
```

```
                              value="MM-dd-yyyy" />
                </bean>
            </set>
        </property>
    </bean>

    <bean id="multipartResolver"
            class="org.springframework.web.multipart.commons.
➡ CommonsMultipartResolver">
    </bean>
</beans>
```

You can use the **maxUploadSize** property of the **multipartResolver** bean
to set the maximum file size that will be accepted. Without this property,
there is no maximum size. Setting no restriction on the file size does not
mean you can upload any size. A very large file will take a long time to
upload and cause the server to time out. To handle very large files, you can
slice the file using the HTML 5 File API and upload each chunk separately.

The JSP Page

The ProductForm.jsp page that you can use to upload an image file is
presented in listing 11.4.

Listing 11.4: The ProductForm.jsp Page

```
<%@ taglib prefix="form"
       uri="http://www.springframework.org/tags/form" %>
<%@ taglib uri="http://java.sun.com/jsp/jstl/core" prefix="c" %>
<!DOCTYPE HTML>
<html>
<head>
<title>Add Product Form</title>
<style type="text/css">@import url("<c:url
       value="/css/main.css"/>");</style>
</head>
<body>

<div id="global">
<form:form commandName="product" action="product_save" method="post"
       enctype="multipart/form-data">
```

```
    <fieldset>
        <legend>Add a product</legend>
        <p>
            <label for="name">Product Name: </label>
            <form:input id="name" path="name"
                cssErrorClass="error"/>
            <form:errors path="name" cssClass="error"/>
        </p>
        <p>
            <label for="description">Description: </label>
            <form:input id="description" path="description"/>
        </p>
        <p>
            <label for="price">Price: </label>
            <form:input id="price" path="price"
                cssErrorClass="error"/>
        </p>
        <p>
            <label for="image">Product Image: </label>
            <input type="file" name="images[0]"/>
        </p>
        <p id="buttons">
            <input id="reset" type="reset" tabindex="4">
            <input id="submit" type="submit" tabindex="5"
                value="Add Product">
        </p>
    </fieldset>
</form:form>
</div>
</body>
</html>
```

Pay attention to the input element of type file in the form. That will be rendered as a button for selecting files to upload.

Submitting the Product form will invoke the **product_save** method. If this method completes successfully, the user will be forwarded to the ProductDetails.jsp page in Listing 11.5.

Listing 11.5: The ProductDetails.jsp Page

```
<%@ taglib uri="http://java.sun.com/jsp/jstl/core" prefix="c" %>
<!DOCTYPE HTML>
<html>
```

```
<head>
<title>Save Product</title>
<style type="text/css">@import url("<c:url
    value="/css/main.css"/>");</style>
</head>
<body>
<div id="global">
    <h4>The product has been saved.</h4>
    <p>
        <h5>Details:</h5>
        Product Name: ${product.name}<br/>
        Description: ${product.description}<br/>
        Price: $$ {product.price}
        <p>Following files are uploaded successfully.</p>
        <ol>
        <c:forEach items="${product.images}" var="image">
            <li>${image.originalFilename}
            <img width="100" src="<c:url value="/image/"/>
            ${image.originalFilename}"/>
            </li>
        </c:forEach>
        </ol>
    </p>
</div>
</body>
</html>
```

The **ProductDetails.jsp** page displays the details of the saved **Product**, including its images.

Testing the Application

To test the application, direct your browser to this URL:

```
http://localhost:8080/app11a/product_input
```

You will see an Add Product form like the one in Figure 11.1. Type in some product information and select a file to upload.

Figure 11.1: A product form that includes a file field

Click Add Product and you'll see something like the web page in Figure 11.2.

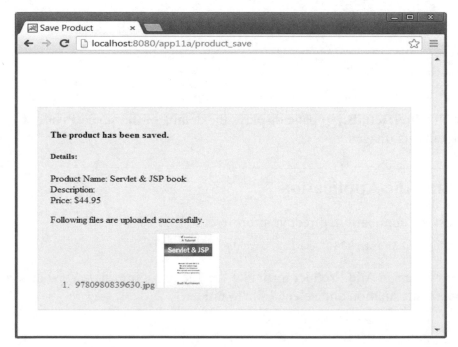

Figure 11.2: Showing the uploaded image

If you look into the **image** directory under the application directory, you'll see the uploaded image.

File Upload with Servlet 3 or Later

With Servlet 3, you don't need the duo Commons FileUpload and Commons IO components. Server side file upload programming in Servlet 3 and later containers centers around the **MultipartConfig** annotation type and the **javax.servlet.http.Part** interface. Servlets that handle uploaded files must be annotated **@MultipartConfig**.

The following are attributes that may appear in the **MultipartConfig** annotation type. All attributes are optional.

- **maxFileSize**. The maximum size for uploaded files. Files larger than the specified value will be rejected. By default, the value of **maxFileSize** is -1, which means unlimited.
- **maxRequestSize**. The maximum size allowed for multipart HTTP requests. By default, the value is -1, which translates into unlimited.
- **location**. The save location when the uploaded file is saved to disk by calling the **write** method on the **Part**.
- **fileSizeThreshold**. The size threshold after which the uploaded file will be written to disk.

The Spring MVC **DispatcherServlet** handles most or all requests. Unfortunately, you cannot annotate the servlet without changing the source code. Fortunately, there is an easier way to make a servlet a **MultipartConfig** servlet in Servlet 3: by passing values to the servlet declaration in the deployment descriptor (the **web.xml** file). The following has the same effect as annotating **DispatcherServlet** with **@MultipartConfig**.

```
<servlet>
    <servlet-name>springmvc</servlet-name>
    <servlet-class>
        org.springframework.web.servlet.DispatcherServlet
    </servlet-class>
```

```
    <init-param>
        <param-name>contextConfigLocation</param-name>
        <param-value>
            /WEB-INF/config/springmvc-config.xml
        </param-value>
    </init-param>
    <multipart-config>
        <max-file-size>20848820</max-file-size>
        <max-request-size>418018841</max-request-size>
        <file-size-threshold>1048576</file-size-threshold>
    </multipart-config>
</servlet>
```

As simple as that. On top of that, you need to use a different multipart resolver in your Spring MVC configuration file. Here it is.

```
<bean id="multipartResolver"
        class="org.springframework.web.multipart.support.
StandardServletMultipartResolver">
</bean>
```

The **app11b** application demonstrates how to handle file upload in a Servlet 3 or later container. It is a rewrite of **app11a**, so the domain and controller classes are very similar. The only difference is the **web.xml** file that now contains a **multipart-config** element. Listing 11.6 shows the **web.xml** file for **app11b**.

Listing 11.6: The web.xml file for app11b

```
<?xml version="1.0" encoding="UTF-8"?>
<web-app version="3.0"
    xmlns="http://java.sun.com/xml/ns/javaee"
    xmlns:xsi="http://www.w3.org/2001/XMLSchema-instance"
    xsi:schemaLocation="http://java.sun.com/xml/ns/javaee
http://java.sun.com/xml/ns/javaee/web-app_3_0.xsd">

    <servlet>
        <servlet-name>springmvc</servlet-name>
        <servlet-class>
            org.springframework.web.servlet.DispatcherServlet
        </servlet-class>
        <init-param>
            <param-name>contextConfigLocation</param-name>
```

```
        <param-value>
            /WEB-INF/config/springmvc-config.xml
        </param-value>
    </init-param>
    <load-on-startup>1</load-on-startup>
    <multipart-config>
        <max-file-size>20848820</max-file-size>
        <max-request-size>418018841</max-request-size>
        <file-size-threshold>1048576</file-size-threshold>
    </multipart-config>
</servlet>

<servlet-mapping>
    <servlet-name>springmvc</servlet-name>
    <url-pattern>/</url-pattern>
</servlet-mapping>
</web-app>
```

Listing 11.7 presents the Spring MVC configuration file for **app11b**.

Listing 11.7: The configuration file for app11b

```
<?xml version="1.0" encoding="UTF-8"?>
<beans xmlns="http://www.springframework.org/schema/beans"
    xmlns:xsi="http://www.w3.org/2001/XMLSchema-instance"
    xmlns:p="http://www.springframework.org/schema/p"
    xmlns:mvc="http://www.springframework.org/schema/mvc"
    xmlns:context="http://www.springframework.org/schema/context"
    xsi:schemaLocation="
        http://www.springframework.org/schema/beans
        http://www.springframework.org/schema/beans/spring-beans.xsd
        http://www.springframework.org/schema/mvc
        http://www.springframework.org/schema/mvc/spring-mvc.xsd
        http://www.springframework.org/schema/context
        http://www.springframework.org/schema/context/spring-
context.xsd">

    <context:component-scan base-package="app11b.controller" />
    <context:component-scan base-package="app11b.formatter" />

    <mvc:annotation-driven conversion-service="conversionService" />

    <mvc:resources mapping="/css/**" location="/css/" />
    <mvc:resources mapping="/*.html" location="/" />
```

```xml
    <mvc:resources mapping="/image/**" location="/image/" />
    <mvc:resources mapping="/file/**" location="/file/" />

    <bean id="viewResolver"
        class="org.springframework.web.servlet.view.
InternalResourceViewResolver">
        <property name="prefix" value="/WEB-INF/jsp/" />
        <property name="suffix" value=".jsp" />
    </bean>

    <bean id="messageSource"
            class="org.springframework.context.support.
ReloadableResourceBundleMessageSource">
        <property name="basename"
                value="/WEB-INF/resource/messages" />
    </bean>

    <bean id="conversionService"
        class="org.springframework.format.support.
FormattingConversionServiceFactoryBean">

        <property name="formatters">
            <set>
                <bean class="app11b.formatter.DateFormatter">
                    <constructor-arg type="java.lang.String"
                            value="MM-dd-yyyy" />
                </bean>
            </set>
        </property>
    </bean>
    <bean id="multipartResolver"
        class="org.springframework.web.multipart.support.
StandardServletMultipartResolver">
    </bean>
</beans>
```

To test the application, direct your browser to this URL.

```
http://localhost:8080/app11b/product_input
```

Upload Clients

While the file upload feature in Servlet 3 makes file upload a breeze to program on the server side, it does nothing to enhance user experience. An HTML form alone will not let you display a progress bar or show the number of files successfully uploaded. Developers have used different techniques to improve the user interface, such as by inquiring the server using a separate browser thread so that upload progress can be reported, or by using third-party technologies such as Java applets, Adobe Flash, or Microsoft Silverlight.

The third-party technologies work. To some extent and with limitation. The first disadvantage of using one of these technologies is that there is no built-in support for them in all major browsers. For example, Java applets can only run if the user has installed Java on his/her computer. While some computer makers, such as Dell and HP, ship their products with Java installed, some others, such as Lenovo, do not. While there are ways to detect if Java is installed on the user's machine and direct the user to install one if none exists, this is a disruption that not all users are willing to tolerate. On top of that, Java applets by default have very restricted access to the local file system unless they are signed. These obviously add costs and complexity to the program.

Flash has the same issues as applets. Flash programs need a player to run and not all platforms support Flash by default. The user will have to install a Flash player to run Flash programs inside a browser. Besides, Apple won't allow Flash to run on iPad and iPhone and Adobe has finally discontinued Flash on mobile platforms.

Microsoft Silverlight also needs a player to run and non-IE browsers do not ship with one. So, basically Silverlight programmers have more or less the same problems as those encountered by applet and Flash developers.

Luckily for us, HTML 5 comes to the rescue.

HTML 5 adds a File API to its DOM to allow local file access. Compared to applets, Flash, and Silverlight, HTML 5 seems ideal as the perfect solution to client side file upload limitations. At time of writing, unfortunately, Internet Explorer 9 does not yet fully support this API. You can test the following example with the latest version of Firefox, Chrome and Opera, however.

To demonstrate the power of HTML 5, the **html5.jsp** page in **app11b** (given in Listing 11.5) uses JavaScript and the HTML 5 File API to provide a progress bar that reports the upload progress. The **app11b** application also contains a copy of the **MultipleUploadsServlet** class to save uploaded files on the server. However, as Javascript is beyond the scope of this book, explanation will only be given cursorily.

In short, we're interested in the **change** event of the HTML 5 **input** element, which is triggered when the value of an **input** element changes. We're also interested in the **progress** event added to the **XMLHttpRequest** object in HTML 5. **XMLHttpRequest** is of course the backbone of AJAX. When the **XMLHttpRequest** object is used asynchronously to upload a file, it triggers the **progress** event continuously until the upload process is complete or canceled or until the process is halted by an error. By listening to the **progress** event, you can easily monitor the progress of a file upload operation.

The **Html5FileUploadController** class in **app11b** has the capability of saving an uploaded file to the **file** directory under the application directory. The **UploadedFile** class in Listing 11.8 shows a simple domain class that contains only one property.

Listing 11.8: The UploadedFile domain class

```
package app11b.domain;
import java.io.Serializable;

import org.springframework.web.multipart.MultipartFile;

public class UploadedFile implements Serializable {
    private static final long serialVersionUID = 72348L;

    private MultipartFile multipartFile;
    public MultipartFile getMultipartFile() {
        return multipartFile;
    }
    public void setMultipartFile(MultipartFile multipartFile) {
```

```
            this.multipartFile = multipartFile;
    }
}
```

The Html5FileUploadController class is given in Listing 11.9.

Listing 11.9: The Html5FileUploadController class

```
package app11b.controller;

import java.io.File;
import java.io.IOException;

import javax.servlet.http.HttpServletRequest;

import org.apache.commons.logging.Log;
import org.apache.commons.logging.LogFactory;
import org.springframework.stereotype.Controller;
import org.springframework.ui.Model;
import org.springframework.validation.BindingResult;
import org.springframework.web.bind.annotation.ModelAttribute;
import org.springframework.web.bind.annotation.RequestMapping;
import org.springframework.web.multipart.MultipartFile;

import app11b.domain.UploadedFile;

@Controller
public class Html5FileUploadController {

    private static final Log logger = LogFactory
            .getLog(Html5FileUploadController.class);

    @RequestMapping(value = "/html5")
    public String inputProduct() {
        return "Html5";
    }

    @RequestMapping(value = "/file_upload")
    public void saveFile(HttpServletRequest servletRequest,
            @ModelAttribute UploadedFile uploadedFile,
            BindingResult bindingResult, Model model) {

        MultipartFile multipartFile =
                uploadedFile.getMultipartFile();
```

```
        String fileName = multipartFile.getOriginalFilename();
        try {
            File file = new File(servletRequest.getServletContext()
                    .getRealPath("/file"), fileName);
            multipartFile.transferTo(file);
        } catch (IOException e) {
            e.printStackTrace();
        }
    }
}
```

The **saveFile** method in **Html5FileUploadController** saves the uploaded file to the **file** directory under the application directory.

The **html5.jsp** page in Listing 11.10 contains JavaScript code that allows the user to select multiple files and upload them in one button click. The files themselves will be uploaded one at a time.

Listing: 11.10: The html5.jsp page

```
<!DOCTYPE HTML>
<html>
<head>
<script>
    var totalFileLength, totalUploaded, fileCount, filesUploaded;

    function debug(s) {
        var debug = document.getElementById('debug');
        if (debug) {
            debug.innerHTML = debug.innerHTML + '<br/>' + s;
        }
    }

    function onUploadComplete(e) {
        totalUploaded += document.getElementById('files').
                files[filesUploaded].size;
        filesUploaded++;
        debug('complete ' + filesUploaded + " of " + fileCount);
        debug('totalUploaded: ' + totalUploaded);
        if (filesUploaded < fileCount) {
            uploadNext();
        } else {
            var bar = document.getElementById('bar');
            bar.style.width = '100%';
```

```
            bar.innerHTML = '100% complete';
            alert('Finished uploading file(s)');
        }
    }

function onFileSelect(e) {
    var files = e.target.files; // FileList object
    var output = [];
    fileCount = files.length;
    totalFileLength = 0;
    for (var i=0; i<fileCount; i++) {
        var file = files[i];
        output.push(file.name, ' (',
                file.size, ' bytes, ',
                file.lastModifiedDate.toLocaleDateString(), ')'
        );
        output.push('<br/>');
        debug('add ' + file.size);
        totalFileLength += file.size;
    }
    document.getElementById('selectedFiles').innerHTML =
        output.join('');
    debug('totalFileLength:' + totalFileLength);
}

function onUploadProgress(e) {
    if (e.lengthComputable) {
        var percentComplete = parseInt(
                (e.loaded + totalUploaded) * 100
                / totalFileLength);
        var bar = document.getElementById('bar');
        bar.style.width = percentComplete + '%';
        bar.innerHTML = percentComplete + ' % complete';
    } else {
        debug('unable to compute');
    }
}

function onUploadFailed(e) {
    alert("Error uploading file");
}

function uploadNext() {
```

```
        var xhr = new XMLHttpRequest();
        var fd = new FormData();
        var file = document.getElementById('files').
                files[filesUploaded];
        fd.append("multipartFile", file);
        xhr.upload.addEventListener(
                "progress", onUploadProgress, false);
        xhr.addEventListener("load", onUploadComplete, false);
        xhr.addEventListener("error", onUploadFailed, false);
        xhr.open("POST", "file_upload");
        debug('uploading ' + file.name);
        xhr.send(fd);
    }

    function startUpload() {
        totalUploaded = filesUploaded = 0;
        uploadNext();
    }
    window.onload = function() {
        document.getElementById('files').addEventListener(
                'change', onFileSelect, false);
        document.getElementById('uploadButton').
                addEventListener('click', startUpload, false);
    }
</script>
</head>
<body>
<h1>Multiple file uploads with progress bar</h1>
<div id='progressBar' style='height:20px;border:2px solid green'>
    <div id='bar'
            style='height:100%;background:#33dd33;width:0%'>
    </div>
</div>
<form>
    <input type="file" id="files" multiple/>
    <br/>
    <output id="selectedFiles"></output>
    <input id="uploadButton" type="button" value="Upload"/>
</form>
<div id='debug'
    style='height:100px;border:2px solid green;overflow:auto'>
</div>
</body>
```

```
</html>
```

The user interface in the **html5.jsp** page consists mainly of a **div** element called **progressBar**, a form, and another **div** element called **debug**. You guessed it right that the **progressBar div** is for showing the upload progress and **debug** is for debugging info. The form has an **input** element of type file and a button.

There are two things to note from the form. First, the **input** element identified as **files** has a **multiple** attribute to support multiple file selection. Second, the button is not a submit button. So, clicking it will not submit the containing form. In fact, the script uses the **XMLHttpRequest** object to do the upload.

Now, let's look at the Javascript code. This assumes some knowledge of the scripting language.

When the script is executed, the first thing it does is allocate space for four variables.

```
var totalFileLength, totalUploaded, fileCount, filesUploaded;
```

The **totalFileLength** variable holds the total length of the files to be uploaded. **totalUploaded** is the number of bytes uploaded so far. **fileCount** contains the number of files to be uploaded, and **filesUploaded** indicates the number of files that have been uploaded.

Then the function assigned to **window.onload** is called after the window completely loads.

```
window.onload = function() {
    document.getElementById('files').addEventListener(
            'change', onFileSelect, false);
    document.getElementById('uploadButton').
            addEventListener('click', startUpload, false);
}
```

This maps the **files input** element's **change** event with the **onFileSelect** function and the button's **click** event with **startUpload**.

The **change** event occurs every time the user changes a different set of files from a local directory. The event handler attached to this event simply prints the names and sizes of the selected files to an output element. Here is the event handler again:

```
function onFileSelect(e) {
    var files = e.target.files; // FileList object
    var output = [];
    fileCount = files.length;
    totalFileLength = 0;
    for (var i=0; i<fileCount; i++) {
        var file = files[i];
        output.push(file.name, ' (',
                file.size, ' bytes, ',
                file.lastModifiedDate.toLocaleDateString(), ')'
        );
        output.push('<br/>');
        debug('add ' + file.size);
        totalFileLength += file.size;
    }
    document.getElementById('selectedFiles').innerHTML =
        output.join('');
    debug('totalFileLength:' + totalFileLength);
}
```

When the user clicks the Upload button, the **startUpload** function is called and it in turns calls the **uploadNext** function. **uploadNext** uploads the next file in the selected file collection. It starts by creating an **XMLHttpRequest** object and a **FormData** object to which the file to be uploaded next is appended to.

```
var xhr = new XMLHttpRequest();
var fd = new FormData();
var file = document.getElementById('files').
        files[filesUploaded];
fd.append("multipartFile", file);
```

The **uploadNext** function then attaches the **progress** event of the **XMLHttpRequest** object to the **onUploadProgress** and the **load** event and the **error** event to **onUploadComplete** and **onUploadFailed**, respectively.

```
xhr.upload.addEventListener(
        "progress", onUploadProgress, false);
xhr.addEventListener("load", onUploadComplete, false);
xhr.addEventListener("error", onUploadFailed, false);
```

Next, it opens a connection to the server and sends the **FormData**.

```
xhr.open("POST", "file_upload");
debug('uploading ' + file.name);
xhr.send(fd);
```

During the upload progress, the **onUploadProgress** function is called repeatedly, giving it the opportunity to update the progress bar. An update involves calculating the ratio of the total bytes already uploaded and the number of bytes of the selected files as well as widening the **div** element within the **progressBar div** element.

```
function onUploadProgress(e) {
    if (e.lengthComputable) {
        var percentComplete = parseInt(
                (e.loaded + totalUploaded) * 100
                / totalFileLength);
        var bar = document.getElementById('bar');
        bar.style.width = percentComplete + '%';
        bar.innerHTML = percentComplete + ' % complete';
    } else {
        debug('unable to compute');
    }
}
```

At the completion of an upload, the **onUploadComplete** function is invoked. This event handler adds to **totalUploaded** the size of the file that has just finished uploading and increments **filesUploaded**. It then checks if all selected files have been uploaded. If yes, a message is displayed telling the user that uploading has completed successfully. If not, it calls **uploadNext** again. The **onUploadComplete** function is reprinted here for reading convenience.

```
function onUploadComplete(e) {
    totalUploaded += document.getElementById('files').
            files[filesUploaded].size;
    filesUploaded++;
    debug('complete ' + filesUploaded + " of " + fileCount);
    debug('totalUploaded: ' + totalUploaded);
    if (filesUploaded < fileCount) {
        uploadNext();
    } else {
```

```
        var bar = document.getElementById('bar');
        bar.style.width = '100%';
        bar.innerHTML = '100% complete';
        alert('Finished uploading file(s)');
    }
}
```

You can test the application using this URL:

```
http://localhost:8080/app11b/html5.jsp
```

Select a couple of files and click the Upload button. You'll see a progress bar and the information on the uploaded files like the screen shot in Figure 11.3.

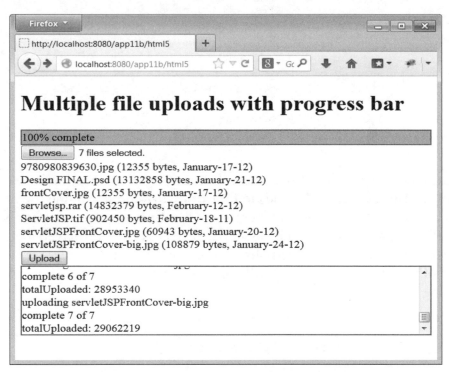

Figure 11.3: File upload with progress bar

Summary

In this chapter you learned how to handle file upload in a Spring MVC application. There are two ways of handling uploaded files, by using the Commons FileUpload component or by taking advantage of the Servlet 3 native file upload feature. The accompanying examples for this chapter showed how to use both approaches.

You also learned how to use HTML 5 to support multiple file upload and enhance user experience on the client side by utilizing the File API.

Chapter 12
File Download

A static resource, such as an image or an HTML file, can be downloaded by simply pointing the browser to the right URL. As long as the resource is located in the application directory or a subdirectory under it and not under **WEB-INF**, the servlet/JSP container will send the resource to the browser. However, sometimes a static resource is stored outside the application directory or in a database, or sometimes you want to control over who can see it and prevent other websites from cross-referencing it. If any of these scenarios applies to you, then you have to send the resource programmatically.

In short, programmatic file download lets you selectively send a file to the browser. This chapter explains what it takes to programmatically send a resource to the browser and presents two examples.

File Download Overview

To send a resource such as a file to the browser, you need to do the following in your controller.

1. Use the **void** return type for your request-handling method and add **HttpServletResponse** as an argument to the method.
2. Set the response's content type to the file's content type. The **Content-Type** header specifies the type of the data in the body of an entity and consists of the media type and subtype identifiers. Visit http://www.iana.org/assignments/media-types for standard content types. If you do not know what the content type is or want the browser to always display the Save As dialog, set it to

APPLICATION/OCTET-STREAM. This value is not case sensitive.

3. Add an HTTP response header named **Content-Disposition** and give it the value **attachment; filename=***fileName*, where *fileName* is the default file name that should appear in the File Download dialog box. This is normally the same name as the file, but does not have to be so.

For instance, this code sends a file to the browser.

```
FileInputStream fis = new FileInputStream(file);
BufferedInputStream bis = new BufferedInputStream(fis);
byte[] bytes = new byte[bis.available()];
response.setContentType(contentType);
OutputStream os = response.getOutputStream();
bis.read(bytes);
os.write(bytes);
```

To send a file programmatically tot he browser, first read the file as a **FileInputStream** and load the content to a byte array. Then, you obtain the **HttpServletResponse**'s **OutputStream** and call its **write** method, passing the byte array.

Example 1: Hiding A Resource

The **app12a** application demonstrates how to send a file to the browser. In this application the **ResourceController** class handles user login and the sending of a **secret.pdf** file to the browser. The **secret.pdf** file is placed under **WEB-INF/data** so that direct access is not possible. Only authorized users can view it. If a user has not logged in, the application will forward to the Login page.

The **ResourceController** class in Listing 12.1 presents a controller responsible for sending the **secret.pdf** file. Access is only granted if the user's **HttpSession** contains a **loggedIn** attribute, which indicates the user has successfully logged in.

Listing 12.1: The ResourceController class

```java
package app12a.controller;

import java.io.BufferedInputStream;
import java.io.File;
import java.io.FileInputStream;
import java.io.IOException;
import java.io.OutputStream;
import javax.servlet.http.HttpServletRequest;
import javax.servlet.http.HttpServletResponse;
import javax.servlet.http.HttpSession;
import org.apache.commons.logging.Log;
import org.apache.commons.logging.LogFactory;
import org.springframework.stereotype.Controller;
import org.springframework.ui.Model;
import org.springframework.web.bind.annotation.ModelAttribute;
import org.springframework.web.bind.annotation.RequestMapping;
import app12a.domain.Login;

@Controller
public class ResourceController {

    private static final Log logger =
    LogFactory.getLog(ResourceController.class);

    @RequestMapping(value="/login")
    public String login(@ModelAttribute Login login, HttpSession
    session, Model model) {
        model.addAttribute("login", new Login());
        if ("paul".equals(login.getUserName()) &&
                "secret".equals(login.getPassword())) {
            session.setAttribute("loggedIn", Boolean.TRUE);
          return "Main";
        } else {
            return "LoginForm";
        }
    }

    @RequestMapping(value="/resource_download")
    public String downloadResource(HttpSession session,
    HttpServletRequest request,
            HttpServletResponse response) {
```

```
if (session == null ||
        session.getAttribute("loggedIn") == null) {
    return "LoginForm";
}
String dataDirectory = request.
        getServletContext().getRealPath("/WEB-INF/data");
File file = new File(dataDirectory, "secret.pdf");
if (file.exists()) {
    response.setContentType("application/pdf");
    response.addHeader("Content-Disposition",
            "attachment; filename=secret.pdf");
    byte[] buffer = new byte[1024];
    FileInputStream fis = null;
    BufferedInputStream bis = null;
    // if using Java 7, use try-with-resources
    try {
        fis = new FileInputStream(file);
        bis = new BufferedInputStream(fis);
        OutputStream os = response.getOutputStream();
        int i = bis.read(buffer);
        while (i != -1) {
            os.write(buffer, 0, i);
            i = bis.read(buffer);
        }
    } catch (IOException ex) {
        // do something,
        // probably forward to an Error page
    } finally {
        if (bis != null) {
            try {
                bis.close();
            } catch (IOException e) {
            }
        }
        if (fis != null) {
            try {
                fis.close();
            } catch (IOException e) {
            }
        }
    }
}
return null;
```

```
        }
}
```

The first method in the controller, **login**, sends the user to the login form.

The **LoginForm.jsp** page is given in Listing 12.2.

Listing 12.2: The LoginForm.jsp page

```
<%@ taglib prefix="form"
        uri="http://www.springframework.org/tags/form" %>
<%@ taglib prefix="c" uri="http://java.sun.com/jsp/jstl/core" %>
<!DOCTYPE HTML>
<html>
<head>
<title>Login</title>
<style type="text/css">@import url("<c:url
        value="/css/main.css"/>");</style>
</head>
<body>
<div id="global">
<form:form commandName="login" action="login" method="post">
    <fieldset>
        <legend>Login</legend>
        <p>
            <label for="userName">User Name: </label>
            <form:input id="userName" path="userName"
                    cssErrorClass="error"/>
        </p>
        <p>
            <label for="password">Password: </label>
            <form:password id="password" path="password"
                cssErrorClass="error"/>
        </p>
        <p id="buttons">
            <input id="reset" type="reset" tabindex="4">
            <input id="submit" type="submit" tabindex="5"
                value="Login">
        </p>
    </fieldset>
</form:form>
</div>
</body>
</html>
```

The user name and password that must be used for a successful login are hardcoded in the **login** method. The username must be **paul** and the password must be **secret**. If the user logs in successfully, he or she will be redirected to the **Main.jsp** page (printed in Listing 12.3). This page contains a link that the user can click to download the document.

Listing 12.2: The Main.jsp page

```
<%@ taglib uri="http://java.sun.com/jsp/jstl/core" prefix="c" %>
<!DOCTYPE HTML>
<html>
<head>
<title>Download Page</title>
<style type="text/css">@import url("<c:url
     value="/css/main.css"/>");</style>
</head>
<body>
<div id="global">
    <h4>Please click the link below.</h4>
    <p>
        <a href="resource_download">Download</a>
    </p>
</div>
</body>
</html>
```

The second method in the **ResourceController** class, **downloadResource**, checks if the user has successfully logged in by verifying the presence of the **loggedIn** session attribute. If the attribute is found, it sends the file to the browser. If not, the user will be sent to the Login page. Note that if you're using Java 7 or later, the new try-with-resources feature is a safer way for handling resources.

You can test the **app12a** application by invoking the **FileDownloadServlet** using this URL:

```
http://localhost:8080/app12a/login
```

Example 2: Preventing Cross-Referencing

Competitors might try to "steal" your web assets by cross-referencing them, i.e. displaying your valuables in their websites as if they were theirs. You can prevent this from happening by programmatically sending the resources only if the **referer** header contains your domain name. Of course the most determined thieves will still be able to download your properties. However, they can't do that without breaking a sweat.

The **app12b** application uses the **ImageController** class in Listing 12.4 to send images to the browser, only if the **referer** header is not null. This will prevent the images from being downloaded directly by typing their URLs in the browser.

Listing 12.4: The ImageController class

```java
package app12a.controller;

import java.io.BufferedInputStream;
import java.io.File;
import java.io.FileInputStream;
import java.io.IOException;
import java.io.OutputStream;
import javax.servlet.http.HttpServletRequest;
import javax.servlet.http.HttpServletResponse;
import org.apache.commons.logging.Log;
import org.apache.commons.logging.LogFactory;
import org.springframework.stereotype.Controller;
import org.springframework.web.bind.annotation.PathVariable;
import org.springframework.web.bind.annotation.RequestHeader;
import org.springframework.web.bind.annotation.RequestMapping;
import org.springframework.web.bind.annotation.RequestMethod;

@Controller
public class ImageController {

    private static final Log logger =
            LogFactory.getLog(ImageController.class);

    @RequestMapping(value="/image_get/{id}", method =
            RequestMethod.GET)
```

```java
public void getImage(@PathVariable String id,
        HttpServletRequest request,
        HttpServletResponse response,
        @RequestHeader String referer) {
    if (referer != null) {
        String imageDirectory = request.getServletContext().
                getRealPath("/WEB-INF/image");
        File file = new File(imageDirectory,
                id + ".jpg");
        if (file.exists()) {
            response.setContentType("image/jpg");
            byte[] buffer = new byte[1024];
            FileInputStream fis = null;
            BufferedInputStream bis = null;
            // if you're using Java 7, use try-with-resources
            try {
                fis = new FileInputStream(file);
                bis = new BufferedInputStream(fis);
                OutputStream os = response.getOutputStream();
                int i = bis.read(buffer);
                while (i != -1) {
                    os.write(buffer, 0, i);
                    i = bis.read(buffer);
                }
            } catch (IOException ex) {
                System.out.println (ex.toString());
            } finally {
                if (bis != null) {
                    try {
                        bis.close();
                    } catch (IOException e) {

                    }
                }
                if (fis != null) {
                    try {
                        fis.close();
                    } catch (IOException e) {

                    }
                }
            }
        }
    }
}
```

```
            }
        }
}
```

In principle the **ImageController** class works like **ResourceController**. The **if** statement at the beginning of the **getImage** method makes sure an image will be sent only if the **referer** header is not null.

You can use the **images.html** file in Listing 12.5 to test the application.

Listing 12.5: The images.html file

```
<!DOCTYPE HTML>
<html>
<head>
    <title>Photo Gallery</title>
</head>
<body>
<img src="image_get/1"/>
<img src="image_get/2"/>
<img src="image_get/3"/>
<img src="image_get/4"/>
<img src="image_get/5"/>
<img src="image_get/6"/>
<img src="image_get/7"/>
<img src="image_get/8"/>
<img src="image_get/9"/>
<img src="image_get/10"/>
</body>
</html>
```

To see **ImageServlet** in action, point your browser to this URL.

```
http://localhost:8080/app12a/images.html
```

Figure 12.1 shows the images sent by **ImageServlet**.

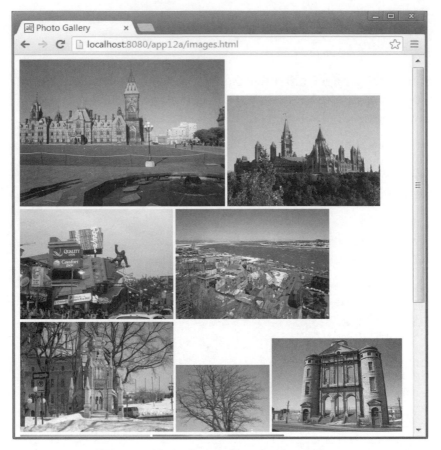

Figure 12.1: ImageServlet in action

Summary

In this chapter you learned how programmatic file download works in Spring MVC applications. You also learned how to select a file and sent it to the browser.

Appendix A
Tomcat

Tomcat is the most popular servlet/JSP container today. It's free, mature, and open-sourced. You need Tomcat 7 or later or another compliant servlet/JSP container to run the sample applications accompanying this book. This appendix provides a quick installation and configuration guide and is by no means a comprehensive tutorial.

Downloading and Configuring Tomcat

You should first download the latest version of Tomcat from http://tomcat.apache.org. You should get the latest binary distribution in either zip or gz. Tomcat 7 and later require Java 6 to run.

After you download the zip or gz file, unpack the file. You will see several directories under the installation directory.

In the **bin** directory, you will find programs to start and stop Tomcat. The **webapps** directory is important because you can deploy your applications there. In addition, the **conf** directory contains configuration files, including the **server.xml** and **tomcat-users.xml** files. The **lib** directory is also of interest since it contains the Servlet and JSP APIs that you need to compile your servlets and custom tags.

After extracting the zip or gz file, set the **JAVA_HOME** environment variable to the JDK installation directory.

For Windows users, it is a good idea to download the Windows installer for easier installation.

Starting and Stopping Tomcat

Once you've downloaded and extracted a Tomcat binary, you can start Tomcat by running the **startup.bat** (on Windows) or the **startup.sh** file (on Unix/Linux/Mac OS). Both files reside under the **bin** directory of Tomcat's installation directory. By default, Tomcat runs on port 8080, so you can test Tomcat by directing your browser to this address:

```
http://localhost:8080
```

To stop Tomcat, run the **shutdown.bat** (on Windows) or **shutdown.sh** file (on Unix/Linux/Mac OS) in the **bin** directory.

Defining A Context

To deploy a servlet/JSP application to Tomcat, you need to define a Tomcat context either explicitly or implicitly. Each Tomcat context represents a web application in Tomcat.

There are several ways of defining a Tomcat context explicitly, including

- Creating an XML file in Tomcat's **conf/Catalina/localhost** directory.
- Adding a **Context** element in Tomcat's **conf/server.xml** file.

If you decide to create an XML file for each context, the file name is important as the context path is derived from it. For example, if you place a **commerce.xml** file in the **conf/Catalina/localhost** directory, the context path of your application will be **commerce** and a resource can be invoked using this URL:

```
http://localhost:8080/commerce/resourceName
```

A context file must contain a **Context** element as its root element. Most of the times the element does not have child elements and is the only element in the file. For example, here is an example context file, consisting of a single line.

```
<Context docBase="C:/apps/commerce" reloadable="true"/>
```

The only required attribute is **docBase**, which specifies the location of the application. The **reloadable** attribute is optional, but if it is present and its value is set to true, Tomcat will monitor the application for any addition, deletion, or update of a Java class file and other resources. When such a change is detected, Tomcat will reload the application. Setting **reloadable** to **true** is recommended during development but not in production.

When you add a context file to the specified directory, Tomcat will automatically load the application. When you delete it, Tomcat will unload the application.

Another way of defining a context is by adding a **Context** element in the **conf/server.xml** file. To do this, open the file and create a **Context** element under the **Host** element. Unlike the previous method, defining a context here requires that you specify the **path** attribute for your context path. Here is an example:

```
<Host name="localhost"  appBase="webapps" unpackWARs="true"
       autoDeploy="true">

   <Context path="/commerce"
           docBase="C:/apps/commerce"
           reloadable="true"
   />
</Host>
```

Generally, managing contexts through **server.xml** is not recommended as updates will only take effect after you restart Tomcat. However, if you have a bunch of applications that you need to test quickly, you may find working with **server.xml** almost ideal as you can manage all your applications in a single file.

Finally, you can also deploy an application implicitly by copying a war file or the whole application to Tomcat's **webapps** directory.

More information on Tomcat contexts can be found here:

```
http://tomcat.apache.org/tomcat-8.0-doc/config/context.html
```

Defining A Resource

You can define a JNDI resource that your application can use in your Tomcat context definition. A resource is represented by the **Resource** element under the **Context** element.

For instance, to add a **DataSource** resource that opens connections to a MySQL database, add this **Resource** element.

```
<Context [path="/appName"] docBase="...">
    <Resource name="jdbc/dataSourceName"
        auth="Container"
        type="javax.sql.DataSource"
        username="..."
        password="..."
        driverClassName="com.mysql.jdbc.Driver"
        url="..."
    />
</Context>
```

More information on the **Resource** element can be found here.

```
http://tomcat.apache.org/tomcat-8.0-doc/jndi-resources-howto.html
```

Installing SSL Certificates

Tomcat supports SSL and you should use it to secure transfer of confidential data such as social security numbers and credit card details. You can generate a public/private key pair using the KeyTool program and pay a trusted authority to create and sign a digital certificate for you.

Once you receive your certificate and import it into your keystore, the next step will be to install it on your server. If you're using Tomcat, simply copy your keystore in a location on the server and configure Tomcat. Then, open your **conf/server.xml** file and add the following **Connector** element under **<service>**.

```
<Connector port="443"
    minSpareThreads="5"
```

```
        maxSpareThreads="75"
        enableLookups="true"
        disableUploadTimeout="true"
        acceptCount="100"
        maxThreads="200"

        scheme="https"
        secure="true"
        SSLEnabled="true"
        keystoreFile="/path/to/keystore"
        keyAlias="example.com"
        keystorePass="01secret02%%%"
        clientAuth="false"
        sslProtocol="TLS"
/>
```

The lines in bold are related to SSL.

Appendix B
Servlets

Servlet is the main technology for developing servlets. Understanding the Servlet API is your gateway to becoming a formidable Java web developer. It is imperative that you be familiar with each of the over seventy types defined in the Servlet API. Seventy may sound a lot but it's not hard if you learn one at a time.

This appendix introduces the Servlet API and teaches you how to write your first servlet.

Servlet API Overview

The Servlet API comes in four Java packages. The packages are as follows.

- **javax.servlet**. Contains classes and interfaces that define the contract between a servlet and a servlet container.
- **javax.servlet.http**. Contains classes and interfaces that define the contract between an HTTP servlet and a servlet container.
- **javax.servlet.annotation**. Contains annotations to annotate servlets, filters, and listeners. It also specifies metadata for annotated components.
- **javax.servlet.descriptor**. Contains types that provide programmatic access to a web application's configuration information.

This chapter focuses on members of **javax.servlet** and **javax.servlet.http**.

The javax.servlet Package

Figure B.1 shows the main types in **javax.servlet**.

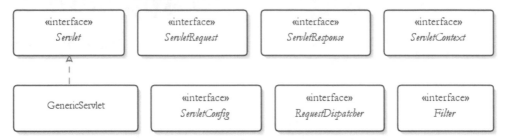

Figure B.1: Prominent members of javax.servlet

At the center of Servlet technology is **Servlet**, an interface that all servlet classes must implement either directly or indirectly. You implement it directly when you write a servlet class that implements **Servlet**. You implement it indirectly when you extend a class that implements this interface.

The **Servlet** interface defines a contract between a servlet and the servlet container. The contract boils down to the promise by the servlet container to load the servlet class into memory and call specific methods on the servlet instance. There can only be one instance for each servlet type in an application.

A user request causes the servlet container to call a servlet's **service** method, passing an instance of **ServletRequest** and an instance of **ServletResponse**. The **ServletRequest** encapsulates the current HTTP request so that servlet developers do not have to parse and manipulate raw HTTP data. The **ServletResponse** represents the HTTP response for the current user and makes it easy to send response back to the user.

For each application the servlet container also creates an instance of **ServletContext**. This object encapsulates the environment details of the context (application). There is only one **ServletContext** for each context. For each servlet instance, there is also a **ServletConfig** that encapsulates the servlet configuration.

Let's first look at the **Servlet** interface. Other interfaces mentioned above will be explained in the other sections of this chapter.

Servlet

The **Servlet** interface defines these five methods.

```
void init(ServletConfig config) throws ServletException

void service(ServletRequest request, ServletResponse response)
        throws ServletException, java.io.IOException

void destroy()

java.lang.String getServletInfo()

ServletConfig getServletConfig()
```

Note that the convention for writing a Java method signature is to use the fully-qualified name for types that are not in the same package as the type containing the method. As such, in the signature of the **service** method **javax.servlet.ServletException**, which is in the same package as **Servlet**, is written without the package information whereas **java.io.Exception** is written fully.

init, **service**, and **destroy** are lifecycle methods. The servlet container invokes these three methods according to these rules.

- **init**. The servlet container invokes this method the first time the servlet is requested. This method is not called at subsequent requests. You use this method to write initialization code. When invoking this method, the servlet container passes a **ServletConfig**. Normally, you will assign the **ServletConfig** to a class level variable so that this object can be used from other points in the servlet class.
- **service**. The servlet container invokes this method each time the servlet is requested. You write the code that the servlet is supposed to do here. The first time the servlet is requested, the servlet container calls the **init** method and the **service** method. For subsequent requests, only **service** is invoked.
- **destroy**. The servlet container invokes this method when the servlet is about to be destroyed. This occurs when the application is unloaded or when the servlet container is being shut down. Normally, you write clean-up code in this method.

The other two methods in **Servlet** are non-life cycle methods: **getServletInfo** and **getServletConfig**.

- **getServletInfo**. This method returns the description of the servlet. You can return any string that might be useful or even **null**.
- **getServletConfig**. This method returns the **ServletConfig** passed by the servlet container to the **init** method. However, in order for **getServletConfig** to return a non-null value, you must have assigned the **ServletConfig** passed to the **init** method to a class level variable. **ServletConfig** is explained in the section "ServletConfig" in this chapter.

An important point to note is thread safety. A servlet instance is shared by all users in an application, so class-level variables are not recommended, unless they are read-only or members of the **java.util.concurrent.atomic** package.

The next section, "Writing A Basic Servlet Application," shows how you can write a **Servlet** Implementation.

Writing A Basic Servlet Application

Writing a servlet application is surprisingly easy. All you have to do is create a directory structure and place your servlet classes in a certain directory. In this section you'll learn how to write a simple servlet application named **b1**. Initially it will contain one servlet, **MyServlet**, which sends a greeting to the user.

You need a servlet container to run your servlets. Tomcat, an open source servlet container, is available free of charge and runs on any platform where Java is available. You should now read Appendix A and install Tomcat if you have not done so.

Writing and Compiling the Servlet Class

After making sure you have a servlet container on your local machine, the next step is to write and compile a servlet class. The servlet class for this example, **MyServlet**, is given in Listing B.1. By convention, the name of a servlet class is suffixed with **Servlet**.

Listing B.1: The MyServlet class

```java
package b1;
import java.io.IOException;
import java.io.PrintWriter;
import javax.servlet.Servlet;
import javax.servlet.ServletConfig;
import javax.servlet.ServletException;
import javax.servlet.ServletRequest;
import javax.servlet.ServletResponse;
import javax.servlet.annotation.WebServlet;

@WebServlet(name = "MyServlet", urlPatterns = { "/my" })
public class MyServlet implements Servlet {

    private transient ServletConfig servletConfig;

    @Override
    public void init(ServletConfig servletConfig)
            throws ServletException {
        this.servletConfig = servletConfig;
    }

    @Override
    public ServletConfig getServletConfig() {
        return servletConfig;
    }

    @Override
    public String getServletInfo() {
        return "My Servlet";
    }

    @Override
```

```
public void service(ServletRequest request,
        ServletResponse response) throws ServletException,
        IOException {
    String servletName = servletConfig.getServletName();
    response.setContentType("text/html");
    PrintWriter writer = response.getWriter();
    writer.print("<html><head></head>"
            + "<body>Hello from " + servletName
            + "</body></html>");
}

@Override
public void destroy() {
}
}
```

The first thing that you may notice when reading the code in Listing B.1 is this annotation.

```
@WebServlet(name = "MyServlet", urlPatterns = { "/my" })
```

The **WebServlet** annotation type is used to declare a servlet. You can name the servlet as well as tell the container what URL invokes the servlet. The **name** attribute is optional and, if present, ordinarily given the name of the servlet class. What's important is the **urlPatterns** attribute, which is also optional but almost always present. In **MyServlet**, **urlPattern** tells the container that the **/my** pattern should invoke the servlet.

Note that a URL pattern must begin with a forward slash.

The servlet's **init** method is called once and sets the private transient **servletConfig** variable to the **ServletConfig** object passed to the method.

```
private transient ServletConfig servletConfig;

@Override
public void init(ServletConfig servletConfig)
        throws ServletException {
    this.servletConfig = servletConfig;
}
```

You only have to assign the passed **ServletConfig** to a class variable if you intend to use the **ServletConfig** from inside your servlet.

The **service** method sends the String "Hello from MyServlet" to the browser. **service** is invoked for every incoming HTTP request that targets the servlet.

To compile the servlet, you have to include the types in the Servlet API in your class path. Tomcat comes with the **servlet-api.jar** file that packages members of the **javax.servlet** and **javax.servlet.http** packages. The jar file is located in the **lib** directory under Tomcat's installation directory.

Application Directory Structure

A servlet application must be deployed in a certain directory structure. Figure B.2 shows the directory structure for this application.

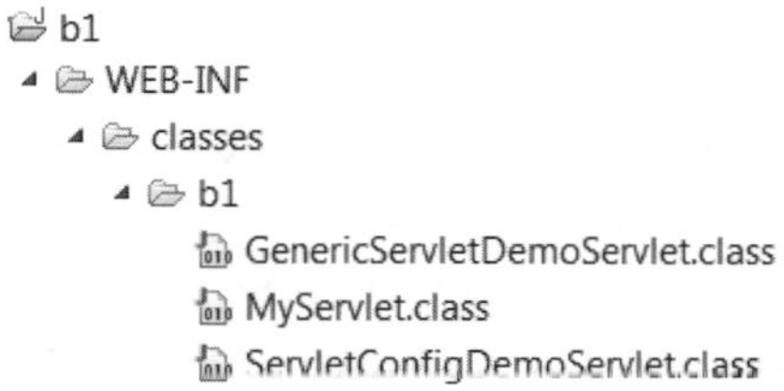

Figure B.2: The application directory of b1

The **b1** directory at the top of the structure is the application directory. Under the application directory is a **WEB-INF** directory. It in turn has two subdirectories:

- **classes**. Your servlet classes and other Java classes must reside here. The directories under classes reflect the class package.
- **lib**. Deploy jar files required by your servlet application here. The Servlet API jar file does not need to be deployed here because the servlet container already has a copy of it. In this application, the **lib** directory is empty. An empty **lib** directory may be deleted.

A servlet/JSP application normally has JSP pages, HTML files, image files, and other resources. These should go under the application directory and are often organized in subdirectories. For instance, all image files can go to an **image** directory, all JSP pages to **jsp**, and so on.

Any resource you put under the application directory is directly accessible to the user by typing the URL to the resource. If you want to include a resource that can be accessed by a servlet but not accessible to the user, put it under **WEB-INF**.

Now, deploy the application to Tomcat. With Tomcat, one way to deploy an application is by copying the application directory to the **webapps** directory under Tomcat installation. You can also deploy an application by editing the **server.xml** file in Tomcat's **conf** directory or deploying an XML file separately in order to avoid editing **server.xml**. Other servlet containers may have different deployment rules. Please refer to Appendix A for details on how to deploy a servlet/JSP application to Tomcat.

The recommended method for deploying a servlet/JSP application is to deploy it as a war file. A war file is a jar file with **war** extension. You can create a war file using the **jar** program that comes with the JDK or tools like WinZip. You can then copy the war file to Tomcat's **webapps** directory. When you start or restart Tomcat, Tomcat will extract the war file automatically. Deployment as a war file will work in all servlet containers.

Invoking the Servlet

To test your first servlet, start or restart Tomcat and direct your browser to the following URL (assuming Tomcat is configured to listen on port 8080, its default port):

```
http://localhost:8080/b1/my
```

The output should be similar to Figure B.3.

Figure B.3: Response from MyServlet

Congratulations. You just wrote your first servlet application.

ServletRequest

For every HTTP request, the servlet container creates an instance of **ServletRequest** and passes it to the servlet's **service** method. The **ServletRequest** encapsulates information about the request.

These are some of the methods in the **ServletRequest** interface.

```
public int getContentLength()
```
Returns the number of bytes in the request body. If the length is not known, this method returns -1.

```
public java.lang.String getContentType()
```
Returns the MIME type of the request body or null if the type is not known.

```
public java.lang.String getParameter(java.lang.String name)
```
Returns the value of the specified request parameter.

```
public java.lang.String getProtocol()
```
Returns the name and version of the protocol of this HTTP request.

getParameter is the most frequently used method in **ServletRequest**. A common use of this method is to return the value of an HTML form field. You'll learn how you can retrieve form values in the section "Working with Forms" later in this chapter.

getParameter can also be used to get the value of a query string. For example, if a servlet is invoked using this URI

```
http://domain/context/servletName?id=123
```

you can retrieve the value of **id** from inside your servlet using this statement:

```
String id = request.getParameter("id");
```

Note that **getParameter** returns null if the parameter does not exist.

In addition to **getParameter**, you can also use **getParameterNames**, **getParameterMap**, and **getParameterValues** to retrieve form field names and values as well as query strings. See the section "HttpServlet" for examples of how to use these methods.

ServletResponse

The **javax.servlet.ServletResponse** interface represents a servlet response. Prior to invoking a servlet's **service** method, the servlet container creates a **ServletResponse** and pass it as the second argument to the **service** method. The **ServletResponse** hides the complexity of sending response to the browser.

One of the methods defined in **ServletResponse** is the **getWriter** method, which returns a **java.io.PrintWriter** that can send text to the client. By default, the **PrintWriter** object uses ISO-8859-1 encoding.

When sending response to the client, most of the time you send it as HTML. You are therefore assumed to be familiar with HTML.

Note
There is also another method that you can use to send output to the browser: **getOutputStream**. However, this method is for sending binary data, so in most cases you will use **getWriter** and not **getOutputStream**.

Before sending any HTML tag, you should set the content type of the response by calling the **setContentType** method, passing "text/html" as an argument. This is how you tell the browser that the content type is HTML. Most browsers by default render a response as HTML in the absence of a content type. However, some browsers will display HTML tags as plain text if you don't set the response content type.

You have used **ServletResponse** in **MyServlet** in Listing B.1. You'll see it used in other applications in this chapter and next chapters.

ServletConfig

The servlet container passes a **ServletConfig** to the servlet's **init** method when the servlet container initializes the servlet. The **ServletConfig** encapsulates configuration information that you can pass to a servlet through **@WebServlet** or the deployment descriptor. Every piece of information so passed is called an initial parameter. An initial parameter has two components: key and value.

To retrieve the value of an initial parameter from inside a servlet, call the **getInitParameter** method on the **ServletConfig** passed by the servlet container to the servlet's **init** method. The signature of **getInitParameter** is as follows.

```
java.lang.String getInitParameter(java.lang.String name)
```

In addition, the **getInitParameterNames** method returns an **Enumeration** of all initial parameter names:

```
java.util.Enumeration<java.lang.String> getInitParameterNames()
```

For example, to retrieve the value of a **contactName** parameter, use this.

```
String contactName = servletConfig.getInitParameter("contactName");
```

On top of **getInitParameter** and **getInitParameterNames**, **ServletConfig** offers another useful method, **getServletContext**. Use this method to retrieve the **ServletContext** from inside a servlet. See the section "ServletContext" later in this chapter for discussion on this object.

As an example of **ServletConfig**, let's add a servlet named **ServletConfigDemoServlet** to **app01a**. The new servlet is given in Listing B.2.

Listing B.2: The ServletConfigDemoServlet class

```java
package b1;
import java.io.IOException;
import java.io.PrintWriter;
import javax.servlet.Servlet;
import javax.servlet.ServletConfig;
import javax.servlet.ServletException;
import javax.servlet.ServletRequest;
import javax.servlet.ServletResponse;
import javax.servlet.annotation.WebInitParam;
import javax.servlet.annotation.WebServlet;

@WebServlet(name = "ServletConfigDemoServlet",
    urlPatterns = { "/servletConfigDemo" },
    initParams = {
        @WebInitParam(name="admin", value="Harry Taciak"),
        @WebInitParam(name="email", value="admin@example.com")
    }
)
public class ServletConfigDemoServlet implements Servlet {
    private transient ServletConfig servletConfig;

    @Override
    public ServletConfig getServletConfig() {
        return servletConfig;
    }

    @Override
    public void init(ServletConfig servletConfig)
            throws ServletException {
        this.servletConfig = servletConfig;
    }

    @Override
    public void service(ServletRequest request,
```

```
        ServletResponse response)
        throws ServletException, IOException {
    ServletConfig servletConfig = getServletConfig();
    String admin = servletConfig.getInitParameter("admin");
    String email = servletConfig.getInitParameter("email");
    response.setContentType("text/html");
    PrintWriter writer = response.getWriter();
    writer.print("<html><head></head><body>" +
            "Admin:" + admin +
            "<br/>Email:" + email +
            "</body></html>");
}

@Override
public String getServletInfo() {
    return "ServletConfig demo";
}

@Override
public void destroy() {
}
}
```

As you can see in Listing B.2, you pass two initial parameters (**admin** and **email**) to the servlet in the **initParams** attribute in **@WebServlet**:

```
@WebServlet(name = "ServletConfigDemoServlet",
    urlPatterns = { "/servletConfigDemo" },
    initParams = {
        @WebInitParam(name="admin", value="Harry Taciak"),
        @WebInitParam(name="email", value="admin@example.com")
    }
)
```

You can invoke **ServletConfigDemoServlet** using this URL:

```
http://localhost:8080/b1/servletConfigDemo
```

The result should be similar to that in Figure B.4.

Figure B.4: ServletConfigDemoServlet in action

Alternatively, you can pass initial parameters in the deployment descriptor. Utilizing the deployment descriptor for this purpose is easier than using **@WebServlet** since the deployment descriptor is a text file and you can edit it without recompiling the servlet class.

The deployment descriptor is discussed in the section "Using the Deployment Descriptor" later in this chapter and in Appendix D, "The Deployment Descriptor."

ServletContext

The **ServletContext** represents the servlet application. There is only one context per web application. In a distributed environment where an application is deployed simultaneously to multiple containers, there is one **ServletContext** object per Java Virtual Machine.

You can obtain the **ServletContext** by calling the **getServletContext** method on the **ServletConfig**.

The **ServletContext** is there so that you can share information that can be accessed from all resources in the application and to enable dynamic registration of web objects. The former is done by storing objects in an internal **Map** within the **ServletContext**. Objects stored in **ServletContext** are called attributes.

The following methods in **ServletContext** deal with attributes:

```
java.lang.Object getAttribute(java.lang.String name)
java.util.Enumeration<java.lang.String> getAttributeNames()
void setAttribute(java.lang.String name, java.lang.Object object)
void removeAttribute(java.lang.String name)
```

GenericServlet

The preceding examples showed how to write servlets by implementing the **Servlet** interface. However, did you notice that you had to provide implementations for all the methods in **Servlet**, even though some of them did not contain code? In addition, you needed to preserve the **ServletConfig** object into a class level variable.

Fortunately, the **GenericServlet** abstract class comes to the rescue. In keeping with the spirit of easier code writing in object-oriented programming, **GenericServlet** implements both **Servlet** and **ServletConfig** and perform the following tasks:

- Assign the **ServletConfig** in the **init** method to a class level variable so that it can be retrieved by calling **getServletConfig**.
- Provide default implementations of all methods in the **Servlet** interface.
- Provide methods that wrap the methods in the **ServletConfig**.

GenericServlet preserves the **ServletConfig** object by assigning it to a class level variable **servletConfig** in the **init** method. Here is the implementation of **init** in **GenericServlet**.

```
public void init(ServletConfig servletConfig)
        throws ServletException {
    this.servletConfig = servletConfig;
    this.init();
}
```

However, if you override this method in your class, the **init** method in your servlet will be called instead and you have to call **super.init(servletConfig)** to preserve the **ServletConfig**. To save you from having to do so, **GenericServlet** provides a second **init** method, which does not take arguments. This method is called by the first **init** method after **ServletConfig** is assigned to **servletConfig**:

```
public void init(ServletConfig servletConfig)
        throws ServletException {
    this.servletConfig = servletConfig;
    this.init();
}
```

This means, you can write initialization code by overriding the no-argument **init** method and the **ServletConfig** will still be preserved by the **GenericServlet** instance.

The **GenericServletDemoServlet** class in Listing B.3 is a rewrite of **ServletConfigDemoServlet** in Listing B.2. Note that the new servlet extends **GenericServlet** instead of implementing **Servlet**.

Listing B.3: The GenericServletDemoServlet class

```
package b1;
import java.io.IOException;
import java.io.PrintWriter;
import javax.servlet.GenericServlet;
import javax.servlet.ServletConfig;
import javax.servlet.ServletException;
import javax.servlet.ServletRequest;
import javax.servlet.ServletResponse;
import javax.servlet.annotation.WebInitParam;
import javax.servlet.annotation.WebServlet;

@WebServlet(name = "GenericServletDemoServlet",
    urlPatterns = { "/generic" },
    initParams = {
        @WebInitParam(name="admin", value="Harry Taciak"),
        @WebInitParam(name="email", value="admin@example.com")
    }
)
public class GenericServletDemoServlet extends GenericServlet {
```

```
        private static final long serialVersionUID = 62500890L;

        @Override
        public void service(ServletRequest request,
                ServletResponse response)
                throws ServletException, IOException {
            ServletConfig servletConfig = getServletConfig();
            String admin = servletConfig.getInitParameter("admin");
            String email = servletConfig.getInitParameter("email");
            response.setContentType("text/html");
            PrintWriter writer = response.getWriter();
            writer.print("<html><head></head><body>" +
                    "Admin:" + admin +
                    "<br/>Email:" + email +
                    "</body></html>");
        }
    }
```

As you can see, by extending **GenericServlet** you do not need to override methods that you don't plan to change. As a result, you have cleaner code. In Listing B.3, the only method overridden is the **service** method. Also, there is no need to preserve the **ServletConfig** yourself.

Invoke the servlet using this URL and the result should be similar to that of **ServletConfigDemoServlet**.

```
http://localhost:8080/b1/generic
```

Even though **GenericServlet** is a nice enhancement to Servlet, it is not something you use frequently, however, as it is not as advanced as **HttpServlet**. **HttpServlet** is the real deal and used in real-world applications. It is explained in the next section, "HTTP Servlets."

HTTP Servlets

Most, if not all, servlet applications you write will work with HTTP. This means, you can make use of the features offered by HTTP. The **javax.servlet.http** package is the second package in the Servlet API that contains classes and interfaces for writing servlet applications. Many of the types in **javax.servlet.http** override those in **javax.servlet**.

Figure B.5 shows the main types in **javax.servlet.http**.

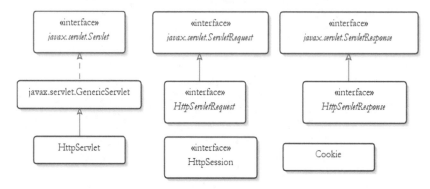

Figure B.5: The more important members of javax.servlet.http

HttpServlet

The **HttpServlet** class overrides the **javax.servlet.GenericServlet** class. When using **HttpServlet**, you will also work with the **HttpServletRequest** and **HttpServletResponse** objects that represent the servlet request and the servlet response, respectively. The **HttpServletRequest** interface extends **javax.servlet.ServletRequest** and **HttpServletResponse** extends **javax.servlet.ServletResponse**.

HttpServlet overrides the **service** method in **GenericServlet** and adds another **service** method with the following signature:

```
protected void service(HttpServletRequest request,
        HttpServletResponse response)
        throws ServletException, java.io.IOException
```

The difference between the new **service** method and the one in **javax.servlet.Servlet** is that the former accepts an **HttpServletRequest** and an **HttpServletResponse**, instead of a **ServletRequest** and a **ServletResponse**.

The servlet container, as usual, calls the original **service** method in **javax.servlet.Servlet**, which in **HttpServlet** is written as follows:

```
public void service(ServletRequest req, ServletResponse res)
        throws ServletException, IOException {
    HttpServletRequest request;
    HttpServletResponse response;
    try {
        request = (HttpServletRequest) req;
        response = (HttpServletResponse) res;
    } catch (ClassCastException e) {
        throw new ServletException("non-HTTP request or response");
    }
    service(request, response);
}
```

The original **service** method downcasts the request and response objects from the servlet container to **HttpServletRequest** and **HttpServletResponse**, respectively, and call the new **service** method. The downcasting is always successful because the servlet container always passes an **HttpServletRequest** and an **HttpServletResponse** when calling a servlet's **service** method, to anticipate the use of HTTP. Even if you are implementing **javax.servlet.Servlet** or extending **javax.servlet.GenericServlet**, you can downcast the servlet request and servlet response passed to the **service** method to **HttpServletRequest** and **HttpServletResponse**, respectively.

The new **service** method in **HttpServlet** then examines the HTTP method used to send the request (by calling **request.getMethod**) and call one of the following methods: **doGet**, **doPost**, **doHead**, **doPut**, **doTrace**, **doOptions**, and **doDelete**. Each of the seven methods represents an HTTP method. **doGet** and **doPost** are the most often used. As such, you rarely need to override the **service** methods anymore. Instead, you override **doGet** or **doPost** or both **doGet** and **doPost**.

To summarize, there are two features in **HttpServlet** that you do not find in **GenericServlet**:

- Instead of the **service** method, you will override **doGet**, **doPost**, or both of them. In rare cases, you will also override any of these methods: **doHead**, **doPut**, **doTrace**, **doOptions**, **doDelete**.
- You will work with **HttpServletRequest** and **HttpServletResponse**, instead of **ServletRequest** and **ServletResponse**.

HttpServletRequest**HttpServletRequest** represents the servlet request in the HTTP environment. It extends the **javax.servlet.ServletRequest** interface and adds several methods. Some of the methods added are as follows.

`java.lang.String getContextPath()`

Returns the portion of the request URI that indicates the context of the request.

`Cookie[] getCookies()`

Returns an array of **Cookie** objects.

`java.lang.String getHeader(java.lang.String name)`

Returns the value of the specified HTTP header.

`java.lang.String getMethod()`

Returns the name of the HTTP method with which this request was made.

`java.lang.String getQueryString()`

Returns the query string in the request URL.

`HttpSession getSession()`

Returns the session object associated with this request. If none is found, creates a new session object.

`HttpSession getSession(boolean create)`

Returns the current session object associated with this request. If none is found and the create argument is **true**, create a new session object.

You will learn to use these methods in the chapters to come.

HttpServletResponse

HttpServletResponse represents the servlet response in the HTTP environment. Here are some of the methods defined in it.

```
void addCookie(Cookie cookie)
```
Adds a cookie to this response object.

```
void addHeader(java.lang.String name, java.lang.String value)
```
Adds a header to this response object.

```
void sendRedirect(java.lang.String location)
```
Sends a response code that redirects the browser to the specified location.

You will learn these methods further in the next chapters.

Working with HTML Forms

A web application almost always contains one or more HTML forms to take user input. You can easily send an HTML form from a servlet to the browser. When the user submits the form, values entered in the form elements are sent to the server as request parameters.

The value of an HTML input field (a text field, a hidden field, or a password field) or text area is sent to the server as a string. An empty input field or text area sends an empty string. As such, **ServletRequest.getParameter** that takes an input field name never returns null.

An HTML select element also sends a string to the header. If none of the options in the select element is selected, the value of the option that is displayed is sent.

A multiple-value select element (a select element that allows multiple selection and is indicated by **<select multiple>**) sends a string array and has to be handled by **ServletRequest.getParameterValues**.

A checkbox is a bit extraordinary. A checked checkbox sends the string "on" to the server. An unchecked checkbox sends nothing to the server and **ServletRequest.getParameter(*fieldName*)** returns null.

Radio buttons send the value of the selected button to the server. If none of the buttons is selected, nothing is sent to the server and **ServletRequest.getParameter(*fieldName*)** returns null.

If a form contains multiple input elements with the same name, all values will be submitted and you have to use **ServletRequest.getParameterValues** to retrieve them. **ServletRequest.getParameter** will only return the last value.

The **FormServlet** class in Listing B.4 demonstrates how to work with an HTML form. Its **doGet** method sends an order form to the browser. Its **doPost** method retrieves the values entered and prints them. This servlet is part of the **b2** application.

Listing B.4: The FormServlet class

```
package b2;
import java.io.IOException;
import java.io.PrintWriter;
import java.util.Enumeration;
import javax.servlet.ServletException;
import javax.servlet.annotation.WebServlet;
import javax.servlet.http.HttpServlet;
import javax.servlet.http.HttpServletRequest;
import javax.servlet.http.HttpServletResponse;

@WebServlet(name = "FormServlet", urlPatterns = { "/form" })
public class FormServlet extends HttpServlet {
    private static final long serialVersionUID = 54L;
    private static final String TITLE = "Order Form";

    @Override
    public void doGet(HttpServletRequest request,
            HttpServletResponse response)
            throws ServletException, IOException {
        response.setContentType("text/html");
        PrintWriter writer = response.getWriter();
        writer.println("<html>");
```

```
writer.println("<head>");
writer.println("<title>" + TITLE + "</title></head>");
writer.println("<body><h1>" + TITLE + "</h1>");
writer.println("<form method='post'>");
writer.println("<table>");
writer.println("<tr>");
writer.println("<td>Name:</td>");
writer.println("<td><input name='name'/></td>");
writer.println("</tr>");
writer.println("<tr>");
writer.println("<td>Address:</td>");
writer.println("<td><textarea name='address' "
        + "cols='40' rows='5'></textarea></td>");
writer.println("</tr>");
writer.println("<tr>");
writer.println("<td>Country:</td>");
writer.println("<td><select name='country'>");
writer.println("<option>United States</option>");
writer.println("<option>Canada</option>");
writer.println("</select></td>");
writer.println("</tr>");
writer.println("<tr>");
writer.println("<td>Delivery Method:</td>");
writer.println("<td><input type='radio' " +
        "name='deliveryMethod'"
        + " value='First Class'/>First Class");
writer.println("<input type='radio' " +
        "name='deliveryMethod' "
        + "value='Second Class'/>Second Class</td>");
writer.println("</tr>");
writer.println("<tr>");
writer.println("<td>Shipping Instructions:</td>");
writer.println("<td><textarea name='instruction' "
        + "cols='40' rows='5'></textarea></td>");
writer.println("</tr>");
writer.println("<tr>");
writer.println("<td> </td>");
writer.println("<td><textarea name='instruction' "
        + "cols='40' rows='5'></textarea></td>");
writer.println("</tr>");
writer.println("<tr>");
writer.println("<td>Please send me the latest " +
        "product catalog:</td>");
```

```java
        writer.println("<td><input type='checkbox' " +
                "name='catalogRequest'/></td>");
        writer.println("</tr>");
        writer.println("<tr>");
        writer.println("<td> </td>");
        writer.println("<td><input type='reset'/>" +
                "<input type='submit'/></td>");
        writer.println("</tr>");
        writer.println("</table>");
        writer.println("</form>");
        writer.println("</body>");
        writer.println("</html>");
    }

    @Override
    public void doPost(HttpServletRequest request,
            HttpServletResponse response)
            throws ServletException, IOException {
        response.setContentType("text/html");
        PrintWriter writer = response.getWriter();
        writer.println("<html>");
        writer.println("<head>");
        writer.println("<title>" + TITLE + "</title></head>");
        writer.println("</head>");
        writer.println("<body><h1>" + TITLE + "</h1>");
        writer.println("<table>");
        writer.println("<tr>");
        writer.println("<td>Name:</td>");
        writer.println("<td>" + request.getParameter("name")
                + "</td>");
        writer.println("</tr>");
        writer.println("<tr>");
        writer.println("<td>Address:</td>");
        writer.println("<td>" + request.getParameter("address")
                + "</td>");
        writer.println("</tr>");
        writer.println("<tr>");
        writer.println("<td>Country:</td>");
        writer.println("<td>" + request.getParameter("country")
                + "</td>");
        writer.println("</tr>");
        writer.println("<tr>");
        writer.println("<td>Shipping Instructions:</td>");
```

```java
writer.println("<td>");
String[] instructions = request
        .getParameterValues("instruction");
if (instructions != null) {
    for (String instruction : instructions) {
        writer.println(instruction + "<br/>");
    }
}
writer.println("</td>");
writer.println("</tr>");
writer.println("<tr>");
writer.println("<td>Delivery Method:</td>");
writer.println("<td>"
        + request.getParameter("deliveryMethod")
        + "</td>");
writer.println("</tr>");
writer.println("<tr>");
writer.println("<td>Catalog Request:</td>");
writer.println("<td>");
if (request.getParameter("catalogRequest") == null) {
    writer.println("No");
} else {
    writer.println("Yes");
}
writer.println("</td>");
writer.println("</tr>");
writer.println("</table>");
writer.println("<div style='border:1px solid #ddd;" +
            "margin-top:40px;font-size:90%'>");

writer.println("Debug Info<br/>");
Enumeration<String> parameterNames = request
        .getParameterNames();
while (parameterNames.hasMoreElements()) {
    String paramName = parameterNames.nextElement();
    writer.println(paramName + ": ");
    String[] paramValues = request
            .getParameterValues(paramName);
    for (String paramValue : paramValues) {
        writer.println(paramValue + "<br/>");
    }
}
writer.println("</div>");
```

```
        writer.println("</body>");
        writer.println("</html>");
    }
}
```

You can invoke the **FormServlet** by using this URL:

```
http://localhost:8080/b2/form
```

The invoked **doGet** method sends this HTML form to the browser.

```
<form method='post'>
<input name='name'/>
<textarea name='address' cols='40' rows='5'></textarea>
<select name='country'>");
    <option>United States</option>
    <option>Canada</option>
</select>
<input type='radio' name='deliveryMethod' value='First Class'/>
<input type='radio' name='deliveryMethod' value='Second Class'/>
<textarea name='instruction' cols='40' rows='5'></textarea>
<textarea name='instruction' cols='40' rows='5'></textarea>
<input type='checkbox' name='catalogRequest'/>
<input type='reset'/>
<input type='submit'/>
</form>
```

The form's method is set to **post** to make sure the HTTP POST method is used when the user submits the form. Its **action** attribute is missing, indicating that the form will be submitted to the same URL used to request it.

Figure B.6 shows an empty order form.

Figure B.6: An empty Order form

Now, fill in the form and click the Submit button. The values you entered in the form will be sent to the server using the HTTP POST method and this will invoke the servlet's **doPost** method. As a result, you'll see the values printed as shown in Figure B.7.

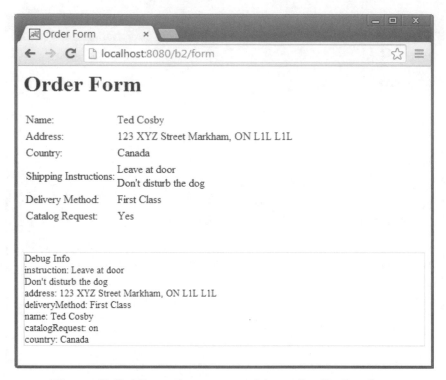

Figure B.7: The values entered into the Order form

Using the Deployment Descriptor

As you can see in the previous examples, writing and deploying a servlet application is easy. One aspect of deployment is configuring the mapping of your servlet with a path. In the examples, you mapped a servlet with a path by using the **WebServlet** annotation type.

Using the deployment descriptor is another way of configuring a servlet application and the deployment descriptor is discussed in detail in Appendix D, "The Deployment Descriptor." The deployment descriptor is always named **web.xml** and located under the **WEB-INF** directory. In this chapter I show you how to create a servlet application named **b3** and write a **web.xml** file for it.

The **b3** has two servlets, **SimpleServlet** and **WelcomeServlet**, and a deployment descriptor to map the servlets. Listings B.5 and B.6 show **SimpleServlet** and **WelcomeServlet**, respectively. Note that the servlet classes are not annotated **@WebServlet**. The deployment descriptor is given in Listing B.7.

Listing B.5: The unannotated SimpleServlet class

```java
package b3;
import java.io.IOException;
import java.io.PrintWriter;
import javax.servlet.ServletException;
import javax.servlet.http.HttpServlet;
import javax.servlet.http.HttpServletRequest;
import javax.servlet.http.HttpServletResponse;

public class SimpleServlet extends HttpServlet {
    private static final long serialVersionUID = 8946L;

    @Override
    public void doGet(HttpServletRequest request,
            HttpServletResponse response)
            throws ServletException, IOException {
        response.setContentType("text/html");
        PrintWriter writer = response.getWriter();
        writer.print("<html><head></head>" +
                    "<body>Simple Servlet</body></html");
    }
}
```

Listing B.6: The unannotated WelcomeServlet class

```java
package app01c;
import java.io.IOException;
import java.io.PrintWriter;
import javax.servlet.ServletException;
import javax.servlet.http.HttpServlet;
import javax.servlet.http.HttpServletRequest;
import javax.servlet.http.HttpServletResponse;

public class WelcomeServlet extends HttpServlet {
    private static final long serialVersionUID = 27126L;

    @Override
```

```
    public void doGet(HttpServletRequest request,
            HttpServletResponse response)
            throws ServletException, IOException {
        response.setContentType("text/html");
        PrintWriter writer = response.getWriter();
        writer.print("<html><head></head>"
                + "<body>Welcome</body></html>");
    }
}
```

Listing B.7: The deployment descriptor

```
<?xml version="1.0" encoding="ISO-8859-1"?>
<web-app xmlns="http://java.sun.com/xml/ns/javaee"
    xmlns:xsi="http://www.w3.org/2001/XMLSchema-instance"
    xsi:schemaLocation="http://java.sun.com/xml/ns/javaee
➡http://java.sun.com/xml/ns/javaee/web-app_3_0.xsd"
    version="3.0">

    <servlet>
        <servlet-name>SimpleServlet</servlet-name>
        <servlet-class>b3.SimpleServlet</servlet-class>
        <load-on-startup>10</load-on-startup>
    </servlet>

    <servlet-mapping>
        <servlet-name>SimpleServlet</servlet-name>
        <url-pattern>/simple</url-pattern>
    </servlet-mapping>


    <servlet>
        <servlet-name>WelcomeServlet</servlet-name>
        <servlet-class>b3.WelcomeServlet</servlet-class>
        <load-on-startup>20</load-on-startup>
    </servlet>

    <servlet-mapping>
        <servlet-name>WelcomeServlet</servlet-name>
        <url-pattern>/welcome</url-pattern>
    </servlet-mapping>
</web-app>
```

There are many advantages of using the deployment descriptor. For one, you can include elements that have no equivalent in **@WebServlet**, such as the **load-on-startup** element. This element loads the servlet at application start-up, rather than when the servlet is first called. Using **load-on-startup** means the first call to the servlet will take no longer than subsequent calls. This is especially useful if the **init** method of the servlet takes a while to complete.

Another advantage of using the deployment descriptor is that you don't need to recompile your servlet class if you need to change configuration values, such as the servlet path.

In addition, you can pass initial parameters to a servlet and edit them without recompiling the servlet class.

The deployment descriptor also allows you to override values specified in a servlet annotation. A **WebServlet** annotation on a servlet that is also declared in the deployment descriptor will have no effect. However, annotating a servlet not in the deployment descriptor in an application with a deployment descriptor will still work. This means, you can have annotated servlets and declare servlets in the deployment descriptor in the same application.

Figure B.8 presents the directory structure of **b3**. The directory structure does not differ much from that of **app01a**. The only difference is that **b3** has a **web.xml** file (the deployment descriptor) in the **WEB-INF** directory.

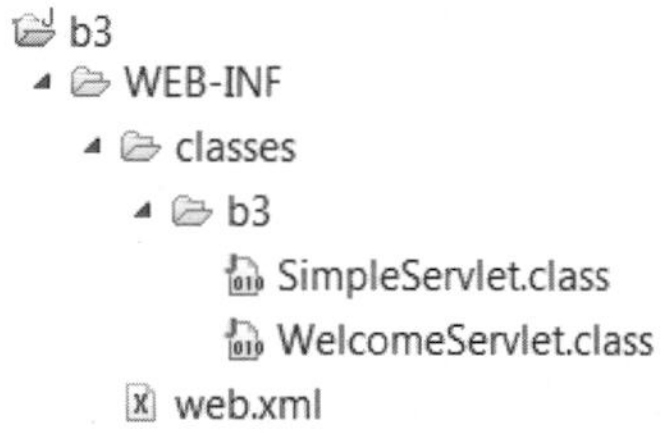

```
b3
  ⊿ WEB-INF
    ⊿ classes
      ⊿ b3
        SimpleServlet.class
        WelcomeServlet.class
    web.xml
```

Figure B.8: Directory structure of b3 with deployment descriptor

Now that **SimpleServlet** and **WelcomeServlet** are declared in the deployment descriptor, you can use these URLs to access them:

```
http://localhost:8080/b3/simple
```

```
http://localhost:8080/b3/welcome
```
For more information on deployment and the deployment descriptor, refer to Appendix D, "The Deployment Descriptor."

Appendix C
JavaServer Pages

You learned in Appendix B, "Servlets" that there are two drawbacks servlets are not capable of overcoming. First, all HTML tags written in a servlet must be enclosed in Java strings, making sending HTTP response a tedious effort. Second, all text and HTML tags are hardcoded; as such, even minor changes to the presentation layer, such as changing a background color, require recompilation.

JavaServer Pages (JSP) solves the two problems in servlets. JSP does not replace Servlet, though. Rather, it complements it. Modern Java web applications use both servlets and JSP pages. The latest version of JSP at the time of writing is 2.2.

This appendix starts with an overview of JSP and discusses in detail comments in JSP pages, implicit objects, and the three syntactic elements (directives, scripting elements, and actions). Error handling is covered towards the end of this appendix.

JSP can be written in standard syntax or XML syntax. JSP pages written in XML syntax are called JSP documents. JSP in XML syntax is very rarely used and is not covered here. In this appendix you learn JSP in standard syntax.

An Overview of JSP

A JSP page is essentially a servlet. However, working with JSP pages is easier than with servlets for two reasons. First, you do not have to compile

JSP pages. Second, JSP pages are basically text files with **jsp** extension and you can use any text editor to write them.

JSP pages run on a JSP container. A servlet container is normally also a JSP container. Tomcat, for instance, is a servlet/JSP container.

The first time a JSP page is requested, a servlet/JSP container does two things:

1. Translate the JSP page into a JSP page implementation class, which is a Java class that implements the **javax.servlet.jsp.JspPage** interface or its subinterface **javax.servlet.jsp.HttpJspPage**. **JspPage** is a subinterface of **javax.servlet.Servlet** and this makes every JSP page a servlet. The class name of the generated servlet is dependent on the servlet/JSP container. You do not have to worry about this because you do not have to work with it directly. If there is a translation error, an error message will be sent to the client.
2. If the translation was successful, the servlet/JSP container compiles the servlet class. The container then loads and instantiates the Java bytecode as well as performs the lifecycle operations it normally does a servlet.

For subsequent requests for the same JSP page, the servlet/JSP container checks if the JSP page has been modified since the last time it was translated. If so, it will be retranslated, recompiled, and executed. If not, the JSP servlet already in memory is executed. This way, the first invocation of a JSP page always takes longer than subsequent requests because it involves translation and compilation. To get around this problem, you can do one of the following:

- Configure the application so that all JSP pages will be called (and, in effect, translated and compiled) when the application starts, rather than at first requests.
- Precompile the JSP pages and deploy them as servlets.

JSP comes with an API that comprises four packages:

- **javax.servlet.jsp**. Contains core classes and interfaces used by the servlet/JSP container to translate JSP pages into servlets. The **JspPage** and **HttpJspPage** interfaces are important members of this package. All JSP page implementation classes must implement either **JspPage** or **HttpJspPage**. In the HTTP environment, **HttpJspPage** is the obvious choice.

- **javax.servlet.jsp.tagext**. Contains types for developing custom tags.
- **javax.el**. Provides the API for the Unified Expression Language.
- **javax.servlet.jsp.el**. Provides classes that must be supported by a servlet/JSP container to support the Expression Language in JSP.

With the exception of **javax.servlet.jsp.tagext**, you rarely have to use the JSP API directly. In fact, when writing a JSP page, you're more concerned with the Servlet API than the JSP API itself. Of course, you also need to master the JSP syntax, which will be explained throughout this appendix. One example where the JSP API is used extensively is when developing a JSP container or a JSP compiler.

You can view the JSP API here:

```
http://download.oracle.com/docs/cd/E17802_01/products/products/jsp/
2.1/docs/jsp-2_1-pfd2/index.html
```

A JSP page can contain template data and syntactic elements. An element is something with a special meaning to the JSP translator. For example, **<%** is an element because it denotes the start of a Java code block within a JSP page. **%>** is also an element because it terminates a Java code block. Everything else that is not an element is template data. Template data is sent as is to the browser. For instance, HTML tags and text in a JSP page are template data.

Listing C.1 presents a JSP page named **welcome.jsp**. It is a simple page that sends a greeting to the client. Notice how simple the JSP page is compared to a servlet that does the same thing?

Listing C.1: The welcome.jsp page

```
<html>
<head><title>Welcome</title></head>
<body>
Welcome
</body>
```

```
</html>
```

In Tomcat, the **welcome.jsp** page is translated into a **welcome_jsp** servlet after the page's first invocation. You can find the generated servlet in a subdirectory under Tomcat's **work** directory The servlet extends **org.apache.jasper.runtime.HttpJspBase**, an abstract class that extends **javax.servlet.http.HttpServlet** and implements **javax.servlet.jsp.HttpJspPage**.

Here is the generated servlet for **welcome.jsp**. Do not worry if you find it too cryptic. You can continue without understanding it, even though it is better if you do.

```java
package org.apache.jsp;
import javax.servlet.*;
import javax.servlet.http.*;
import javax.servlet.jsp.*;

public final class welcome_jsp extends
        org.apache.jasper.runtime.HttpJspBase
        implements org.apache.jasper.runtime.JspSourceDependent {

    private static final javax.servlet.jsp.JspFactory _jspxFactory =
        javax.servlet.jsp.JspFactory.getDefaultFactory();

    private static java.util.Map<java.lang.String,java.lang.Long>
        _jspx_dependants;

    private javax.el.ExpressionFactory _el_expressionfactory;
    private org.apache.tomcat.InstanceManager _jsp_instancemanager;

    public java.util.Map<java.lang.String,java.lang.Long>
        getDependants() {
            return _jspx_dependants;
    }

    public void _jspInit() {
        _el_expressionfactory =
                _jspxFactory.getJspApplicationContext(
                getServletConfig().getServletContext())
                .getExpressionFactory();
        _jsp_instancemanager =
```

```
                    org.apache.jasper.runtime.InstanceManagerFactory
                .getInstanceManager(getServletConfig());
    }

    public void _jspDestroy() {
    }

    public void _jspService(final
        javax.servlet.http.HttpServletRequest request, final
        javax.servlet.http.HttpServletResponse response)
        throws java.io.IOException, javax.servlet.ServletException {

        final javax.servlet.jsp.PageContext pageContext;
        javax.servlet.http.HttpSession session = null;
        final javax.servlet.ServletContext application;
        final javax.servlet.ServletConfig config;
        javax.servlet.jsp.JspWriter out = null;
        final java.lang.Object page = this;
        javax.servlet.jsp.JspWriter _jspx_out = null;
        javax.servlet.jsp.PageContext _jspx_page_context = null;

        try {
            response.setContentType("text/html");
            pageContext = _jspxFactory.getPageContext(this, request,
                response, null, true, 8192, true);
            _jspx_page_context = pageContext;
            application = pageContext.getServletContext();
            config = pageContext.getServletConfig();
            session = pageContext.getSession();
            out = pageContext.getOut();
            _jspx_out = out;

            out.write("<html>\n");
            out.write("<head><title>Welcome</title></head>\n");
            out.write("<body>\n");
            out.write("Welcome\n");
            out.write("</body>\n");
            out.write("</html>");
        } catch (java.lang.Throwable t) {
            if (!(t instanceof
                    javax.servlet.jsp.SkipPageException)){
                out = _jspx_out;
                if (out != null && out.getBufferSize() != 0)
```

```
            try {
                out.clearBuffer();
            } catch (java.io.IOException e) {
            }
        if (_jspx_page_context != null)
            _jspx_page_context.handlePageException(t);
        }
    } finally {
        _jspxFactory.releasePageContext(_jspx_page_context);
    }
  }
}
```

As you can see in the code above, the body of the JSP page is translated into a **_jspService** method. This method is defined in **HttpJspPage** and is called from the implementation of the **service** method in **HttpJspBase**. Here is from the **HttpJspBase** class.

```
public final void service(HttpServletRequest request,
        HttpServletResponse response) throws ServletException,
        IOException {
    _jspService(request, response);
}
```

To override the **init** and **destroy** methods, you can declare methods as explained in the section "Scripting Elements" later in this appendix.

Another aspect where a JSP page differs from a servlet is the fact that the former does not need to be annotated or mapped to a URL in the deployment descriptor. Every JSP page in the application directory can be invoked by typing the path to the page in the browser. Figure C.1 shows the directory structure of **c1**, a JSP application accompanying this appendix.

```
📁 c1
  ▷ 📂 WEB-INF
    📄 welcome.jsp
```

Figure C.1: The directory structure of c1

With only one JSP page, the structure of the **app03a** application is very simple, consisting of an empty **WEB-INF** directory and a **welcome.jsp** page.

You can invoke the **welcome.jsp** page using this URL:

```
http://localhost:8080/c1/welcome.jsp
```

Note
You do not need to restart Tomcat after adding a new JSP page.

Listing C.2 shows how to use Java code in JSP to produce a dynamic page. The **todaysDate.jsp** page in Listing C.2 shows today's date.

Listing C.2: The todaysDate.jsp page

```
<%@page import="java.util.Date"%>
<%@page import="java.text.DateFormat"%>
<html>
<head><title>Today's date</title></head>
<body>
<%
    DateFormat dateFormat =
            DateFormat.getDateInstance(DateFormat.LONG);
    String s = dateFormat.format(new Date());
    out.println("Today is " + s);
%>
</body>
</html>
```

The **todaysDate.jsp** page sends a couple of HTML tags and the string "Today is" followed by today's date to the browser.

There are two things to note. First, Java code can appear anywhere in a JSP page and is enclosed by **<%** and **%>**. Second, to import a Java type used in a JSP page, you use the **import** attribute of the **page** directive. Without importing a type, you have to write the fully-qualified name of the Java type in your code.

The **<% ... %>** block is called a scriptlet and is discussed further in the section "Scripting Elements" later in this appendix. The **page** directive is explained in detail in the section "Directives" later in this appendix.

You can invoke the **todaysDate.jsp** page using this URL:

```
http://localhost:8080/c1/todaysDate.jsp
```

Comments

Adding comments to a JSP page is good practice. There are two types of comments that can appear in a JSP page:

1. JSP comments, which are comments documenting what the page is doing.
2. HTML/XHTML comments, which are comments that will be sent to the browser.

A JSP comment starts with **<%--** and ends with **--%>**. For instance, the following is a JSP comment:

```
<%-- retrieve products to display --%>
```

A JSP comment is not sent to the browser and cannot be nested.

An HTML/XHTML comment has the following syntax:

```
<!-- [comments here] -->
```

An HTML/XHTML comment is not processed by the container and is sent to the browser as is. One use of the HTML/XHTML comment is to identify the JSP page itself:

```
<!-- this is /jsp/store/displayProducts.jspf -->
```

This is particularly useful when working with an application that has many JSP fragments. The developer can easily find out which JSP page or fragment generated a certain HTML section by viewing the HTML source in the browser.

Implicit Objects

The servlet container passes several objects to the servlets it is running. For instance, you get an **HttpServletRequest** and an **HttpServletResponse** in the servlet's **service** method and a **ServletConfig** in the **init** method. In addition, you can obtain an **HttpSession** by calling **getSession** on the **HttpServletRequest** object.

In JSP you can retrieve those objects by using implicit objects. Table C.1 lists the implicit objects.

Object	Type
request	javax.servlet.http.HttpServletRequest
response	javax.servlet.http.HttpServletResponse
out	javax.servlet.jsp.JspWriter
session	javax.servlet.http.HttpSession
application	javax.servlet.ServletContext
config	javax.servlet.ServletConfig
pageContext	javax.servlet.jsp.PageContext
page	javax.servlet.jsp.HttpJspPage
exception	java.lang.Throwable

Table C.1: JSP Implicit Objects

For example, the **request** implicit object represents the **HttpServletRequest** passed by the servlet/JSP container to the servlet's **service** method. You can use **request** as if it was a variable reference to the **HttpServletRequest**. For instance, the following code retrieves the **userName** parameter from the **HttpServletRequest** object.

```
<%
    String userName = request.getParameter("userName");
%>
```

pageContext refers to the **javax.servlet.jsp.PageContext** created for the page. It provides useful context information and access to various servlet-related objects via its self-explanatory methods, such as **getRequest**, **getResponse**, **getServletContext**, **getServletConfig**, and **getSession**. These methods are not very useful in scriptlets since the objects they return can be accessed more directly through the implicit objects **request**, **response**, **session**, and **application**.

Another set of interesting methods offered by **PageContext** are those for getting and setting attributes, the **getAttribute** and **setAttribute** methods. Attributes can be stored in one of four scopes: page, request, session, and application. The page scope is the narrowest scope and attributes stored here are only available in the same JSP page. The request scope refers to the current **ServletRequest**, the session scope the current **HttpSession**, and the application scope the **ServletContext**.

The **setAttribute** method in **PageContext** has the following signature:

```
public abstract void setAttribute(java.lang.String name,
        java.lang.Object value, int scope)
```

The value of *scope* can be one of the following static final **int**s in **PageContext**: **PAGE_SCOPE**, **REQUEST_SCOPE**, **SESSION_SCOPE**, and **APPLICATION_SCOPE**.

Alternatively, to store an attribute in the page scope, you can use this **setAttribute** overload:

```
public abstract void setAttribute(java.lang.String name,
        java.lang.Object value)
```

For example, the following scriptlet stores an attribute in the **ServletRequest**.

```
<%
    // product is a Java object
    pageContext.setAttribute("product", product,
            PageContext.REQUEST_SCOPE);
%>
```

The Java code above has the same effect as this:

```
<%
    request.setAttribute("product", product);
%>
```

The **out** implicit object references a **javax.servlet.jsp.JspWriter**, which is similar to the **java.io.PrintWriter** you get from calling **getWriter()** on the **HttpServletResponse**. You can call its **print** method overloads just as you would a **PrintWriter** to send messages to the browser. For instance:

```
out.println("Welcome");
```

The **implicitObjects.jsp** page in Listing C.3 demonstrates the use of some of the implicit objects.

Listing C.3: The implicitObjects.jsp page

```
<%@page import="java.util.Enumeration"%>
<html>
<head><title>JSP Implicit Objects</title></head>
<body>
<b>Http headers:</b><br/>
<%
    for (Enumeration<String> e = request.getHeaderNames();
            e.hasMoreElements(); ) {
        String header = e.nextElement();
        out.println(header + ": " + request.getHeader(header) +
                "<br/>");
    }
%>
<hr/>
<%
    out.println("Buffer size: " + response.getBufferSize() +
        "<br/>");
    out.println("Session id: " + session.getId() + "<br/>");
    out.println("Servlet name: " + config.getServletName() +
        "<br/>");
    out.println("Server info: " + application.getServerInfo());
%>
</body>
</html>
```

You can invoke the **implicitObjects.jsp** page with this URL:

```
http://localhost:8080/c1/implicitObjects.jsp
```

The page produces the following text on your browser:

Http headers:
```
host: localhost:8080
user-agent: Mozilla/5.0 (Macintosh; Intel Mac OS X 10_5_8)
        AppleWebKit/534.50.2 (KHTML, like Gecko) Version/5.0.6
        Safari/533.22.3
accept:text/html,application/xhtml+xml,application/xml;q=0.9,*/*;q=
0.8
accept-language: en-us
```

```
accept-encoding: gzip, deflate
connection: keep-alive

Buffer size: 8192
Session id: 561DDD085ADD99FC03F70BDEE87AAF4D
Servlet name: jsp
Server info: Apache Tomcat/7.0.14
```

What exactly you see in your browser depend on the browser you're using and your environment.

Note that by default the JSP compiler sets the content type of a JSP page to **text/html**. If you're sending a different type, you must set the content type by calling **response.setContentType()** or by using the **page** directive (discussed in the section "Directives"). For example, the following sets the content type to text/json:

```
response.setContentType("text/json");
```

Note also that the **page** implicit object represents the current JSP page and is not normally used by the JSP page author.

Directives

Directives are the first type of JSP syntactic elements. They are instructions for the JSP translator on how a JSP page should be translated into a servlet. There are several directives defined in JSP 2.2, but only the two most important ones, **page** and **include**, are discussed in this appendix.

The page Directive

You use the **page** directive to instruct the JSP translator on certain aspects of the current JSP page. For example, you can tell the JSP translator the size of the buffer that should be used for the **out** implicit object, what content type to use, what Java types to import, and so on.

The **page** directive has the following syntax:

```
<%@ page attribute1="value1" attribute2="value2" ... %>
```

The space between *@* and **page** is optional and *attribute1*, *attribute2*, and so on are the **page** directive's attributes. Here is the list of attributes for the **page** directive.

- **import**. Specifies a Java type or Java types that will be imported and useable by the Java code in this page. For example, specifying **import="java.util.List"** imports the **List** interface. You can use the wildcard * to import the whole package, such as in **import="java.util.*"**. To import multiple types, separate two types with a comma, such as in **import="java.util.ArrayList, java.util.Calendar, java.io.PrintWriter"**. All types in the following packages are implicitly imported: **java.lang**, **javax.servlet**, **javax.servlet.http**, **javax.servlet.jsp**.
- **session**. A value of **true** indicates that this page participates in session management, and a value of **false** indicates otherwise. By default, the value is **true**, which means the invocation of a JSP page will cause a **javax.servlet.http.HttpSession** instance to be created if one does not yet exist.
- **buffer**. Specifies the buffer size of the **out** implicit object in kilobytes. The suffix **kb** is mandatory. The default buffer size is 8kb or more, depending on the JSP container. It is also possible to assign **none** to this attribute to indicate that no buffering should be used, which will cause the output to be written directly to the corresponding **PrintWriter**.
- **autoFlush**. A value of **true**, the default value, indicates that the buffered output should be flushed automatically when the buffer is full. A value of **false** indicates that the buffer is only flushed if the **flush** method of the **response** implicit object is called. Consequently, an exception will be thrown in the event of buffer overflow.
- **isThreadSafe**. Indicates the level of thread safety implemented in the page. JSP authors are advised against using this attribute as it could result in a generated servlet containing deprecated code.
- **info**. Specifies the return value of the **getServletInfo** method of the generated servlet.

- **errorPage**. Indicates the page that will handle errors that may occur in this page.
- **isErrorPage**. Indicates if this page is an error handler.
- **contentType**. Specifies the content type of the **response** implicit object of this page. By default, the value is **text/html**.
- **pageEncoding**. Specifies the character encoding for this page. By default, the value is **ISO-8859-1**.
- **isELIgnored**. Indicates whether EL expressions are ignored. EL, which is short for expression language.
- **language**. Specifies the scripting language used in this page. By default, its value is **java** and this is the only valid value in JSP 2.2.
- **extends**. Specifies the superclass that this JSP page's implementation class must extend. This attribute is rarely used and should only be used with extra caution.
- **deferredSyntaxAllowedAsLiteral**. Specifies whether or not the character sequence #{ is allowed as a String literal in this page and translation unit. The default value is false. #{ is important because it is a special character sequence in the Expression Language.
- **trimDirectiveWhitespaces**. Indicates whether or not template text that contains only white spaces is removed from the output. The default is false; in other words, not to trim white spaces.

The **page** directive can appear anywhere in a page. The exception is when it contains the **contentType** or the **pageEncoding** attribute, in which case it must appear before any template data and before sending any content using Java code. This is because the content type and the character encoding must be set prior to sending any content.

The **page** directive can also appear multiple times. However, an attribute that appears in multiple **page** directives must have the same value. An exception to this rule is the **import** attribute. The effect of the **import** attribute appearing in multiple **page** directives is cumulative. For example, the following page directives import both **java.util.ArrayList** and **java.io.File**.

```
<%@page import="java.util.ArrayList"%>
<%@page import="java.util.Date"%>
```

This is the same as

```
<%@page import="java.util.ArrayList, java.util.Date"%>
```

As another example, here is a **page** directive that sets the **session** attribute to **false** and allocates 16KB to the page buffer:

```
<%@page session="false" buffer="16kb"%>
```

The include Directive

You use the **include** directive to include the content of another file in the current JSP page. You can use multiple **include** directives in a JSP page. Modularizing a particular content into an include file is useful if that content is used by different pages or used by a page in different places.

The syntax of the **include** directive is as follows:

```
<%@ include file="url"%>
```

where the space between **@** and **include** is optional and *url* represents the relative path to an include file. If *url* begins with a forward slash (/), it is interpreted as an absolute path on the server. If it does not, it is interpreted as relative to the current JSP page.

The JSP translator translates the **include** directive by replacing the directive with the content of the include file. In other words, if you have written the **copyright.jspf** file in Listing C.4.

Listing C.4: The copyright.jspf include file

```
<hr/>
&copy;2012 BrainySoftware
<hr/>
```

And, you have the **main.jsp** page in Listing C.5.

Listing C.5: The main.jsp page

```
<html>
<head><title>Including a file</title></head>
<body>
This is the included content: <hr/>
```

```
<%@ include file="copyright.jspf"%>
</body>
</html>
```

Using the **include** directive in the **main.jsp** page has the same effect as writing the following JSP page.

```
<html>
<head><title>Including a file</title></head>
<body>
This is the included content: <hr/>
<hr/>
&copy;2014 BrainySoftware
<hr/>
</body>
</html>
```

For the above **include** directive to work, the **copyright.jspf** file must reside in the same directory as the including page.

By convention an include file has **jspf** extension, which stands for JSP fragment. Today JSP fragments are called JSP segments but the **jspf** extension is still retained for consistency.

Note that you can also include static HTML files.

The **include** action, discussed in the section "Actions" later in this appendix, is similar to the include directive. The subtle difference is explained in the section "Actions" and it is important you understand the difference between the two.

Scripting Elements

The second type of JSP syntactic elements, scripting elements incorporate Java code into a JSP page. There are three types of scripting elements: scriptlets, declarations, and expressions. They are discussed in the following subsections.

Scriptlets

A scriptlet is a block of Java code. A scriptlet starts with **<%** and ends with **%>**. For example, the **scriptletTest.jsp** page in Listing C.6 uses scriptlets.

Listing C.6: Using a scriplet (scriptletTest.jsp)

```
<%@page import="java.util.Enumeration"%>
<html>
<head><title>Scriptlet example</title></head>
<body>
<b>Http headers:</b><br/>
<%-- first scriptlet --%>
<%
    for (Enumeration<String> e = request.getHeaderNames();
            e.hasMoreElements(); ) {
        String header = e.nextElement();
        out.println(header + ": " + request.getHeader(header) +
                "<br/>");
    }
    String message = "Thank you.";
%>
<hr/>
<%-- second scriptlet --%>
<%
    out.println(message);
%>
</body>
</html>
```

There are two scriptlets in the JSP page in Listing C.6. Note that variables defined in a scriptlet is visible to the other scriptlets below it.

It is legal for the first line of code in a scriptlet to be in the same line as the **<%** tag and for the **%>** tag to be in the same line as the last line of code. However, this would result in a less readable page.

Expressions

An expression is evaluated and its result fed to the **print** method of the **out** implicit object. An expression starts with **<%=** and ends with **%>**. For example, the text in bold in the following line is an expression:

```
Today is <%=java.util.Calendar.getInstance().getTime()%>
```

Note that there is no semicolon after an expression.

With this expression, the JSP container first evaluates **java.util.Calendar.getInstance().getTime()**, and then passes the result to **out.print()**. This is the same as writing this scriptlet:

```
Today is
<%
    out.print(java.util.Calendar.getInstance().getTime());
%>
```

Declarations

You can declare variables and methods that can be used in a JSP page. You enclose a declaration with **<%!** and **%>**. For example, the declarationTst.jsp page in Listing C.7 shows a JSP page that declares a method named **getTodaysDate**.

Listing C.7: Using a declaration (declarationTest.jsp)

```
<%!
    public String getTodaysDate() {
        return new java.util.Date();
    }
%>
<html>
<head><title>Declarations</title></head>
<body>
Today is <%=getTodaysDate()%>
</body>
</html>
```

A declaration can appear anywhere in a JSP page and there can be multiple declarations in the same page.

You can use declarations to override the **init** and **destroy** methods in the implementation class. To override **init**, declare a **jspInit** method. To override **destroy**, declare a **jspDestroy** method. The two methods are explained below.

- **jspInit**. This method is similar to the **init** method in **javax.servlet.Servlet**. **jspInit** is invoked when the JSP page is initialized. Unlike the **init** method, **jspInit** does not take arguments. You can still obtain the **ServletConfig** object through the **config** implicit object.
- **jspDestroy**. This method is similar to the **destroy** method in **Servlet** and is invoked when the JSP page is about to be destroyed.

Listing C.8 presents the **lifeCycle.jsp** page that demonstrates how you can override **jspInit** and **jspDestroy**.

Listing C.8: The lifeCycle.jsp page

```
<%!
    public void jspInit() {
        System.out.println("jspInit ...");
    }
    public void jspDestroy() {
        System.out.println("jspDestroy ...");
    }
%>
<html>
<head><title>jspInit and jspDestroy</title></head>
<body>
Overriding jspInit and jspDestroy
</body>
</html>
```

The **lifeCycle.jsp** page will be translated into the following servlet:

```
package org.apache.jsp;
import javax.servlet.*;
import javax.servlet.http.*;
import javax.servlet.jsp.*;
```

```java
public final class lifeCycle_jsp extends
        org.apache.jasper.runtime.HttpJspBase
        implements org.apache.jasper.runtime.JspSourceDependent {

    public void jspInit() {
        System.out.println("jspInit ...");

    }

    public void jspDestroy() {
        System.out.println("jspDestroy ...");
    }

    private static final javax.servlet.jsp.JspFactory _jspxFactory =
            javax.servlet.jsp.JspFactory.getDefaultFactory();

    private static java.util.Map<java.lang.String,java.lang.Long>
        _jspx_dependants;

    private javax.el.ExpressionFactory _el_expressionfactory;
    private org.apache.tomcat.InstanceManager _jsp_instancemanager;

    public java.util.Map<java.lang.String,java.lang.Long>
            getDependants() {
        return _jspx_dependants;
    }

    public void _jspInit() {
        _el_expressionfactory =
                _jspxFactory.getJspApplicationContext(
                getServletConfig().getServletContext())
                .getExpressionFactory();
        _jsp_instancemanager =
                org.apache.jasper.runtime.InstanceManagerFactory
                .getInstanceManager(getServletConfig());
    }

    public void _jspDestroy() {
    }

    public void _jspService(final
            javax.servlet.http.HttpServletRequest request, final
```

```
        javax.servlet.http.HttpServletResponse response)
        throws java.io.IOException,
        javax.servlet.ServletException {

final javax.servlet.jsp.PageContext pageContext;
javax.servlet.http.HttpSession session = null;
final javax.servlet.ServletContext application;
final javax.servlet.ServletConfig config;
javax.servlet.jsp.JspWriter out = null;
final java.lang.Object page = this;
javax.servlet.jsp.JspWriter _jspx_out = null;
javax.servlet.jsp.PageContext _jspx_page_context = null;

try {
    response.setContentType("text/html");
    pageContext = _jspxFactory.getPageContext(this, request,
        response, null, true, 8192, true);
    _jspx_page_context = pageContext;
    application = pageContext.getServletContext();
    config = pageContext.getServletConfig();
    session = pageContext.getSession();
    out = pageContext.getOut();
    _jspx_out = out;

    out.write("\n");
    out.write("<html>\n");
    out.write("<head><title>jspInit and jspDestroy" +
            "</title></head>\n");
    out.write("<body>\n");
    out.write("Overriding jspInit and jspDestroy\n");
    out.write("</body>\n");
    out.write("</html>");
} catch (java.lang.Throwable t) {
    if (!(t instanceof
            javax.servlet.jsp.SkipPageException)){
        out = _jspx_out;
        if (out != null && out.getBufferSize() != 0)
            try {
                out.clearBuffer();
            } catch (java.io.IOException e) {
            }
        if (_jspx_page_context != null)
            _jspx_page_context.handlePageException(t);
```

```
        }
    } finally {
        _jspxFactory.releasePageContext(_jspx_page_context);
    }
    }
}
```

Notice that the **jspInit** and **jspDestroy** methods in the generated servlet?

You can invoke **lifeCycle.jsp** by using this URL:

```
http://localhost:8080/c1/lifeCycle.jsp
```

You will see "jspInit ..." on your console when you first invoke the JSP page, and "jspDestroy ..." when you shut down your servlet/JSP container.

Disabling Scripting Elements

With the advance of the Expression Language in JSP 2.0, the recommended practice is to use the EL to access server-side objects and not to write Java code in JSP pages. For this reason, starting JSP 2.0 scripting elements may be disabled by defining a **scripting-invalid** element within **<jsp-property-group>** in the deployment descriptor.

```
<jsp-property-group>
    <url-pattern>*.jsp</url-pattern>
    <scripting-invalid>true</scripting-invalid>
</jsp-property-group>
```

Actions

Actions are the third type of syntactic element. They are translated into Java code that performs an operation, such as accessing a Java object or invoking a method. This section discusses standard actions that must be supported by all JSP containers. In addition to standard actions, you can also create custom tags that perform certain operations.

The following are some of the standard actions.

useBean

This action creates a scripting variable associated with a Java object. It was one of the earliest efforts to separate presentation and business logic. Thanks to other technologies such as custom tags and the Expression Language, **useBean** is now rarely used.

As an example, the **useBeanTest.jsp** page in Listing C.9 creates an instance of **java.util.Date** and associates it with scripting variable **today**, which then be used in an expression.

Listing C.9: The useBeanTest.jsp page

```
<html>
<head>
    <title>useBean</title>
</head>
<body>
<jsp:useBean id="today" class="java.util.Date"/>
<%=today%>
</body>
</html>
```

The action will be translated into this code in Tomcat.

```
java.util.Date today = null;
today = (java.util.Date) _jspx_page_context.getAttribute("today",
        javax.servlet.jsp.PageContext.REQUEST_SCOPE);
if (today == null) {
    today = new java.util.Date();
    _jspx_page_context.setAttribute("today", today,
            javax.servlet.jsp.PageContext.REQUEST_SCOPE);
}
```

Running this page prints the current date and time in your browser.

setProperty and getProperty

The **setProperty** action sets a property in a Java object and **getProperty** prints a Java object's property. As an example, the **getSetPropertyTest.jsp** page in Listing C.11 sets and gets the **firstName** property of an instance of the **Employee** class, defined in Listing C.10.

Listing C.10: The Employee class

```
package app03a;
public class Employee {
    private String id;
    private String firstName;
    private String lastName;

    public String getId() {
        return id;
    }
    public void setId(String id) {
        this.id = id;
    }
    public String getFirstName() {
        return firstName;
    }
    public void setFirstName(String firstName) {
        this.firstName = firstName;
    }
    public String getLastName() {
        return lastName;
    }
    public void setLastName(String lastName) {
        this.lastName = lastName;
    }
}
```

Listing C.11: The getSetPropertyTest.jsp

```
<html>
<head>
<title>getProperty and setProperty</title>
</head>
<body>
<jsp:useBean id="employee" class="app03a.Employee"/>
<jsp:setProperty name="employee" property="firstName"
        value="Abigail"/>
First Name: <jsp:getProperty name="employee" property="firstName"/>
</body>
</html>
```

include

The **include** action is used to include another resource dynamically. You can include another JSP page, a servlet, or a static HTML page. For example, the **jspIncludeTest.jsp** page in Listing C.12 uses the **include** action to include the **menu.jsp** page.

Listing C.12: The jspIncludeTest.jsp page

```
<html>
<head>
<title>Include action</title>
</head>
<body>
<jsp:include page="jspf/menu.jsp">
    <jsp:param name="text" value="How are you?"/>
</jsp:include>
</body>
</html>
```

It is important that you understand the difference between the **include** directive and the **include** action. With the **include** directive, inclusion occurs at page translation time, i.e. when the JSP container translates the page into a generated servlet. With the **include** action, inclusion occurs at request time. As such, you can pass parameters using the **include** action, but not the **include** directive.

The second difference is that with the **include** directive, the file extension of the included resource does not matter. With the include action, the file extension must be jsp for it to be processed as a JSP page. Using jspf in the **include** action, for example, will make the JSP segment be treated as a static file.

forward

The **forward** action forwards the current page to a different resource. For example, the following forward action forwards the current page to the **login.jsp** page.

```
<jsp:forward page="jspf/login.jsp">
```

```
    <jsp:param name="text" value="Please login"/>
</jsp:forward>
```

Error Handling

Error handling is well supported in JSP. Java code can be handled using the **try** statement, however you can also specify a page that will be displayed should any of the pages in the application encounters an uncaught exception. In such events, your users will see a well designed page that explains what happened, and not an error message that makes them frown.

You make a JSP page an error page by using the **isErrorPage** attribute of the **page** directive. The value of the attribute must be **true**. Listing C.13 shows such an error handler.

Listing C.13: The errorHandler.jsp page

```
<%@page isErrorPage="true"%>
<html>
<head><title>Error</title></head>
<body>
An error has occurred. <br/>
Error message:
<%
    out.println(exception.toString());
%>
</body>
</html>
```

Other pages that need protection against uncaught exceptions will have to use the **errorPage** attribute of the **page** directive, citing the path to the error handling page as the value. For example, the **buggy.jsp** page in Listing C.14 uses the error handler in Listing C.13.

Listing C.14: The buggy.jsp page

```
<%@page errorPage="errorHandler.jsp"%>
Deliberately throw an exception
<%
    Integer.parseInt("Throw me");
%>
```

If you run the **buggy.jsp** page, it will throw an exception. However, you will not see an error message generated by the servlet/JSP container. Instead, the content of the **errorHandler.jsp** page is displayed.

Summary

JSP is the second technology for building web applications in Java, invented to complement Servlet technology and not to replace it. Well designed Java web applications use both servlets and JSP.

In this appendix you've learned how JSP works and how to write JSP pages. By now, you should know all there is to know about the implicit objects and be able to use the three syntactic elements that can be present in a JSP page, directives, scripting elements, and actions.

Appendix D
The Deployment Descriptor

Deploying a Servlet 3 application is a breeze. Thanks to the servlet annotation types and depending on how complex your application is, you can deploy a servlet/JSP application without the deployment descriptor. Having said that, the deployment descriptor is still needed in many circumstances where more refined configuration is needed. When the deployment descriptor is present, it must be named **web.xml** and located under the **WEB-INF** directory. Java classes must reside in **WEB-INF/classes** and Java libraries in **WEB-INF/lib**. All application resources must then be packaged into a single file with war extension. A war file is basically a jar file.

This appendix discusses deployment and the deployment descriptor, which is an important component of an application.

Deployment Descriptor Overview

Before Servlet 3 deployment always involved a **web.xml** file, the deployment descriptor, in which you configured various aspects of your application. With Servlet 3 the deployment descriptor is optional because you can use annotations to map a resource with a URL pattern. However, the deployment descriptor is needed if one of these applies to you.

- You need to pass initial parameters to the **ServletContext**.
- You have multiple filters and you want to specify the order in which the filters are invoked.
- You need to change the session timeout.

- You want to restrict access to a resource collection and provide a way for the user to authenticate themselves.

Listing D. 1 shows the skeleton of the deployment descriptor. It must be named **web.xml** and reside in the **WEB-INF** directory of the application directory.

Listing D.1: The skeleton of the deployment descriptor

```
<?xml version="1.0" encoding="ISO-8859-1"?>
<web-app xmlns="http://java.sun.com/xml/ns/javaee"
    xmlns:xsi="http://www.w3.org/2001/XMLSchema-instance"
    xsi:schemaLocation="http://java.sun.com/xml/ns/javaee
➡http://java.sun.com/xml/ns/javaee/web-app_3_0.xsd"
    version="3.0"
    [metadata-complete="true|false"]
>

    ...

</web-app>
```

The **xsi:schemaLocation** attribute specifies the location of the schema against which the deployment descriptor can be validated. The **version** attribute specifies the version of the Servlet specification.

The optional **metadata-complete** attribute specifies whether the deployment descriptor is complete. If its value is true, the servlet/JSP container must ignore servlet-specific annotations. If this element is set to false or if it's not present, the container must examine the class files deployed with the application for servlet-specific annotations and scan for web fragments.

The **web-app** element is the root element and can have subelements for specifying:

- servlet declarations
- servlet mappings
- **ServletContext** initial parameters
- session configuration
- listener classes

- filter definitions and mappings
- MIME type mappings
- welcome file list
- error pages
- JSP-specific settings
- JNDI settings

The rules for each of the elements that may appear in a deployment descriptor are given in the **web-app_3_0.xsd** schema that can be downloaded from this site.

```
http://java.sun.com/xml/ns/javaee/web-app_3_0.xsd
```

The **web-app_3.0.xsd** schema includes another schema (**web-common_3_0.xsd**) that contains most of the information. The other schema can be found here.

```
http://java.sun.com/xml/ns/javaee/web-common_3_0.xsd
```

In turn, **web-common_3_0.xsd** includes two other schemas:

- **javaee_6.xsd**, which defines common elements shared by other Java EE 6 deployment types (EAR, JAR and RAR)
- **jsp_2_2.xsd**, which defines elements for configuring the JSP part of an application according to JSP 2.2 specification

The rest of this section lists servlet and JSP elements that may appear in the deployment descriptor. It does not include Java EE elements that are not in the Servlet or JSP specification.

Core Elements

This section discusses the more important elements in detail. Subelements of <web-app> can appear in any order. Certain elements, such as **session-config**, **jsp-config**, and **login-config**, can appear only once. Others, such as **servlet**, **filter**, and **welcome-file-list**, can appear many times.

The more important elements that can appear directly under **<web-app>** are given a separate subsection. To find the description of an element which is not directly under **<web-app>**, trace its parent element. For example, the **taglib** element can be found under the subsection "jsp-config" and the **load-on-startup** element under "servlet." The subsections under this section are presented in alphabetical order.

context-param

The **context-param** element passes values to the **ServletContext**. These values can be read from any servlet/JSP page. This element contains a name/value pair that can be retrieved by calling the **getInitParameter** method on the **ServletContext**. You can have multiple **context-param** elements as long as the parameter names are unique throughout the application. **ServletContext.getInitParameterNames()** returns all **ServletContext** parameter names.

The **context-param** element must contain a **param-name** element and a **param-value** element. The **param-name** element contains the parameter name, and the **param-value** element the parameter value. Optionally, a **description** element also can be present to describe the parameter.

The following are two example **context-param** elements.

```
<context-param>
    <param-name>location</param-name>
    <param-value>localhost</param-value>
</context-param>
<context-param>
    <param-name>port</param-name>
    <param-value>8080</param-value>
    <description>The port number used</description>
</context-param>
```

distributable

If present, the **distributable** element indicates that the application is written to be deployed into a distributed servlet/JSP container. The **distributable** element must be empty. For example, here is a **distributable** element.

```
<distributable/>
```

error-page

The **error-page** element contains a mapping between an HTTP error code to a resource path or between a Java exception type to a resource path. The **error-page** element dictates the container that the specified resource should be returned in the event of the HTTP error or if the specified exception is thrown.

This element must contain the following subelements.

- **error-code**, to specify an HTTP error code
- **exception-type**, to specify the fully-qualified name of the Java exception type to be captured
- **location**, to specify the location of the resource to be displayed in the event of an error or exception. The **location** element must start with a /.

For example, the following is an **error-page** element that tells the servlet/JSP container to display the **error.html** page located at the application directory every time an HTTP 404 error code occurs:

```
<error-page>
    <error-code>404</error-code>
    <location>/error.html</location>
</error-page>
```

The following is an **error-page** element that maps all servlet exceptions with the **exceptions.html** page.

```
<error-page>
    <exception-type>javax.servlet.ServletException</exception-type>
    <location>/exception.html</location>
</error-page>
```

filter

This element specifies a servlet filter. At the very minimum, this element must contain a **filter-name** element and a **filter-class** element. Optionally, it can also contain the following elements: **icon**, **display-name**, **description**, **init-param**, and **async-supported**.

The **filter-name** element defines the name of the filter. The filter name must be unique within the application. The **filter-class** element specifies the fully qualified name of the filter class. The **init-param** element is used to specify an initial parameter for the filter and has the same element descriptor as **<context-param>**. A **filter** element can have multiple **init-param** elements.

The following are two **filter** elements whose names are **Upper Case Filter** and **Image Filter**, respectively.

```
<filter>
    <filter-name>Upper Case Filter</filter-name>
    <filter-class>com.example.UpperCaseFilter</filter-class>
</filter>
<filter>
    <filter-name>Image Filter</filter-name>
    <filter-class>com.example.ImageFilter</filter-class>
    <init-param>
        <param-name>frequency</param-name>
        <param-value>1909</param-value>
     </init-param>
    <init-param>
        <param-name>resolution</param-name>
        <param-value>1024</param-value>
    </init-param>
</filter>
```

filter-mapping

The **filter-mapping** element specifies the resource or resources a filter is applied to. A filter can be applied to either a servlet or a URL pattern. Mapping a filter to a servlet causes the filter to work on the servlet. Mapping a filter to a URL pattern makes filtering occur to any resource whose URL matches the URL pattern. Filtering is performed in the same order as the appearance of the **filter-mapping** elements in the deployment descriptor.

The **filter-mapping** element contains a **filter-name** element and a **url-pattern** element or a **servlet-name** element.

The **filter-name** value must match one of the filter names declared using the **filter** elements.

The following are two **filter** elements and two **filter-mapping** elements:

```
<filter>
    <filter-name>Logging Filter</filter-name>
    <filter-class>com.example.LoggingFilter</filter-class>
</filter>
<filter>
    <filter-name>Security Filter</filter-name>
    <filter-class>com.example.SecurityFilter</filter-class>
</filter>

<filter-mapping>
    <filter-name>Logging Filter</filter-name>
    <servlet-name>FirstServlet</servlet-name>
</filter-mapping>
<filter-mapping>
    <filter-name>Security Filter</filter-name>
    <url-pattern>/*</url-pattern>
</filter-mapping>
```

listener

The **listener** element registers a listener. It contains a **listener-class** element, which defines the fully qualified name of the listener class. Here is an example.

```
<listener>
    <listener-class>com.example.AppListener</listener-class>
</listener>
```

locale-encoding-mapping-list and locale-encoding-mapping

The **locale-encoding-mapping-list** element contains one or more **locale-encoding-mapping** elements. A **locale-encoding-mapping** element maps a locale name with an encoding and contains a **locale** element and an **encoding** element. The value for **<locale>** must be either a language-code defined in ISO 639, such as "en", or a language-code_country-code, such as "en_US". When a language-code_country-code is used, the country-code part must be one of the country codes defined in ISO 3166.

For instance, here is a **locale-encoding-mapping-list** that contains a **locale-encoding-mapping** element that maps the Japanese language to Shift_JIS encoding.

```
<locale-encoding-mapping-list>
    <locale-encoding-mapping>
        <locale>ja</locale>
        <encoding>Shift_JIS</encoding>
    </locale-encoding-mapping>
</locale-encoding-mapping-list>
```

login-config

The **login-config** element is used to specify the authentication method used to authenticate the user, the realm name, and the attributes needed by the form login mechanism if form-based authentication is used. A **login-config** element has an optional **auth-method** element, an optional **realm-name** element, and an optional **form-login-config** element.

The **auth-method** element specifies the access authentication method. Its value is one of the following: **BASIC**, **DIGEST**, **FORM**, or **CLIENT-CERT**.

The **realm-name** element specifies the realm name to use in Basic access authentication and Digest access authentication.

The **form-login-config** element specifies the login and error pages that should be used in form-based authentication. If form-based authentication is not used, these elements are ignored.

The **form-login-config** element has a **form-login-page** element and a **form-error-page** element. The **form-login-page** element specifies the path to a resource that displays a Login page. The path must start with a / and is relative to the application directory.

The **form-error-page** element specifies the path to a resource that displays an error page when login fails. The path must begin with a / and is relative to the application directory.

As an example, here is an example of the **login-config** element.

```
<login-config>
    <auth-method>DIGEST</auth-method>
    <realm-name>Members Only</realm-name>
</login-config>
```

And, here is another example.

```
<login-config>
    <auth-method>FORM</auth-method>
    <form-login-config>
        <form-login-page>/loginForm.jsp</form-login-page>
        <form-error-page>/errorPage.jsp</form-error-page>
    </form-login-config>
</login-config>
```

mime-mapping

The **mime-mapping** element maps a MIME type to an extension. It contains an **extension** element and a **mime-type** element. The **extension** element describes the extension and the **mime-type** element specifies the MIME type. For example, here is a **mime-mapping** element.

```
<mime-mapping>
    <extension>txt</extension>
    <mime-type>text/plain</mime-type>
</mime-mapping>
```

security-constraint

The **security-constraint** element allows you to restrict access to a collection of resources declaratively.

The **security-constraint** element contains an optional **display-name** element, one or more **web-resource-collection** elements, an optional **auth-constraint** element, and an optional **user-data-constraint** element.

The **web-resource-collection** element identifies a collection of resources to which access needs to be restricted. In it you can define the URL pattern(s) and the restricted HTTP method or methods. If no HTTP method is present, the security constraint applies to all HTTP methods.

The **auth-constraint** element specifies the user roles that should have access to the resource collection. If no **auth-constraint** element is specified, the security constraint applies to all roles.

The **user-data-constraint** element is used to indicate how data transmitted between the client and servlet/JSP container must be protected.

A **web-resource-collection** element contains a **web-resource-name** element, an optional **description** element, zero or more **url-pattern** elements, and zero or more **http-method** elements.

The **web-resource-name** element contains a name associated with the protected resource.

The **http-method** element can be assigned one of the HTTP methods, such as GET, POST, or TRACE.

The **auth-constraint** element contains an optional **description** element and zero or more **role-name** element. The **role-name** element contains the name of a security role.

The **user-data-constraint** element contains an optional **description** element and a **transport-guarantee** element. The **transport-guarantee** element must have one of the following values: **NONE**, **INTEGRAL**, or **CONFIDENTIAL**. **NONE** indicates that the application does not require transport guarantees. **INTEGRAL** means that the data between the server and the client should be sent in such a way that it can't be changed in transit. **CONFIDENTIAL** means that the data transmitted must be encrypted. In most cases, Secure Sockets Layer (SSL) is used for either **INTEGRAL** or **CONFIDENTIAL**.

The following example uses a **security-constraint** element to restrict access to any resource with a URL matching the pattern **/members/***. Only a user in the **payingMember** role will be allowed access. The **login-config** element requires the user to log in and the Digest access authentication method is used.

```
<security-constraint>
    <web-resource-collection>
        <web-resource-name>Members Only</web-resource-name>
        <url-pattern>/members/*</url-pattern>
    </web-resource-collection>
    <auth-constraint>
        <role-name>payingMember</role-name>
    </auth-constraint>
</security-constraint>

<login-config>
    <auth-method>Digest</auth-method>
    <realm-name>Digest Access Authentication</realm-name>
</login-config>
```

security-role

The **security-role** element specifies the declaration of a security role used in security constraints. This element has an optional **description** element and a **role-name** element. The following is an example **security-role** element.

```
<security-role>
    <role-name>payingMember</role-name>
</security-role>
```

servlet

The **servlet** element is used to declare a servlet. It can contain the following elements.

- an optional **icon** element
- an optional **description** element
- an optional **display-name** element
- a **servlet-name** element
- a **servlet-class** element or a **jsp-file** element
- zero or more **init-param** elements

- an optional **load-on-startup** element
- an optional **run-as** element
- an optional **enabled** element
- an optional **async-supported** element
- an optional **multipart-config** element
- zero or more **security-role-ref** elements

At a minimum a **servlet** element must contain a **servlet-name** element and a **servlet-class** element, or a **servlet-name** element and a **jsp-file** element. The **servlet-name** element defines the name for that servlet and must be unique throughout the application.

The **servlet-class** element specifies the fully qualified class name of the servlet.

The **jsp-file** element specifies the full path to a JSP page within the application. The full path must begin with a /.

The **init-param** subelement can be used to pass an initial parameter name and value to the servlet. The element descriptor of **init-param** is the same as **context-param**.

You use the **load-on-startup** element to load the servlet automatically into memory when the servlet/JSP container starts up. Loading a servlet means instantiating the servlet and calling its **init** method. You use this element to avoid delay in the response for the first request to the servlet, caused by the servlet loading to memory. If this element is present and a **jsp-file** element is specified, the JSP file is precompiled into a servlet and the resulting servlet is loaded.

load-on-startup is either empty or has an integer value. The value indicates the order of loading this servlet when there are multiple servlets in the same application. For example, if there are two **servlet** elements and both contain a **load-on-startup** element, the servlet with the lower **load-on-startup** value is loaded first. If the value of the **load-on-startup** is empty or is a negative number, it is up to the web container to decide when to load the servlet. If two servlets have the same **load-on-startup** value, the loading order between the two servlets cannot be determined.

Defining **run-as** overrides the security identity for calling an Enterprise JavaBean by that servlet in this application. The role name is one of the security roles defined for the current web application.

The **security-role-ref** element maps the name of the role called from a servlet using **isUserInRole(*name*)** to the name of a security role defined for the application. The **security-role-ref** element contains an optional **description** element, a **role-name** element, and a **role-link** element.

The **role-link** element is used to link a security role reference to a defined security role. The **role-link** element must contain the name of one of the security roles defined in the **security-role** elements.

The **async-supported** element is an optional element that can have a true or false value. It indicates whether or not this servlet supports asynchronous processing.

The **enabled** element is also an optional element whose value can be true or false. Setting this element to false disables this servlet.

For example, to map the security role reference "PM" to the security role with role-name "payingMember," the syntax would be as follows.

```
<security-role-ref>
    <role-name>PM</role-name>
    <role-link>payingMember</role-link>
</security-role-ref>
```

In this case, if the servlet invoked by a user belonging to the "payingMember" security role calls **isUserInRole("payingMember")**, the result would be true.

The following are two example **servlet** elements:

```
<servlet>
    <servlet-name>UploadServlet</servlet-name>
    <servlet-class>com.brainysoftware.UploadServlet</servlet-class>
    <load-on-startup>10</load-on-startup>
</servlet>
<servlet>
    <servlet-name>SecureServlet</servlet-name>
    <servlet-class>com.brainysoftware.SecureServlet</servlet-class>
    <load-on-startup>20</load-on-startup>
```

```
</servlet>
```

servlet-mapping

The **servlet-mapping** element maps a servlet to a URL pattern. The **servlet-mapping** element must have a **servlet-name** element and a **url-pattern** element.

The following **servlet-mapping** element maps a servlet with the URL pattern **/first**.

```
<servlet>
    <servlet-name>FirstServlet</servlet-name>
    <servlet-class>com.brainysoftware.FirstServlet</servlet-class>
</servlet>
<servlet-mapping>
    <servlet-name>FirstServlet</servlet-name>
    <url-pattern>/first</url-pattern>
</servlet-mapping>
```

session-config

The **session-config** element defines parameters for **javax.servlet.http.HttpSession** instances. This element may contain one or more of the following elements: **session-timeout**, **cookie-config**, or **tracking-mode**.

The **session-timeout** element specifies the default session timeout interval in minutes. This value must be an integer. If the value of the **session-timeout** element is zero or a negative number, the session will never time out.

The **cookie-config** element defines the configuration of the session tracking cookies created by this servlet/JSP application.

The **tracking-mode** element defines the tracking mode for sessions created by this web application. Valid values are **COOKIE**, **URL**, or **SSL**.

The following **session-config** element causes the **HttpSession** objects in the current application to be invalidated after twelve minutes of inactivity.

```
<session-config>
```

```
    <session-timeout>12</session-timeout>
</session-config>
```

welcome-file-list

The **welcome-file-list** element specifies the file or servlet that is displayed when the URL entered by the user in the browser does not contain a servlet name or a JSP page or a static resource.

The **welcome-file-list** element contains one or more **welcome-file** elements. The **welcome-file** element contains the default file name. If the file specified in the first **welcome-file** element is not found, the web container will try to display the second one, and so on.

Here is an example **welcome-file-list** element.

```
<welcome-file-list>
    <welcome-file>index.htm</welcome-file>
    <welcome-file>index.html</welcome-file>
    <welcome-file>index.jsp</welcome-file>
</welcome-file-list>
```

The following example uses a **welcome-file-list** element that contains two **welcome-file** elements. The first **welcome-file** element specifies a file in the application directory called **index.html**; the second defines the welcome servlet under the servlet directory, which is under the application directory:

```
<welcome-file-list>
    <welcome-file>index.html</welcome-file>
    <welcome-file>servlet/welcome</welcome-file>
</welcome-file-list>
```

JSP-Specific Elements

The **jsp-config** element under **<web-app>** contains elements specific to JSP. It can have zero or more **taglib** elements and zero or more **jsp-property-group** elements. The **taglib** element is explained in the first subsection of this section and the **jsp-property-group** element in the second subsection.

taglib

The **taglib** element describes a JSP custom tag library. The **taglib** element contains a **taglib-uri** element and a **taglib-location** element.

The **taglib-uri** element specifies the URI of the tag library used in the servlet/JSP application. The value for **<taglib-uri>** is relative to the location of the deployment descriptor.

The **taglib-location** element specifies the location of the TLD file for the tag library.

The following is an example **taglib** element.

```
<jsp-config>
    <taglib>
        <taglib-uri>
            http://brainysoftware.com/taglib/complex
        </taglib-uri>
        <taglib-location>/WEB-INF/jsp/complex.tld
    </taglib-location>
  </taglib>
</jsp-config>
```

jsp-property-group

The **jsp-property-group** element groups a number of JSP files so they can be given global property information. You can use subelements under **<jsp-property-group>** to do the following.

- Indicate whether EL is ignored
- Indicate whether scripting elements are allowed
- Indicate page encoding information
- Indicate that a resource is a JSP document (written in XML)
- Prelude and code automatic includes

The **jsp-property-group** element has the following subelements.

- an optional **description** element
- an optional **display-name** element

- an optional **icon** element
- one or more **url-pattern** elements
- an optional **el-ignored** element
- an optional **page-encoding** element
- an optional **scripting-invalid** element
- an optional **is-xml** element
- zero or more **include-prelude** elements
- zero or more **include-code** elements

The **url-pattern** element is used to specify a URL pattern that will be affected by the property settings.

The **el-ignored** element can have a boolean value of true or false. A value of true means that the EL expressions will not evaluated in the JSP pages whose URL match the specified URL pattern(s). The default value of this element is false.

The **page-encoding** element specifies the encoding for the JSP pages whose URL match the specified URL pattern(s). The valid value for **page-encoding** is the same as the value of the **pageEncoding** attribute of the **page** directive used in a matching JSP page. There will be a translation-time error to name a different encoding in the **pageEncoding** attribute of the **page** directive of a JSP page and in a JSP configuration element matching the page. It is also a translation-time error to name a different encoding in the prolog or text declaration of a document in XML syntax and in a JSP configuration element matching the document. It is legal to name the same encoding through multiple mechanisms.

The **scripting-invalid** element accepts a boolean value. A value of true means that **scripting** is not allowed in the JSP pages whose URLs match the specified pattern(s). By default, the value of the **scripting-invalid** element is false.

The **is-xml** element accepts a boolean value and true indicates that the JSP pages whose URLs match the specified pattern(s) are JSP documents.

The **include-prelude** element is a context-relative path that must correspond to an element in the servlet/JSP application. When the element is present, the given path will be automatically included (as in an **include** directive) at the beginning of each JSP page whose URL matches the specified pattern(s).

The **include-coda** element is a context-relative path that must correspond to an element in the application. When the element is present, the given path will be automatically included (as in the **include** directive) at the end of each JSP page in this **jsp-property-group** element.

For example, here is a **jsp-property-group** element that causes EL evaluation in all JSP pages to be ignored.

```
<jsp-config>
    <jsp-property-group>
        <url-pattern>*.jsp</url-pattern>
        <el-ignored>true</el-ignored>
    </jsp-property-group>
</jsp-config>
```

And, here is a **jsp-property-group** element that is used to enforce script-free JSP pages throughout the application.

```
<jsp-config>
    <jsp-property-group>
        <url-pattern>*.jsp</url-pattern>
        <scripting-invalid>true</scripting-invalid>
    </jsp-property-group>
</jsp-config>
```

Deployment

Deploying a Servlet/JSP application has always been easy since the first version of Servlet. It has just been a matter of zipping all application resources in its original directory structure into a war file. You can either use the jar tool in the JDK or a popular tool such as WinZip. All you need is make sure the zipped file has war extension. If you're using WinZip, rename the result once it's done.

You must include in your war file all libraries and class files as well as HTML files, JSP pages, images, copyright notices (if any), and so on. Do not include Java source files. Anyone who needs your application can simply get a copy of your war file and deploy it in a servlet/JSP container.

Web Fragments

Servlet 3 adds web fragments, a new feature for deploying plug-ins or frameworks in an existing web application. Web fragments are designed to complement the deployment descriptor without having to edit the **web.xml** file. A web fragment is basically a package (jar file) containing the usual web objects, such as servlets, filter, and listeners, and other resources, such as JSP pages and static images. A web fragment can also have a descriptor, which is an XML document similar to the deployment descriptor. The web fragment descriptor must be named **web-fragment.xml** and reside in the **META-INF** directory of the package. A web fragment descriptor may contain any elements that may appear under the **web-app** element in the deployment descriptor, plus some web fragment-specific elements. An application can have multiple web fragments.

Listing D.2 shows the skeleton of the web fragment descriptor. The text printed in bold highlights the difference between it and the deployment descriptor. The root element in a web fragment is, unsurprisingly, **web-fragment**. The **web-fragment** element can even have the **metadata-complete** attribute. If the value of the **metadata-complete** attribute is true, annotations in the classes contained by the web fragment will be skipped.

Listing D.2: The skeleton of a web-fragment.xml file

```
<?xml version="1.0" encoding="ISO-8859-1"?>
<web-fragment xmlns="http://java.sun.com/xml/ns/javaee"
    xmlns:xsi="http://www.w3.org/2001/XMLSchema-instance"
    xsi:schemaLocation="http://java.sun.com/xml/ns/javaee
➥http://java.sun.com/xml/ns/javaee/web-fragment_3_0.xsd"
    version="3.0"
    [metadata-complete="true|false"]
>
```

```
    ...
```

```
</web-fragment>
```

As an example, the **d1** application contains a web fragment in a jar file named **fragment.jar**. The jar file has been imported to the **WEB-INF/lib** directory of **d1**. The focus of this example is not on **d1** but rather on the **webfragment** project, which contains a servlet (**fragment.servlet.FragmentServlet**, printed in Listing D.3) and a **web-fragment.xml** file (given in Listing D.4).

Listing D.3: The FragmentServlet class

```java
package fragment.servlet;
import java.io.IOException;
import java.io.PrintWriter;
import javax.servlet.ServletException;
import javax.servlet.http.HttpServlet;
import javax.servlet.http.HttpServletRequest;
import javax.servlet.http.HttpServletResponse;

public class FragmentServlet extends HttpServlet {

    private static final long serialVersionUID = 940L;

    public void doGet(HttpServletRequest request,
       HttpServletResponse response)
            throws ServletException, IOException {

        response.setContentType("text/html");
        PrintWriter out = response.getWriter();
        out.println("A plug-in");
    }
}
```

Listing D.4: The web fragment descriptor in project webfragment

```xml
<?xml version="1.0" encoding="ISO-8859-1"?>
<web-fragment xmlns="http://java.sun.com/xml/ns/javaee"
    xmlns:xsi="http://www.w3.org/2001/XMLSchema-instance"
    xsi:schemaLocation="http://java.sun.com/xml/ns/javaee
➡http://java.sun.com/xml/ns/javaee/web-fragment_3_0.xsd"
    version="3.0"
>
```

```
<servlet>
    <servlet-name>FragmentServlet</servlet-name>
    <servlet-class>fragment.servlet.FragmentServlet</servlet-
  class>
</servlet>
<servlet-mapping>
    <servlet-name>FragmentServlet</servlet-name>
    <url-pattern>/fragment</url-pattern>
</servlet-mapping>
</web-fragment>
```

FragmentServlet is a simple servlet that sends a string to the browser. The **web-fragment.xml** file registers and maps the servlet. The structure of the **fragment.jar** file is depicted in Figure D.1.

Figure D.1: The structure of the fragment.jar file

You can test the **Fragment** servlet by invoking using this URL:

```
http://localhost:8080/d1/fragment
```

You should see the output from the **Fragment** servlet.

Summary

This appendix explained how you can configure and deploy your servlet/JSP applications. The appendix started by introducing the directory structure of a typical application and then moved to an explanation of the deployment descriptor.

After the application is ready for deployment, you can deploy it by retaining the files and directory structure of your application. Alternatively, you can package the application into a WAR file and deploy the whole application as a single file.

Index